D0803507

Business and Crime Prevention

Business and Crime Prevention

edited by

Marcus Felson and Ronald V. Clarke

* * *

Criminal Justice Press

Monsey, New York

1997

NATIONAL UNIVERSITY
LIBRARY   SAN DIEGO

© Copyright 1997 by
Willow Tree Press, Inc.
All rights reserved.

Printed in the United States of America. No part of this book may be reproduced in any manner whatsoever without written permission, except for brief quotations embodied in critical articles and reviews. For information, contact Willow Tree Press, Inc., P.O. Box 249, Monsey, NY 10952 U.S.A.

Library of Congress Cataloging-in-Publication Data

Business and crime prevention / edited by Marcus Felson and Ronald V. Clarke
    p. cm.
Proceedings of a conference held at Rutgers University in May 1996.
Includes bibliographical references.
ISBN: 1-881798-09-7
1. Corporations--Security measures--Congresses. 2. Industries--Security measures--Congresses. 3. Retail trade--Security measures--Congresses. 4. Crime prevention--Congresses. I. Felson, Marcus,
HV8290.B88 1997
658.4'7--dc21

96-30023
CIP

NATIONAL UNIVERSITY
SAN DIEGO
LIBRARY

Contents

Foreword
Jeremy Travis vii

Contributing
Authors ix

Editors' Introduction: Business and Crime
Marcus Felson and Ronald V. Clarke 1

Criminology and Business Crime: Building the Bridge
John Burrows 13

Will Crime Prevention Ever Be a Business Priority?
Dennis Challinger 35

Measuring Crime and Its Impact in the
Business Environment
Richard C. Hollinger 57

Technology, Business, and Crime
Marcus Felson 81

Towards Effective Public-Private Partnerships in
Crime Control: Experiences in the Netherlands
Jan J.M. van Dijk 97

Do Premises Liability Suits Promote Business
Crime Prevention?
John E. Eck 125

Crime Prevention and the Insurance Industry
Roger A. Litton 151

continued

A Brief History of the Security Industry in the
United States
Robert D. McCrie 197

Unrecognized Origins of the New Policing: Linkage
between Private and Public Policing
Clifford Shearing 219

Real Estate Development and Crime Prevention Needs
Richard B. Peiser 231

Financial Analysis of Retail Crime Prevention
Robert DiLonardo 249

Preventing Pay Phone Damage
Cressida Bridgeman 263

Insurance Industry Analyses and the Prevention of
Motor Vehicle Theft
Kim Hazelbaker 283

FOREWORD

This book arose out of my discussions with one of the editors, Ronald Clarke, when he was a Visiting Fellow at the National Institute of Justice. We discovered a mutual interest in the role of business and industry in the production and the prevention of crime — and a shared regret that these topics have attracted so little interest from criminologists.

When scholars have studied business, they have tended to focus on crimes committed by corporations. Few studies exist on the many other ways in which business and industry relate to crime, including the vital role of small businesses in maintaining the stability of marginal neighborhoods, ways that new business products and services can create or reduce crime opportunities, and the nature of crimes suffered by businesses, their customers and their employees. Above all, there has been little research into the effectiveness of the wide range of crime preventive practices pursued by business and little discussion of the ways in which criminological knowledge could assist in preventing business crime.

It is tempting to dismiss private prevention as non-public in its significance, but a different view is taken here. When small businesses lose a good share of their potential profits to shoplifting and employee theft, this can contribute to their bankruptcy with consequent harm to their employees and the wider community they serve. When a clerk in a convenience store is harmed by robbers, or when fear of victimization affects employees or their families, this harm extends beyond the business itself. Conversely, businesses that do not take into account the nature of the communities they serve may contribute to nearby alcohol and drug problems or other crimes. Often they suffer from the consequences of crime, but may not realize that they could be playing a role in creating the problems or, indeed, in their solution.

Greater communication between criminologists and business would not only assist business crime prevention, as well as the wider society, but academic criminology would have much to gain from greater familiarity with the crime problems faced by business and the efforts being taken to deal with these problems. Another fertile field of research is the role of business in creating new crime opportunities, or prevention possibilities, through the provision of new products, technologies and services.

These potential benefits seemed worthy of further exploration and, as a first step, I invited Ronald Clarke and Marcus Felson, his Rutgers colleague who had previously undertaken an NIJ-funded study of business crime prevention, to work with the National Institute of Justice in arranging a small research conference on the subject of Business and Crime Prevention. This would showcase the work of a small group of pioneers working in this country and overseas and would explore the scope for further study. In particular, it might help define a role for the National Institute of Justice in this field involving, as it does, the novel element of partnerships between the private and public sectors.

The conference held at Rutgers University in May 1996 proved to be very stimulating. The international group of participants included a handful of academic criminologists who have undertaken studies of business crime and its prevention, experts from the security industry, trained criminologists holding employment in retailing and insurance, business intellectuals who have analyzed crime or developed preventive policies, government researchers with an interest in crime prevention, and a senior civil servant from Europe who has taken a leading role in promoting crime prevention partnerships between the public and private sectors. Many of these participants combined expertise in criminology with knowledge of business and business crime prevention.

This book is largely the proceedings of that meeting and I hope its contents will help demonstrate to a broader audience of criminologists that rigorous and challenging work in this field can be undertaken. In the meanwhile, we at the National Institute of Justice will continue to explore the role of government-sponsored research in this field, seeking, in particular, to identify partners among government and private agencies willing to share in the funding of new studies.

Jeremy Travis

**Director,
U.S. National Institute of Justice**

CONTRIBUTING AUTHORS

Cressida Bridgeman, Home Office Police Research Group, 50 Queen Anne's Gate, London, SW1H 9AT U.K.

John Burrows, Morgan Harris Burrows—Consultants, 84 Wilberforce Road, London N4 2SR U.K.

Dennis Challinger, Corporate Security and Loss Prevention, Coles Myer Ltd., P.O. Box 2000, Tooronga, Victoria 3146, Australia.

Ronald V. Clarke, School of Criminal Justice, Rutgers-The State University of New Jersey, 15 Washington Street, Newark, NJ 07102.

Robert DiLonardo, 2882 Sandpiper Place, Clearwater, FL 34622.

John E. Eck, Department of Criminology and Criminal Justice, University of Maryland, 2220 LeFrak Hall, College Park, MD 20742.

Marcus Felson, School of Criminal Justice, Rutgers-The State University of New Jersey, 15 Washington Street, Newark, NJ 07102.

Kim Hazelbaker, Senior Vice President, Highway Loss Data Institute, 1005 North Glebe Road, Arlington, VA 22201.

Richard C. Hollinger, University of Florida, 3360 Turlington Hall, Gainesville, FL 32611.

Roger A. Litton, Smithson Mason Ltd., Insurance Brokers, SMG House, 31 Clarendon Road, Leeds LS2 9PA U.K.

Robert D. McCrie, John Jay College of Criminal Justice, 899 Tenth Avenue, New York, NY 10019.

continued

Richard B. Peiser, Lusk Center for Real Eastate, School of Urban and Regional Planning, Von Kleinsmid Center 351, University of Southern California, University Park, CA 90089.

Clifford Shearing, Centre of Criminology, University of Toronto, 130 St. George St., Room 8001, Toronto, Ontario M5S 3H1 Canada.

Jan J.M. van Dijk, Ministerie van Justitie, Directie Beleid, P.O. Box 20301, 2500 EH the Hague, the Netherlands.

EDITORS' INTRODUCTION: BUSINESS AND CRIME

by Marcus Felson and Ronald V. Clarke

Rutgers, The State University of New Jersey

INTRODUCTION

Reading through most of the standard criminology literature, one would hardly guess that the United States has a private-enterprise economy. Such articles and books seldom mention business as the target of much crime or business facilities as the location of crime (although it is not unusual to see research emphasizing business offenders). Nor does the standard business administration literature feature crime among the business problems to be solved. Only on the periphery of criminology and business administration does one find security management and business crime prevention. Yet these important efforts seldom feed back into the mainstream of the two fields or link these fields to one another. Something new is needed to bridge this gap and to assemble the scattered efforts already found.

Our purpose here is to foster a broader dialogue among criminologists, business intellectuals and practicing business managers. We would be glad to see the growth of a new field entitled "business and crime." Yet, we would not want this to become simply another specialty of criminology or business, isolated from the mainstream of both. In our view, business should become a central theme in criminology while crime prevention should be a core concern among business intellectuals and practitioners. Business is central to understanding crime because it is at the core of the economy and the very organization of everyday life. Crime is an essential topic for business because it threatens profits while interfering with business goals and relations to a larger society. If criminologists join hands with business, both fields will be well served, as will society.

WHY BUSINESS CRIME IS IMPORTANT FOR LARGER SOCIETY

Some people may be tempted to dismiss business and crime as a topic only relevant to business itself. This approach has two fallacies: (1) ignoring how business losses affect the larger community and society; and (2) missing the extent to which business organizes community life and, hence, sets the stage for a good deal of crime for which business is not itself the direct target.

To take up the first fallacy, the substantial crime victimization of business, detailed in Hollinger's chapter in this book, has significance beyond business itself. Business losses to crime (as well as costs of security) are passed on to customers and to shareholders, including the employee profit-sharing plans and the pension funds supporting many of our elderly people. These added costs of doing business can play a strong role in driving many businesses to bankruptcy, especially in marginal areas that can least afford to lose providers of jobs, goods and services. This can serve to drive up costs to consumers. It is difficult to believe that the additional jobs provided by the security industry offset these community losses. Moreover, a nation with high wage rates has enough difficulty competing with other nations in industrial production, without adding crime and security expenses.

The second fallacy is to neglect business as society's main organizer of everyday activities, within which crime carves its niche. Its schedules, facilities, employment patterns, deliveries, customer patterns, all set the stage for a good deal of crime, even when business is not itself the direct target. Several industries find their employees highly vulnerable to victimization, whether on the way to or from work or on the job. Some occupations are especially at risk of victimization (see, for example, Block et al., 1985; National Institute for Occupational Health and Safety, 1996). Crime vulnerability can interfere with recruitment of workers from other areas and produce extra problems and fears for workers' families. In some cases, entry of a business to an area may foster additional theft or other crime by producing more targets or even bringing in more offenders.

On a more positive note, entry of new businesses to otherwise high-crime areas often gives them additional "eyes on the street" and more "capable guardians" through diversity of age; in the process, lower crime rates are generated. As a new business contributes to "gentrification," it may assist crime reduction. This is a complicated topic worthy of research and analysis, surely posing a challenge.

Not only does a business influence crime on the way to and from work and in the vicinity of business establishments, but many businesses control facilities within which customers, clients and employees, as well as their property, are highly vulnerable to illegal attack. Indeed, almost implicit in the definition of business is the need to attract these people. Hotels and motels have strangers entering and leaving day and night, sometimes in large numbers. Public entertainment businesses — including bars, restaurants and theaters — generate crowds and concomitant crime risks. Industrial parks, malls and other retail trade establishments find people and property at risk in their parking lots. In addition, private ownership and management of apartments and condominiums involves business in residential victimization. The private sector is most of the economy. Most of us work in business settings. Even purely public settings are close to and influenced by business settings.

Business scheduling of activities, from restaurant closing to flexitime, has major significance for where people are going, including after dark. Are there many stragglers subject to physical attack? Are there cars on the street with few people around to stop them from being stolen? Are businesses themselves readily broken into on evenings and weekends? These questions are largely answered by the scheduling structure of the private businesses involved. This does not mean that all business scheduling creates more crime. Indeed, some scheduling may reduce crime significantly for all concerned. Once more, we see that business decisions are very important in their externalities, just as they are important for businesses themselves. Nor should we ignore the impact that public-agency regulations on business have on these very problems. British researchers have concluded that uniform pub-closing hours dump too many drunk people out on the town center at the same time, contributing to crime problems in the vicinity. Those problems originate with public policy to which the businesses probably object.

On the other hand, many public-sector decisions are designed to increase the volume of business; any impact on crime can only be understood by considering business as well. For example, the construction and management of public parking structures is largely oriented to providing customers for businesses in town cores. The design and management of roads in a private-enterprise economy has a strong business purpose but also serves to increase or decrease crime. Criminology cannot deny that business and crime is a core topic in a private-enterprise society.

BUSINESS IS CENTRAL FOR IMPROVING PUBLIC POLICY

The broad significance of business applies not only to crime problems but also to solutions. It seems that criminologists and civil servants are years (if not decades) behind many businesses in recognizing the limitations of public agencies for reducing crime. Indeed, any crime prevention program depending upon "making human beings better" has yet to prove itself on a large scale. Certain changes in policy prescriptions have already gained some ground in other nations (see Garland, 1996) and are, at least, discussed in the United States. These include community policing, problem-oriented policing and situational crime prevention. Community policing is not sharply defined, but it implies that police become more attuned to local community needs and make better use of community resources in dealing with crime. A more focused policy prescription is problem-oriented policing. This emphasizes more precise analysis of a crime problem in a given place, avoiding non-strategic arrests and taking more creative steps to solving the problem (Goldstein, 1990). For example, the public sector can re-route traffic away from a drug market and, thus, may greatly reduce the problem without overburdening the local jails. The "broken windows" approach to policing emphasizes the day-to-day management of small crime problems to prevent larger ones from developing (Kelling and Coles, 1996).

Business is generally quite responsive to creative invitations by the public sector to join in problem-oriented policing. For example, owners of apartment buildings or shopping centers have cooperated with police in expelling drug dealers or, more simply, in keeping down noise. More generally, cooperation with local business is essential to the efficient policing of a community. That is why business is so central to any public-policy changes. An expanded concern with the new forms of community and problem-oriented policing will be informed by a "business and crime" perspective. Indeed, the central theme of Shearing's chapter in this volume is that this "new policing" has its origins in the emergence and recent rapid development of private policing and private security.

Business can play an essential role in breaking the public-sector monopoly on the crime issue. In the United States, crime policy has been virtually monopolized by the criminal justice system. Police, prosecutors, lawyers, jails, prisons and executions — these are the core of American discussion about crime and its prevention. In reality, these have little to do with most ordinary crime. It occurs in private life. It occurs on streets, in parking lots, in stores and other places where there is no policeman. If a report is made at all, it is long after the offender has fled and the trail is cold. The shift to preventive thinking is essential. Even here, the public sector — the schools, social services, public housing authorities — gets disproportionate attention. Yet, the private sector is where most human activity occurs, including crime prevention. The private sector has enormous potential for a creative synergy between modern management principles and crime prevention, as shown by Bridgeman's analysis in this volume of successful efforts by telephone companies in Britain and Australia to deal with pay-phone vandalism.

Even manufacturers have an important role in crime prevention (see Felson's and Hazelbaker's chapters). Automatic teller machines are now produced with keyboards sloped so a thief cannot see the access code as it is entered. Car radios and tape players have engineered out the very theft problem they produced, allowing the owner to key in a code or to pull out the activating part and put it in purse or pocket. Mobile phones have been designed to make thefts of calls difficult or a stolen phone useless. Ink tags have been attached to make garments not worth stealing. That reduces dependence on arresting people.

More generally, the fact that business has a practical bent puts it at the core of crime prevention. It has the capacity to do something for itself and others.

BUSINESS CAN IMPROVE CRIMINOLOGY

The essential point is that business knows as much about crime and crime prevention as government, or even criminology. Business expertise can be applied by others, but that requires increased communications with businesses to learn what they have been doing.

Criminologists have traditionally traded knowledge about policy issues with those in the criminal justice system. Business people have been rather unlikely to articulate their knowledge about crime, perhaps because they are busy with practical tasks, or because they get no particular rewards for writing. When business intellectuals do write, they are not likely to come to the attention of government officials or criminologists. We have tried to bridge that gap in this volume. Litton's chapter on how the insurance industry can attempt to influence crime-preventive action is one example. A second is provided by DiLonardo's chapter on financial analysis that shows how one group of business professionals tracks goods and money to prevent crime. Inventories, layouts of stores, stockroom management and other methods have been pioneered by business, not criminology. One of us (R.V.C.) has recently edited an entire issue of *Security Journal* (Vol. 7, No. 1, April 1996) on retail crime prevention, detailing many of the methods of preventing crime with problem-orientated and situational approaches and a similar publication has recently appeared in Britain (Gill, 1994). Business efforts to discourage drug dealing by relocating pay phones offer another example of how business has much to share with criminology (Natarajan et al., 1995).

We have noted that a very large proportion of crime in modern Western nations is committed against business. This includes much more than shoplifting from retail firms. Indeed, the great variety of offenses and business types involved in such victimizations itself justifies a substantial sharing of information and development of principles.

As criminologists learn more about business crime, they might respond with some changes in criminology. Several ideas come to mind. First, their emphasis on business offenders will likely be reduced with recognition of business as victims, and the consequence of business victimization for citizens and communities. Second, by studying business and crime, criminologists may learn more about how society delivers temptations to offenders. Third, criminologists are likely to discern non-punitive means for preventing crime in common business practices. Fourth, criminologists may learn more from business about how fear of crime has its impact independent of objective crime, as well as about methods for reducing fear. Fifth, criminologists may come to recognize the significance of business for generating and preventing crime against other victims. Sixth, business expertise can help improve calculations of the direct and indirect financial costs of crime.

The most important general point is that criminologists should be interested in business for scientific and preventive reasons.

BUSINESS CAN BENEFIT FROM CRIMINOLOGY

We should not exaggerate the degree of business innovation in crime prevention. Most businesses put security systems in late, rather than early, relying on expensive technology or guards rather than inexpensive situational prevention. Many guards seek to catch people in the act of stealing rather than designing systems that prevent stealing in the first place. This is why business itself has something to learn.

Many situational prevention methods (Clarke, 1995) cost little or nothing. Most methods for designing buildings and facilities low in crime cost no more, sometimes less, than standard methods. Criminologists aware of these methods, such as Challinger and Burrows (see their chapters in this volume), can assist business in reducing losses to crime, without compromising their scientific role. When some rigor must be given up, knowledge can still be gained that will help in calculating costs and deciding what preventive action to take.

Conventional security is a labor-intensive activity. Banks, retailers, insurers, pubs and clubs, entertainment complexes and many other business organizations spend large sums of money protecting themselves, their employees and their customers from a wide range of crime. Most large companies have their own security divisions. In addition, a whole private security industry has developed, offering such specialized products as alarms and surveillance cameras and such specific services as cash transportation or guarding of facilities (see McCrie's chapter). The number of people employed in this industry greatly exceeds the numbers of sworn law enforcement officers. Perhaps the security industry itself lacks incentives to emphasize low-cost prevention. Criminologists can offer independent assessments and ideas for prevention at lower costs. Universities can train such people and, thus, contribute to lower crime risks while helping business save money.

Moreover, criminology can help business to analyze crime costs more broadly and to see how business decisions produce more, or less, crime for the community as a whole. For example, what size establishments have what consequences for crime in the vicinity? How does crime in the vicinity influence customers and recruitment? How do business decisions affect lawsuits by crime victims (see Calder and Sipes, 1992, and Eck's chapter in this volume)? How does objective crime lead to fear of crime?

How does fear of crime reduce business assets (see Peiser's chapter on the real estate industry)?

These considerations should not be taken in a purely selfish and short-term perspective. Businesses that neglect their communities may allow crime to grow, with problems feeding back on themselves. Yet, increasing experience indicates that expensive means for protecting a community or insulating an organization from it can often be replaced with inexpensive design or redesign. Even so extreme a case as the Port Authority Bus Terminal in New York City saw substantial crime reductions through ingenuity, with few additional security measures (Felson et al., 1996). Cooperation among nearby businesses often reduces costs for all. Links between government and business for local problem-oriented prevention is also feasible. Criminologists in universities have some time to gather relevant information and write about it. With communications among business, government and universities, all can gain something.

BETTER COMMUNICATIONS AND FEWER CONFRONTATIONS

One of us has proposed a "crime prevention extension service" to help link criminologists to businesses (Felson, 1994). Following the well-known agricultural model, this would employ university experts in crime prevention to help local businesses solve their crime problems while feeding knowledge back to the universities. Communications are the essential means for achieving the three goals we have mentioned: helping criminology to improve, helping business to reduce crime and guiding government towards more effective public policy.

We have avoided regulation as the main method for achieving crime reduction where business is involved. If regulations are developed, we believe this should be accomplished cooperatively. For example, one California community assembled business, police and public planning representatives to design a new crime prevention ordinance. Initial resistance by business faded away as they were properly consulted. The ordinance passed. A counter example is found with the convenience store industry, which had initiated a multi-point plan to reduce robberies. Florida crime prevention specialists added to this plan a requirement for two employees in each store at night (Hunter and Jeffrey, 1992). Although this is highly defensible from a crime prevention standpoint, the costs in antagonizing the industry against crime prevention may have offset any gains.

If criminologists are primarily in search of a stick to beat business, that will kill cooperation and thwart prevention. Given the powers of business in American society, regulation may succeed in one case but fail in ten others. Even if businesses have something to gain in money, that will probably not suffice if they have to go through a gauntlet of insults to secure the savings. For this reason, we must analyze closely when and how crime prevention benefits business and offer it emotional, as well as monetary incentives to proceed accordingly. This support must be accompanied with academic independence and the ability to make constructive criticism. Many past approaches to crime prevention have achieved little success and university scholars must maintain sufficient independence to note any problems.

Yet, this same independence cannot be used as a shield against providing viable solutions that serve practical purposes. In particular, business crime prevention must emphasize improvement in profits. Only if this happens quickly can business be expected to make an initial outlay of funds and to show much interest in criminologists. The net financial benefit must exceed what would result from the same outlay to alternative activities, such as marketing the product (see chapter by DiLonardo). This is why situational crime prevention becomes strategically important, with its promise of quick results at little or no cost.

ISSUES FOR THE FUTURE

As criminologists, business intellectuals and businesses communicate, a number of important issues are sure to arise. Each of these is worth discussing in colloquia, courses and over cocktails. We offer no simple answers; indeed none is possible given the huge diversity of enterprises falling under the rubric of private business. Nevertheless, we feel that the questions themselves demonstrate the richness of the potential future inquiry.

First, is crime prevention a threat to business? This question involves whether and when crime prevention undermines profits, including whether crime information will undermine business confidence. It also points to the need for more sophisticated assessment of the social and financial costs and benefits of crime prevention.

Second, does business have a public responsibility to prevent crime generated by its products and practices? This leads to further inquiry into business incentives for such responsibility, the role of litigation for encouraging crime prevention and the role of legislation and regulation.

Third, what is the government's role in promoting crime prevention activity by business? This suggests various possibilities, ranging from laissez faire to benign regulation, cooperation to confrontation and disregard to concern for other business goals. The use of public resources (including police) to prevent private business crime is an important issue. Public-private partnerships in prevention and government encouragement of cooperation among businesses come to the fore, along with linkages between public police and private security. Of particular interest is keeping crime prevention from becoming nothing more than a public-relations exercise. How is that to be avoided? And can business be persuaded to act more easily by appeals to civic responsibility or to profit (see Burrows, 1991)? At the conference giving rise to this book, van Dijk was forthright on this issue, by urging: "Talk morality, not money." In his paper included here, he describes government experience in the Netherlands of forging a crime prevention partnership with business, but the issues raised need to be revisited for the United States and other countries.

Fourth, how can the divide between criminologists and business be bridged? This, in turn, poses questions about how the business community can educate the academic community about its particular problems and practices, and how it can obtain advice on preventing specific crime problems from the academic community. The academic community in turn needs to gain entry into the business community and to find full-time jobs for its progeny as criminologists in business loss prevention. Challinger and Burrows, themselves distinguished criminologists, show in this volume how they seek to be valuable employees in business, but a wider range of experience in these practical roles needs to be accumulated and evaluated.

Fifth, how can the necessary crime prevention research be undertaken? Should it be carried out by individual businesses, trade associations, or universities? How should it financed? Government agencies may refuse funding on the grounds that private industry should take care of its own needs. This ignores the benefits for the local community and the general public brought about by reduced crime against businesses. In any case, most businesses are far too small to fund such research. One of the conference participants, Burrows, reported that 95 percent of retail establishments in Britain employ fewer than five people. Another source of difficulty is that criminologists want to publish what they find while businesses might fear that publication will create embarrassment or give commercial advantage to competitors. Opening business databases to academic research raises similar issues of compromising proprietary interests. Infusing applied business crime prevention with rigorous analysis and measurement is another important issue meriting discussion.

Sixth, how can crime prevention knowledge be shared among the business community? Can trade associations help to spread this knowledge? What are the respective roles of business schools and schools of criminal justice? Should crime prevention training be expanded among security professionals? Can extra crime prevention training be extended to those out of school? How can the security industry be encouraged to think more broadly about crime prevention, instead of relying so heavily on guards and alarms? Many of the best prevention methods are inexpensive and provide no profit; therefore, the security industry has limited incentive to offer these methods unless businesses insist.

Some of these questions have no single or final answer, but progress can and will be made if we begin to address them. We believe it is both timely and essential to develop "business and crime" as a core topic in criminology as well as a field of concern for business. The contributions collected together in this volume address many of the topics comprising the field, but there are large gaps reflecting the patchy criminological interest in business crime. For example, the specific crime problems of many business sectors have received little or no attention from criminologists. This lack of consistent coverage has made it difficult to group the following chapters into discrete sections. Instead we have tried to follow a logic of presentation that proceeds from very general issues of criminological involvement in business (Chapters 2-5) through discussions of the role of key institutions — the law, the insurance and security industries — in preventing business crime (Chapters 6-10) and, finally, to the crime prevention activity of specific business sectors (Chapters 11-14). We hope this volume will stimulate inquisitive minds to find new and fruitful areas for exploration, filling the gaps and extending the reach of business and crime.

* * *

Acknowledgments: We wish to thank Dr. Martha Smith, Research Director of the Center for Crime Prevention Studies at Rutgers, for her invaluable help in the editorial work for this volume.

REFERENCES

Block, R., M. Felson and C.R. Block (1985). "Crime Victimization Rates for Incumbents of 246 Occupations." *Sociology and Social Research* 69:442-451.

Burrows, J. (1991). *Making Crime Prevention Pay: Initiatives from Business.* Crime Prevention Unit Paper 27. London, UK: Home Office.

Calder, J.D. and D.D. Sipes (1992). "Crime, Security, and Premises Liability: Toward Precision in Security Expert Testimony." *Security Journal* 3:66-82.

Clarke, R.V. (1995). "Situational Crime Prevention." In: M. Tonry and D.P. Farrington (eds.), *Building a Safer Society: Strategic Approaches to Crime Prevention.* Crime and Justice: A Review of Research, vol. 19. Chicago, IL: University of Chicago Press.

Felson, M. (1994). "A Crime Prevention Extension Service." In: RV. Clarke (ed.), *Crime Prevention Studies*, vol. 3. Monsey, NY: Criminal Justice Press.

——— M.E. Belanger, G.M. Bichler, C.D. Bruzinski, G.S. Campbell, C.L. Fried, K.C. Grofik, I.S. Mazur, A.B. O'Regan, P.J. Sweeney, A.L. Ullman and L.M. Williams (1996). "Redesigning Hell: Preventing Crime and Disorder at the Port Authority Bus Terminal." In: R.V. Clarke (ed.), *Preventing Mass Transit Crime.* Crime Prevention Studies, vol. 6. Monsey, NY: Criminal Justice Press.

Garland, D. (1996). "The Limits of the Sovereign State: Strategies of Crime Control in Contemporary Society." *British Journal of Criminology* 36:445-471.

Gill, M. (1994). *Crime at Work: Studies in Security and Crime Prevention.* Leicester, UK: Perpetuity Press.

Goldstein, H. (1990). *Problem-Oriented Policing.* New York, NY: McGraw Hill.

Hunter, R.D. and C.R. Jeffrey (1992). "Preventing Convenience Store Robbery Through Environmental Design." In: R.V. Clarke (ed.), *Situational Crime Prevention: Successful Case Studies.* Albany, NY: Harrow and Heston.

Kelling, G. and C Coles. (1996). *Fixing Broken Windows.* New York, NY: Free Press.

Natarajan, M., R.V. Clarke and B.D. Johnson. (1995). "Telephones as Facilitators of Drug Dealing: A Research Agenda." *European Journal of Criminal Policy and Research* 3(3):137-153.

U.S. National Institute for Occupational Health and Safety (1996). *Violence in the Workplace. Risk Factors and Prevention Strategies.* Current Intelligence Bulletin 57. Washington, DC: U.S. Department of Health and Human Services.

CRIMINOLOGY AND BUSINESS CRIME: BUILDING THE BRIDGE

by John Burrows
Morgan Harris Burrows (MHB), Consultants

Abstract: *This paper argues that poor communication between criminologists and the business community is, to a large extent, symptomatic of the low priority attached to crime against business by those responsible for law enforcement and crime prevention. As a means of understanding the government and police position on business crime, the paper attempts to outline the key developments in business criminology in the U.K. since 1986 and to highlight both what this work has achieved and what it has failed to address. The main lessons from this small, but not insignificant, body of research are then summarized. The research shows, in particular, the very high rates of victimization suffered by those in business, their clear concerns about the problem, and a growing rejection of the prevailing view that businesses must "look after themselves" in preventing crime. Various arguments in favor of partnerships between businesses and the police are then presented. In conclusion, it is argued that criminologists in the U.K. have considerable scope to become more involved in the field of business crime, and may have a particular opportunity at present to assist businesses and the police to work together more effectively in preventing crime.*

The theme of the May 1996 conference on business and crime prevention was the lack of attention given to business crime by academic criminologists, the case for greater communication between criminologists and business, and the benefits that might accrue from such an association. These are wide issues, but this paper seeks to broaden them still further and address the relationship that exists between the government and government agencies (particularly the police service) and business on this topic in the United Kingdom. It does so in the belief that in many respects the differences between criminologists and business are a *symptom* of policies and attitudes prevailing among those responsible for law enforcement and crime prevention, who are, of course, highly influential in directing criminologists' research activities.

This crucial relationship has received very little attention: indeed, many aspects of the relationship would not be easily amenable to research. But the assertion that police and businesses "ought to" cooperate more widely has probably been the one common message characterizing all the various working parties and committees that have addressed aspects of this relationship in the U.K. context and emerges regularly from the pages of the limited research literature. Few, however, have sought to dissect either what stands in the way of cooperation or the benefits of greater partnership.

This paper endeavors to take some initial steps in this direction. First, it addresses the work that government groups and criminologists have carried out in this area and seeks to identify common strands in this activity. Second, drawing on the key findings of the research activities, attention is given first to the belief — held by many in the business world — that they are expected to deal with crime on their own and then to the case for greater involvement with the police. Finally, the paper tries to suggest productive areas where criminologists might help develop crime prevention activities involving business, particularly in supporting the small, but growing, movement toward collaborative work in the U.K.

"Business crime" is a wide phrase. Felson and Clarke, in their introduction, make the useful distinction between: (1) businesses as crime "generators" (to use the term developed by Brantingham and Brantingham (1995)), either of offenses against themselves as businesses or of crime opportunities (by their creation of new services and products); and (2) businesses as "victims" and active agents in crime prevention. These different roles are not easily separated and there can be little doubt that government and police attitudes about businesses as "crime generators" strongly color their attitudes to them as victims. The primary (but not exclusive) focus of the paper, however, will be on business *as victims*.

CRIME AGAINST BUSINESS IN THE U.K.

While there can be few who could argue that business crime has secured proper — or even adequate — attention from either criminologists or the government in the U.K., it would be a mistake to assume that no such work had been carried out. Moreover, there are compelling and obvious reasons for arguing that knowledge of this earlier work should strongly influence the scope and direction of future activities by criminologists.

It is unfortunate that there is no existing account to which we can turn. Compiling any comprehensive account would, of course, be very difficult — requiring details of the activities of police forces, crime prevention agencies and (above all) businesses that simply do not exist. But an abbreviated history of the principal activities at the national level (including significant publications) would be a more modest undertaking and would serve to give a taste of the major themes pursued. Taking the last ten years as a convenient cut-off point, such an account is provided below in the Appendix. What follows in the next section is an assessment of the ground covered — and neglected.

Common Themes

Taking a global view of the events set out in the Appendix is instructive. The choice of key events is naturally subjective and, were the exercise to be completed for other countries, the implications drawn may be widely different. In the U.K., we have witnessed the following key events:

(1) a comparatively small, but nonetheless significant, investment in research into certain aspects of business crime by the Home Office (particularly in the late 1980s), with such work heavily geared at examining the policing implications;

(2) relatively little work initiated and conducted by academic institutions on their own;

(3) a historical legacy of short-term working groups commissioned to investigate high-profile aspects of business crime, with a trend now toward a more restricted number of permanent committees (albeit with the same ill-defined "advisory" remit);

(4) a recent growth in survey work to gauge the extent of business crime that was initiated by business itself but (most significantly) is now taken up by government;

(5) a growing interest in crime prevention by business trade associations (particularly those in retailing), often championed by a small number of industry leaders, but frequently *only* able to speak for major businesses;

(6) a similar small, but growing, interest by risk management and security experts in major businesses to promote professionalism and their links with academic research;

(7) a small nucleus of academic institutions (with Leicester University as the front runner) building valuable links with businesses and conducting research for them, but with the primary purpose of such work being normally to provide "live environments" for students in courses and with the results not always being published; and

(8) the first signs that Health and Safety authorities expect businesses whose employees face high risks of violence to demonstrate that they have taken "reasonable" actions to prevent such crime.

Many of these are positive signs, but, of course, any list of the *deficiencies* of this activity could be very much longer. Limiting this list to the most obvious, there has been little evidence of:

(1) any criminological enquiry into offenders' perspectives — such as who commits crime against businesses, why and how they do so (particularly their methods of disposing of stolen goods), and whether they engage in such offending as part of a criminal career that also embraces offenses against the personal victim;

(2) study and analysis of the response the police service makes to crimes against business and of the implications of this on police workloads;

(3) scrutiny of the effects of high victimization on local retailers and other service providers and the impact of the closure of such businesses on the wider community; and

(4) any significant effort to encourage, draw together, and disseminate the evaluation of crime prevention measures taken by business.

RESEARCH FINDINGS ON BUSINESS CRIME AND THEIR IMPLICATIONS ON THE POLICING OF THIS CRIME

The Lessons of Research

The program of activities described above encompasses a small, but not insignificant, body of research into crime against U.K. businesses. It is, of course, far from comprehensive. The range of crimes affecting business is large, and businesses' experience varies dramatically according to factors such the type of trade they engage in and their trading location. Despite these differences, some common findings can be drawn and are discussed below.

First, on average, and where comparisons can be drawn, businesses have proved to face much higher crime risks than households. For example, the Commercial Victimisation Survey (CVS) showed that the chances of retail or manufacturing premises being burgled was six times higher than for a home; that there were four times as many thefts of vehicles per hundred owners (comparing commercial and domestic owners); and that businesses were twice as likely to have their premises vandalized in some way (Mirrlees-Black and Ross, 1995).

Second, despite these higher risks, for most types of crime, businesses account for a relatively small proportion of total crime victimization. This is for the simple reason that there are so few businesses relative to domestic premises. The principal exception here is that the number of "witnessed" thefts by customers in the retail sector is enormous — extrapolated to number 5.8 million by the CVS (about the same as the total number of notifiable offenses recorded by the police annually in England and Wales). Indeed the "true" total has been estimated by the British Retail Consortium (BRC) to be of the order of about 16 million incidents if "unwitnessed" incidents were also to be taken into account (Speed et al., 1995).

Third, there is evidence of considerable crime concentration. The CVS found that 3% of retailers experienced 59% of all retail crimes, and that 8% of manufacturing premises accounted for 63% of the full crime count against this sector (Mirrlees-Black and Ross, 1995). The extent of concentration is, in fact, higher than that believed to affect the "personal/household" field in England and Wales — where the finding that only 4% of personal victims of crime account for 44% of victimization has initiated a radical new focus on the issue of repeat victimization.

Four, crime-recording systems within the police service are typically not capable of separately identifying crimes against business or their risk of victimization. Despite a significant investment in crime-analysis facilities, very few police forces are able to break down recorded crime according to the attributes of the victims of crime. In many respects, it is this weakness that has necessitated the investment in survey work, rather than low reporting levels (see Mirrlees-Black and Ross, 1995, and point eight below). By the same token, individual police forces do not have access to data on the numbers of businesses (or any other potential victims) in their areas that will enable them to calculate risk.

Five, crime is viewed as "a serious problem" by many businesses. Forty-four percent (44%) of retail respondents and 36% of manufacturers cited crime as a "fairly serious" or "serious" problem when asked by the CVS (Mirrlees-Black and Ross, 1995). Overall, crime was viewed by business as a relatively more serious concern than other traditional problems such as parking and "teenagers hanging around."

Six, the costs of crime victimization are high. The CVS showed that the cost per incident of crime to the retailer or manufacturer is considerably higher than for domestic premises. It also reported that the cost of crime born by manufacturers in England and Wales totaled £275 million for the manufacturing sector and £780 million for the retail industry. Both are high figures, but the comparable (second sweep) of the BRC survey put the total U.K. retail losses as much higher still — at some £2,149 million (equivalent to 21% of the profitability of U.K. retailers) (Speed et al., 1995). The main difference in the CVS and BRC figures is that the BRC surveys *also* put a figure on the scale of loss apportioned by retail companies to customer and staff theft (*not* simply their "shrinkage") although it was not directly witnessed by them.[1]

Seven, businesses typically invest heavily in crime prevention. The CVS found that the average annual running costs of security measures was £1,040 for retail premises and £2,070 for manufacturing — and put the total spending for the two sectors at £260 million and £180 million, respectively (Mirrlees-Black and Ross, 1995).

Eight, businesses tend to report a higher proportion of crime to the police than the "personal" victim. This tends to hold true for the majority of crimes where comparisons can be drawn — such as burglary, vandalism and thefts from vehicles — and is probably primarily attributable to the insurance requirements placed on businesses. Across the board, the CVS estimated that manufacturers reported an estimated 60% of crime to the police compared to 41% reported by householders. The figure for retailers was lower — an estimated 26% — because of the low number of customer thefts (shoplifting) reported by them.

Nine, a significant minority of victims are dissatisfied with the police. The CVS found that about a quarter of respondents (24% of retailers and 25% of manufacturers) were "very" or "fairly" dissatisfied with the way the police dealt with local crime problems (Mirrlees-Black and Ross, 1995).

The Implications of Recent Research on the Policing of Business Crime

The point has been made earlier that the trend towards victimization surveys in the U.K. started within the businesses community itself. The relevance of these survey findings have — quite properly — tended to be eclipsed by the more comprehensive coverage (and more appropriate "premises" methodology — see note 1) provided by the Commercial Victimisation Survey, but it is important not to lose sight of what persuaded the trade associations to mount such surveys in the first instance. Although never publicly expressed as such, it was done — quite bluntly — to "make the case" that crime against business is widespread and often more serious than supposed. While this message was certainly directed at businesses themselves, its primary target audience was the government and the police service as a signal to them that the problem *also needs their attention.*

In other words, the promotion of victimization surveys (and, indeed, much of the other national activity in the U.K.) has been part of a reaction against the perception — within the business community — that the authorities believe businesses can be held independently responsible for preventing and dealing with all crime in and around the workplace. A useful collection of papers on crime at work published in 1994 (Gill, 1994:4) had to revert to secondary sources to find this view expressed in reasonably direct terms: "While prepared to tender guidance through Crime Prevention Officers, the view officially expressed by a spokesman for the Association of Chief Police Officers is that 'industry must put its own house in order' and 'responsibility for the safeguarding of property is that of the owner.'"

An interesting investigation initiated by the Risk and Security Management Forum (RSMF) (see "Key Developments" in the Appendix) into the extent to which business crime warrants priority in the formal objectives of individual police forces (Willis and Beck, 1994) bears witness to this approach. While unable to obtain the formal objectives of all 43 forces in England and Wales, the researchers found references to business-related, commercial, or retail crime to be almost totally absent in the force objectives they examined.

The real facts about how much the police service assists business, and vice versa, could be hotly disputed: the police service could, quite fairly, point to the high priority they give, for example, to dealing with intruder alarm activations at business premises. There are undoubtedly a significant number of flourishing local partnerships between different business sectors and the police service, often developed by charismatic leaders in one or both parties. And indeed businesses could be found that could demonstrate their track record, and continued ability, to "keep their own house in order." Such a debate would be largely sterile. The point is that, in the U.K. currently, much of the effort of government advisory groups and trade associations is aimed at developing the cooperation between the police and business that is widely perceived to be at a low ebb.

The case for developing a stronger involvement by the police service in *some aspects* of business crime rests on a number of contentions. The most important themes (a total of seven) are discussed below.

First, not all businesses are big enough to afford to adequately protect themselves against crime. Those in smaller businesses often feel keenly that many in the public sector regard all businesses as profitable and see the smaller as able to protect themselves as well as the larger corporations do. In reality, of course, businesses with dedicated security personnel are very much the exception and the high number of business failures each year[2] indicate that many will be so pre-occupied with the business of survival that they will find it difficult to allocate significant thought, or the necessary financial resources, to crime prevention (despite the dividends that could accrue). There is no reliable means of assessing companies' "ability to protect themselves." However, the statistics on the sizes of businesses in the U.K. paint a picture of an economy where small businesses are major players. In the U.K., "micro" and "small" businesses —

defined as those with staffs of fewer than nine and 99 workers, respectively — account for 94% of all businesses and over 50% of non-government employment (DTI, 1995). In international terms, the U.K. has relatively fewer small firms that Germany, Japan and the U.S.A. Many of these smaller firms operate in a volatile environment where they are highly vulnerable to market pressures and closure (although, in the U.K. and U.S.A., it is worth noting that smaller firms are regularly net creators of jobs, with the impact of job losses in economic downturns being felt by larger businesses).

Second, victimization rates are high. Few will contest too vigorously the view that the limited resources of the criminal justice system should be directed to offer support to those who suffer most from crime. The data derived from the growing body of crime surveys in the business sector reinforce what many businesses have felt for some time: they, indeed, face risks of crime quite disproportionate to the personal individual.

Third, high-risk rates promise the police service much greater chances of apprehending offenders — with the promise of a "knock on" effect on domestic crime. Not only does recent survey research clearly indicate the very high risks faced by many businesses, but it also show that the levels of repeat victimization, too, are very much higher. So, for example, while the CVS shows that for burglary with entry, the percentage of victims is six times higher among both retailers and manufactures than it is for domestic premises, it shows too that — when repeats are taken into account — *the number of incidents is nine times higher for businesses* (Mirrlees-Black and Ross, 1995). This picture is little different for burglaries without entry and several other types of crime.

Fourth, crime against business — particularly retailers — is consistently shown to be at the start of the "learning curve" for those who engage in criminality. This is a lesson of a number of "cohort studies" that aim to identify what personal or social factors shape or steer people into crime (see, for example, West and Farrington, 1977). It implies that if effective steps can be taken to identify and divert offenders at an early stage of criminal careers, this may also have a considerable payback in reducing other, more serious, offenses that these individuals might otherwise "graduate" to.

Five, crime against business imposes a heavy load on the criminal justice system. While many businesses in the U.K. are, quite properly, "policing their own estate" independently of the criminal justice system, the scale of the demands they make on the police service can still be substantial. For example, in England and Wales, the offense of "theft from a shop" only accounts for some 23% of incidents in the overall number of "thefts," but this same offense consistently accounts for *nearly half of all persons dealt with for theft* (for the simple reason that the crime is seldom reported without the shopkeeper presenting the police with a suspect). Cutting these numbers by instituting preventive actions could present the criminal justice system with a considerable reduction in workload.

Six, fear and anxiety is experienced by very many who work in business — and has a "multiplier" effect. Those in the public sector typically tend to separate "personal victims" from the "corporate victim," and sympathies inevitably tend to lie with the former. This overlooks the obvious point that the employees of corporate victims (of businesses, and indeed local authorities, hospitals and schools) *are also individuals*. The evidence available indicates that these employees do not feel that crime against business is qualitatively different or that the anxiety and fear that crime may present in the workplace is by any means remote. Burglaries in small businesses have been found to have an impact on employees in much the same way as they affect domestic victims — bringing the same sense of invasion of private space (Johnston et al., 1994) — and, of course, affect a greater number of people than a domestic crime. Moreover, research into the impact of crime against small shops has demonstrated how news of such crime spreads quickly, having a significant impact on perceptions of local safety (Hibberd and Shapland, 1993).

Finally, crime against businesses (especially the smaller ones who are the main employers) threatens their existence and, thus, jobs along with the social fabric of local communities. This is a concern that planning authorities and others in the U.K. are now thinking about much more seriously. In particular, the concern is that when faced with serious and persistent crime, the larger, more profitable businesses can move on to more secure environments. The smaller players generally do not have this option.

BUILDING THE BRIDGE BETWEEN BUSINESSES AND THE CRIMINOLOGIST

This short review of some of the developments relating to business crime in the U.K. will convey mixed messages to those who believe that there should be greater involvement by criminologists in this area. Despite the growing evidence of the substantial crime risks faced by many in business, the services of criminologists have patently not been called on *by business*. Generally their involvement to date has been restricted to executing research paid for by the government and looking primarily at aspects of business crime that affect public policing. Despite this, there are reasonable grounds for believing that, in the U.K., the scope for further work is considerable.

These "grounds" might be broadly summarized along the following lines. Awareness of crime among business is now relatively high, owing, in no small part, to the messages conveyed by the application of victimization survey methods. The message being promoted by many business leaders is that crime is a manageable problem — yielding one of the most accessible routes available to many businesses to restore profitability (CBI/Crime Concern, 1990). The approaches advocated involve critical analysis of crime data, the development of solutions specifically tailored to the presenting problem, regular monitoring and staged evaluations: in short, much of the "stock in trade" of those implementing situational crime prevention. Added to this, there is a significant movement that challenges the assumption — whether real or imagined — that businesses should be able to deal with their own problems in isolation from the police service and other parts of the criminal justice system.

The scope for activity exists in various forms, three of which are listed below. Within each form, the question of "who pays" is a key dimension that, in turn, raises critical — and unresolved — questions about the respective responsibilities of business and government in dealing with crime.

Work Where Business Crime and Public Policing Meet

This is a sphere of work where criminologists in the U.K. have established a considerable track record, where the present reaction against the philosophy that "businesses must look after themselves" is likely to create new demands on their expertise, and which can serve as a useful springboard for working directly with business. Funding for this sort of work has tended (without much debate) to fall to the government and other public service agencies who are well used to dealing with the criminologist.

From the perspective of this paper — which focuses on businesses "as victims" — there are a number of priorities. There is an urgent need to develop police systems for crime recording and analysis — which, in the past, have proved as poorly suited to identifying businesses as victims as they have in identifying repeat victimization — so the police can effectively monitor risks to different types of victims. There is a need to develop our understanding of how those committing crime against the business target operate — from their initial selection of targets through to their actions in finding markets for stolen goods. Given the many innovative local partnerships between police and local businesses, much would be gained if these issues could be subjected to considered evaluation. And, of course, more light needs to be shed on the role of small business in the social fabric of local communities and on how crime can affect their operation and survival.

Work with Groups of Businesses Affected by Crime

In the U.K., the scope for work is clearly opening up in the direction of working with groups of businesses affected by crime. As described above, in the last three or four years several trade associations have started to develop survey work. Some have gone further and actively sought to promote crime-prevention partnership activities between their members and with the police. Across the board there is evidence of a greater readiness to share experience and the evaluations of preventive activities (although not often in the form required by academe). In these limited numbers of cases, trade associations, banks and even charities have proved willing to fund activities, although often with the expectation that their "investment" will have the effect of eliciting more support from the government and the criminal justice system.

The scope for further work remains. Despite their progress, victimization surveys have in the main focused on the retail industry and, to a lesser extent, manufacturing — leaving the impact of crime on many other sectors unexplored. Criminological expertise is an essential requisite to ensure such work is carried out to the necessary standard.

Work Directly with, or for, the Single Business

The ability to draw on specialist skill in crime management is a luxury only the biggest businesses can afford. Undoubtedly, the expertise and professionalism of security practitioners serving larger companies has developed a great deal in recent years. Indeed, so too has the standard of the consultancy support on which major businesses occasionally draw. But, in the U.K., relationships between single businesses and criminologist remain a rarity.

Opportunities clearly exist on this front, but — from the perspective of the single business — the criminologist will more often than not lack the familiarity with business methods and systems (such as retail EPoS and EFTPoS systems[3]) that are central in providing both the opportunities for crime and its prevention, which the commercial consultant can furnish. The question of "who pays" is also much more clearly defined. In the final reckoning, businesses are not interested in understanding crime as an objective in its own right — unlike the criminologist — but only as a means to prevent it. Many businesses may be willing to support criminological enquiries into their activities and problems if they are asked to do no more than serve as "test beds" for research. But to the extent they are required to pay for criminological expertise, they will expect those providing this expertise to act as active practitioners in solving their problems rather than as impartial observers or evaluators. How far criminologists themselves will want to assume this mantle is uncertain.

CONCLUSION

In sum, this commentator's assessment is that U.K. businesses are increasingly open to working with the criminologist and that a small, but growing, number of businesses recognize the direct two-way relationship between their own activities and those within the communities in which they operate. Businesses are likely to be increasingly receptive to the lessons of situational crime prevention, with its promise to reduce the impact of crime on their business — even to the extent of paying for such expertise! But, beyond this, their social responsibility will (with probably some justification) wane. The notion that governments should "own" the responsibility for the economic and social causes of criminality is one to which business (like virtually every other group in society) is strongly attached.

* * *

NOTES

1. Mirrlees-Black and Ross (1995) provided a useful summary of the relative merits of the two different methodologies for measuring business crime: "premises" surveys (like the CVS) and "Head Office surveys (like those of the BRC). They argue that the "premises" approach yields more reliable estimates of victimization, but that "Head Office" approaches are probably more appropriate for measuring full costs.

2. There were 3.6 million businesses in the U.K. at the end of 1993. During 1994, some 422,000 (12%) closed. The number of business start-ups in 1994 (446,000) exceeded the number of closures, but the short lifespan of many businesses is not widely understood by many in the public sector.

3. "EPoS" stands for "Electronic Point of Sale" while "EFTPoS" stands for "Electronic Funds Transfer at Point of Sale."

REFERENCES

Austin, C. (1988). *The Prevention of Robbery at Building Society Branches.* Crime Prevention Series, Paper No. 14. London, UK: Home Office.

Bamfield, J. (1994). *National Survey of Retail Theft and Security, 1994.* Moulton Park, Northampton, UK: Nene College.

Brantingham, P.L. and P.J. Brantingham (1995) "Criminality of Place: Crime Generators and Crime Attractors." *European Journal of Criminal Policy and Research* 3:5-26.

Brooks, C. and C. Cross. (1996). *Retail Crime Costs, 1994/5 Survey.* London, UK: British Retail Consortium.

Buckle, A., D.P. Farrington, J. Burrows, M. Speed, and T. Burns-Howell. (1992). "Measuring Shoplifting by Repeated Systematic Counting." *Security Journal* 3:137-145.

Burrows, J. (1988). *Retail Crime: Prevention through Crime Analysis.* Crime Prevention Series, Paper No. 11. London, UK: Home Office.

—— (1991). *Making Crime Prevention Pay: Initiatives from Business.* Crime Prevention Series, Paper No. 27. London, UK: Home Office.

—— and M. Speed (1994). *Retail Crime Costs, 1992/3 Survey.* London, UK: British Retail Consortium.

Confederation of British Industry(CBI)/Crime Concern (1990). *Crime: Managing the Business Risk.* London, UK: CBI.

Department of Trade and Industry (DTI) (1995). *Small Firms in Britain, 1995.* London, UK: Her Majesty's Stationery Office.

Ekblom, P. (1986). *The Prevention of Shop Theft: An Approach through Crime Analysis.* Crime Prevention Series Paper No. 5. London, UK: Home Office.

—— (1987). *Preventing Robberies at Sub-Post Offices: An Evaluation of a Security Initiative.* Crime Prevention Series Paper No. 9. London, UK: Home Office.

—— and F. Simon (1988). *Crime Prevention and Racial Harassment in Asian-Run Small Shops: The Scope for Prevention.* Crime Prevention Series Paper No. 15. London, UK: Home Office.

Farrington, D.P. and J. Burrows (1993). "Did Shoplifting Really Decrease?" *British Journal of Criminology* 33:57-69.

Gill, M. (ed.) (1994). *Crime at Work: Studies in Security and Crime Prevention.* Leicester, UK: Perpetuity Press.

Health and Safety Executive (HSE) (1993). *Preventing Violence to Staff in Banks and Building Societies.* Sudbury, UK: HSE.

—— (1995). *Preventing Violence to Retail Staff.* London, UK: HSE Books.

Hibberd, M. and J. Shapland (1993). *Violent Crime in Small Shops.* London, UK: Police Foundation.

Johnston, V., M. Leitner, J. Shapland, and P. Wiles (1994). *Crime on Industrial Estates.* Crime Prevention Series Paper No. 54. London, UK: Home Office.

Levi, M. (1988). *The Prevention of Fraud*. Crime Prevention Series Paper No. 17. London, UK: Home Office.

—— P. Bissel and T. Richardson (1991). *The Prevention of Cheque and Credit Card Fraud*. Crime Prevention Series Paper No. 26. London, UK: Home Office.

Mayhew, P., D. Elliott and L. Dowds (1989). *The 1988 British Crime Survey*. Home Office Research Study No. 111. London, UK: Home Office.

Mirrlees-Black, C. and A. Ross (1995). *Crime against Retail and Manufacturing Premises: Findings from the 1994 Commercial Victimisation Survey*. Home Office Research Study No. 146. London, UK: Home Office.

Phillips, S. and R. Cochrane (1988). *Crime and Nuisance in the Shopping Centre: A Case Study in Crime Prevention*. Crime Prevention Series Paper No. 16. London, UK: Home Office.

Southall, D. and P. Ekblom (1986). *Designing for Car Security: Towards a Crime-Free Car*. Crime Prevention Series Paper No. 4. London, UK: Home Office.

Speed, M., J. Burrows and J. Bamfield (1995). *Retail Crime Costs, 1993/4 Survey* London, UK: British Retail Consortium.

Tilley, N. (1993). *The Prevention of Crime against Small Businesses: The Safer Cities Experience*. Crime Prevention Series Paper No. 45. London, UK: Home Office.

U.K. Home Office (1988). *Report of the Working Group on the Costs of Crime*. London, UK: Home Office Standing Conference on Crime Prevention.

West, D.J. and D.P. Farrington (1977). *The Delinquent Way of Life*. Cambridge Studies in Criminology. London, UK: Heinemann.

Willis, A. and A. Beck (1994). *An Analysis of Policing Charters*. Leicester, UK: Centre for the Study of Public Order, Leicester University.

Wood, J., G. Wheelwright and J. Burrows (forthcoming). *Tackling Crime against Small Businesses: The Small Business and Crime Initiative*. Swindon, UK: Crime Concern.

APPENDIX

Key Developments Relating to Business Criminology in the U.K., 1986-96

1986

• "The Prevention of Shop Theft" (Ekblom, 1986) — a Home Office[A1] analysis of shop theft in London's Oxford Street that focused on the considerable police effort directed at dealing with shoplifters at one major store, questioning its merchandising policies

• "Designing for Car Security: Towards a Crime-Free Car" (Southall and Ekblom, 1986) — a Home Office examination of how technological improvements could reduce car crime

1987

• "Preventing Robberies at Sub-Post Offices" (Ekblom, 1987) — a Home Office evaluation of the security precautions taken at post offices to prevent robbery attacks

1988

• "Crime and Racial Harassment in Asian-Run Small Shops" (Ekblom and Simon, 1988) — assessed these problems in shops in two areas of London

• "Retail Crime: Prevention Through Crime Analysis" (Burrows, 1988) — an account of the crime analysis techniques employed by a major chain of electrical stores to institute preventive actions, published by the Home Office

• "Report of the Home Office Working Party on the Costs of Crime" (U.K. Home Office, 1988) — included the results of a small survey of the costs of crime victimization among the top 100 U.K. businesses

• "Crime and Nuisance in the Shopping Centre" (Phillips and Cochrane, 1988) — Home Office-funded examination of crime in a Midlands shopping center

• "The Prevention of Fraud" (Levi, 1988) — Home Office-funded account of the scale and characteristics of the problem of credit card fraud and ways of reducing loss

• "The Prevention of Robbery at Building Society Branches" (Austin, 1988) — the Home Office explored how to prevent attacks at these mutually owned banks

1989

• Evidence from the third British Crime survey (Mayhew et al., 1989) pointed out that seven out of ten thefts of workers' property take place in the workplace

1990

• Report of the Confederation of British Industry (CBI) and Crime Concern Working Party on Business Crime[A2] published — promoted the need to consider crime as a "mainstream" business issue, principally through "crime audits" and the application of normal management disciplines to its control (including analysis, monitoring and evaluation)

• Establishment of the Risk and Security Management Forum (RSMF) to promote the professionalism of risk and security management, to share information and to monitor and evaluate new ideas and approaches — set up by a group of senior security professionals in the private and public sector

1991

• "Making Crime Prevention Pay: Initiatives from Business" (Burrows, 1991) — a Home Office-funded account of the cost-effective actions taken by a range of large businesses (and groups of businesses) to tackle crime

• "The Prevention of Cheque and Credit Card Fraud" (Levi et al., 1991) picked up the preventive lessons from the Home Office's earlier (Levi, 1988) work (see above)

1992

• Publication of the evaluation of the first of a number of experiments in reducing shoplifting (Buckle et al., 1992)

1993

• Publication of policy advice from the Health and Safety Executive to deal with violence to staff in the financial services sector (HSE, 1993)

• The British Retail Consortium (BRC)[A3] set up their Retail Crime Initiative — aimed at collecting data from retailers on their experience of crime and encouraging collaborative action against crime

• The Home Office set up the Retail Action Group (RAG) — an advisory group to the National Board for Crime Prevention (which remains in existence)

• The Forum of Private Businesses started to collect data on the crime problems experienced by its members

• "The Prevention of Crime Against Small Businesses" (Tilley, 1993) — a Home Office summary of both the actions taken by the government's "Safer City" schemes to prevent crimes against businesses and their impact

• "Did Shoplifting Really Decrease?" (Farrington and Burrows, 1993) — used victimization data to challenge police crime statistics showing a dramatic decrease in the offense of "theft from shops"

• "Violent Crime in Small Shops" (Hibberd and Shapland, 1993) — documented the serious problems faced by such units through localized crime surveys in London and the West Midlands.

1994

• "Retail Crime Costs, 1992/3" (Burrows and Speed, 1994) — the first broad-ranging victimization survey of the retail sector (via Head Offices) by the BRC

• "Retail Shrinkage" (Bamfield, 1994) — another major survey of crime in the retail sector

• Decision by the Home Office to mount their first victimization survey of businesses, focusing on 3,000 business premises

• RAG started to issue a series of crime prevention guides for small businesses, with the first on robbery

• "Crime on Industrial Estates" (Johnston et al., 1994) — a partially Home Office-funded description of the crime problems faced by manufacturers and industrial units on five industrial estates in the north of England

• "Crime at Work" (Gill, 1994) — a collection of fourteen studies by academic and independent researchers into aspects of crime in the workplace

1995

• Publication of policy advice from the Health and Safety Executive to deal with violence to staff in the retail sector (HSE, 1995)

• Publication of the results of the 1994 Commercial Victimisation Survey (CVS) by the Home Office (Mirrlees-Black and Ross, 1995) — covering crime experience in the retail and manufacturing sectors

• "Retail Crime Costs, 1993/4" (Speed et al., 1995) — the second sweep of the retail (Head Office) victimization survey by the BRC

• Establishment of the Small Business and Crime Initiative — a three-year action research program aimed at understanding the crime problems faced by small businesses in two project areas, including implementing crime prevention activity there with an evaluation (Wood et al., forthcoming)

1996

• "Retail Crime Costs, 1994/5" (Brooks and Cross, 1996) — the third sweep of the Head Office-focused crime survey by the BRC

Appendix Notes

A1. The Home Office is the British government department responsible for crime and policing policy. Two sections within it conduct, or fund, criminological research: (1) the Research and Planning Unit (now the Research and Statistics Directorate), which, for example, conducts the British Crime Survey; and (2) the Crime Prevention Unit's Police Research Group, which has initiated many of the focused studies listed here.

A2. The CBI represents the U.K.'s major employers. Crime Concern is a major charity set up by the government to promote crime prevention.

A3. The BRC is a trade association representing — directly or through its links with other retail groups — 90% of U.K. retailers.

WILL CRIME PREVENTION EVER BE A BUSINESS PRIORITY?

by Dennis Challinger

Corporate Security & Loss Prevention, Coles Myer Ltd

Abstract: *Business profits could be enhanced if losses due to crime were reduced. However, business does not usually focus on managing down its crime losses even though it takes crime in general quite seriously. This occurs because business people are generally ignorant of how crime prevention can benefit them and because it is difficult to quantify losses from crime (especially in the critical area of internal crime). Without solid figures on losses, the crucial cost-benefit calculations for implementing a crime prevention initiative in a business setting cannot be completed. Actual experiences of promoting crime prevention in business are used to canvass difficulties and issues that arise in practice. Business will act against crime affecting them when it becomes demonstrably major or visible or when economics dictates that action is necessary. It will also occur to avoid negative customer reactions, to ensure customer safety, or to improve staff morale. The ensuing action would be called crime prevention by a criminologist, but a business leader would simply call it good business. Fruitful areas for business and criminology to work positively together include reducing opportunities for crime, giving clear leadership to staff on crime matters and improving the workplace culture.*

Businesses exist to make profits. Businesses obviously set priorities that are oriented toward increasing those profits, and they generally do that by finding new or better ways of doing more business. As it becomes harder to find those new or better ways, businesses usually try to reduce their costs because that improves their percentage profit. They tend not to focus on reducing the losses they suffer from crime, a strategy that would also have an immediate positive effect on their profits. This may be because, even when they can very accurately measure their other costs, all too often the extent of their losses from crime is unknown.

I do not make these statements lightly, but as a result of having worked as an applied criminologist in two different profit-making companies, four years in the telecommunications industry (Telecom Australia) and three years to date in retailing (Coles Myer Ltd). This paper reflects some of my experiences and draws upon academic research that has helped me advance the crime prevention perspective in the business[1] environment.

BUSINESS ATTITUDES TO CRIME

It would be wrong to suggest that business does not take crime seriously. No business would fail to use some physical security measures to protect its fixed assets. However, a notable event might be necessary to ensure that adequate attention is paid even to physical security. For instance, in 1987, an offender gained access to underground telephone cables in central Sydney, severed many of them in various locations and caused massive disruption to voice and data communications. This accelerated Telecom's efforts to secure manholes and pit covers in city streets.

On a community level, Australian business has been a generous supporter of crime prevention initiatives such as Neighbourhood Watch, Crime Stoppers and the Safety House program. Businesses have also supported initiatives geared toward preventing particular crime problems affecting them. For instance, Telecom provided schools with project materials encouraging responsible telephone usage and discouraging vandalism, and Coles Myer, with other retailers, funded the introduction of an anti-shoplifting program — "Not Bought, You're Caught" — developed by the police and youth groups and now used in hundreds of Australian schools.

It is when business falls victim to crime, however, that its attitude becomes less forthright. While it is quite realistic for business to acknowledge that it cannot avoid suffering some crime, why are its attempts to control or prevent those crimes the exceptions rather than the rule? There are numerous reasons, but I would argue that the main one is that understanding crime is not something about which business people learn.

It is not unreasonable to describe business executives, engineers, merchants, or accountants as ignorant about crime prevention. The topic is not generally a major part of their professional education. Indeed, a student of retailing, using a typical and prominent college text of over 600 pages (Levy and Weitz, 1995), will find only five pages dealing with inventory shrinkage, theft and loss prevention.

Shapland (1995) suggested that using more recognizable "business phrases," such as loss control or risk management, would focus business on its crime losses, but they are euphemisms for crime prevention. The phrase must be introduced into the business setting. At Telecom, my job title purposely included the words "crime prevention," allowing me to quickly establish that my responsibilities were to prevent or reduce losses to the company from crime or misconduct.

Without analyzing the specifics of crime and its prevention, it is not difficult to see how business actively, and perhaps unwittingly, provides opportunities for people to be dishonest. Two real-life examples illustrate this. The first is a practice best described as *application fraud*. It occurs when a person arranges for the installation or activation of a telephone service by verbally providing fraudulent identifying details over a telephone to a Telecom operator. The service is installed and unlimited credit is therefore provided to a voice over a telephone. When the first bill for the telephone usage is issued, it is not paid; and, invariably, it is found that no one at the address where the phone was installed will admit to having the name provided by the voice that had initiated the service.

The second is the practice of *refund fraud*, a major problem for Coles Myer and retailers around the world who offer customers the ability to refund merchandise they had purchased but with which they were later not happy. Not only does this allow unscrupulous people to use, for instance, an expensive ball gown once and then return it — an effective free hire (rental) — but it also allows offenders to fraudulently claim a full refund for goods they have stolen, sometimes from within the store in which they seek the refund.

Each of these two opportunities was offered to customers for perfectly sound business reasons. The first provides hassle-free service quickly and conveniently while the second provides a guarantee of satisfaction that should attract customers to shop at particular stores. The possibility that these opportunities will be abused and that some customers (and staff) are dishonest appears beyond the comprehension of some business people. However, believing that the customer is always right is criminologically naive. What a criminologist in business can do is to highlight the ways in which existing or planned systems or procedures may provide opportunities for the dishonest.

In practice, business people may simply not see the potential risks that a criminologist might see. A good example is provided by Telecom's introduction in 1989 of the Phonecard, a plastic debit card used instead of cash in pay phones. The engineers developed the Phonecard technology in a highly secure environment with restricted access control, requiring all technical data to remain on site. They believed that these safeguards would prevent unauthorized reverse engineering that could compromise the product. However, a criminological consideration of the Phonecard project identified a major crime risk arising from the card reader, the key to the technology, being readily accessible in every public pay phone cabinet. Within weeks of the Phonecard's release, a pay phone cabinet was stripped of the telephone unit incorporating the card-reader, and others followed. Fake or re-charged Phonecards did start to circulate during 1993, but a technical fix quickly made them useless.

The Phonecard provided other new public crime possibilities. First, it provided a new target for petty thieves in the small shops and outlets from which Phonecards were sold. However, any losses resulting from these thefts were borne by those shops, not Telecom. Second, it allowed confidence tricksters to sell recycled cards that they claimed to have recharged in some way. The losers, in these cases, were the people who greedily bought worthless cards at a big discount.

This illustrates how a business development can actually and unwittingly generate crime, a difficult proposition for some business people to grasp, but a proposition they need to acknowledge. A recent example is provided by Carter et al. (1995), who found that promotional activities for certain products in a retail store not only stimulated customers to buy more of them, but also encouraged thieves to steal more of them. In fact, thefts increased by a greater percentage than sales.

INTERNAL CRIME

It is not possible to discuss crime against business without referring to crimes committed by employees, usually called internal crime. Coles Myer is a unique company in Australia for publicly acknowledging this problem as long ago as 1986, when its Annual Report (Coles Myer Ltd, 1986:6) stated that 1,450 of its then 139,243 employees "were detected stealing from the company" during the previous year. While it is no longer company policy to publish specific figures, the company remains active in addressing this problem.

This is not true for many other companies that seem to need convincing that internal crime is a major problem. They ignore the large volume of published research on the topic of workplace deviance (see, for instance, Hollinger and Clark, 1983; Hogan and Hogan, 1989; Analoui and Kakabadse, 1991). They also ignore industry-sponsored research showing the extent of the problem. For instance, annual surveys of American supermarket employees' behavior have reported consistently high levels of internal crime over the last five years and, in 1995, reported 43% of the staff queried admitted to stealing cash or property at work (Boye et al., 1995).

The contribution of internal crime to the financial losses from crime in any business can only be estimated. The retailing industry probably has the best estimates because it conducts regular stocktakes of inventory that quantify unexplained losses and, after analysis of other business data, allow sources of those losses to be estimated. The best Australian estimates are that 40% of retailers' losses result from internal theft and deviance, a further 40% from external theft and the remainder from what is called paperwork error (administrative errors with pricing, invoicing and the like). A higher estimate for internal theft would be expected in a workplace where there is a workplace culture that effectively condones theft. This is not uncommon as research shows that many of those who steal from work do not regard themselves as thieves (Altheide et al., 1978) — a most important consideration for a crime prevention practitioner.

Distinguishing between internal and external crime is not always clear. For instance, internal thieves can be involved in what are thought to be external problems. Consider the two frauds introduced above. An application fraud could occur as a result of a Telecom operator having telephone services installed in locations requested by friends or others by simply inserting fictional details into the system, the bills remaining unpaid because no such person exists.[2] In the refund fraud case, a store employee could manufacture details of a non-existent request for a refund and remove the cash from the register.[3]

The involvement of employees in both internal and external deviance is further illustrated by a commentator on the American fast-food business who stated that "90% of all financial losses are on the inside," and "approximately 64% of armed robbery experiences involve current or former employees" (Sympson, 1995:80). Obviously, initiating crime prevention programs that focus on internal crime would be beneficial in any business, and they should be relatively easy to implement as they are entirely in-house. However, before that is done, a business must acknowledge that internal deviance is a major problem for it.

QUANTIFYING LOSSES

Getting business to acknowledge that a crime problem exists at all is the first hurdle for a crime prevention practitioner to clear. Then it is necessary to get agreement that it makes good business sense to do something about it. In practical terms, these comprise the first three steps recommended for a situational crime prevention project — collecting data, analyzing conditions, and suggesting preventive approaches (Clarke, 1992:5). For business, the crucial data are the losses suffered by business as a result of the crime occurring and more pointedly, the costs of doing something about it.

Quantifying the losses that a business suffers from crime is actually very difficult. Even in retailing, where periodic stocktakes of inventory provide possibly the best measures of loss in any industry, those measures are out of date insofar as they reflect what may have happened up to six months earlier. A more reliable measure of losses from retail stores is to count stock very frequently, an approach used in some criminological research (Masuda, 1992; Buckle et al., 1992). I have tried using the value of empty packaging found discarded in a store to approximate crime losses there, but that has not been fruitful. This is mainly because the measure only reflects a particular sort of theft, where the contents of the packaging can be immediately well concealed by the thief, and that sort of theft does not constitute a stable fraction of all thefts.

Most of the time, the best that can be done in any business is to estimate the losses from crime. For instance, the cost of the telephone application frauds are buried in the bad debts reported in the company's financial records. However, there are some data available to make a sound estimate of the impact of the offense. They include admissions by some householders that they used false names to avoid payment, successful convictions for fraud and records from known addresses where successive customers who cannot be located have had telephone services installed.

The full impact of refund frauds is similarly embedded in a retail store's records of its refunding activity, the vast majority of which are quite legitimate. There two good estimates can be made on the basis of successful convictions of refund fraudsters: (1) identified instances when a person has appeared a number of times for refunds in a short period of time; and (2) oral evidence from the sales floor of refund applicants leaving hurriedly when their identification is sought. Unfortunately, these store-based data are not able to be used scientifically because they are intermittent and depend on store staff faithfully recording incidents.

When it comes to putting dollar values to those losses, there are further complications. Take the example of what are known as telephone call-selling scams. In these, a person will fraudulently apply for a telephone service and then allow others to make international phone calls from those services on payment to them, often in cash, at a rate much discounted from the official tariff. When a bill arrives, the person absconds. If the unpaid bills amounted to say $200,000, the criminologist would count that amount as the loss to the business — after all, the person, if detected, would be charged with a fraud for that value. A communications engineer might argue that the loss is only the 50 cents of electricity required to make the calls. The account executive might argue that some of the callers would have made their calls (probably shorter in duration) anyway, so the loss may be only half that amount.

In the retail area, the same sort of perceptual problem may exist. Retail accountants assess the value of merchandise at its cost price so that, if a garment is bought for $50 to sell at $75 and it is stolen, the accountant sees that as a loss of $50, while the criminologist counts it as a $75 loss. If the thief then makes a fraudulent refund at the same store, the loss to the retail business is certainly $75, but now the garment is back in stock so there is no apparent loss of merchandise.

Particular problems are caused when attempts are made to measure trends in losses because invariably some change or other will have occurred, meaning that there is no longer a common basis for comparison. For instance, a retailer might institute new procedures to measure its waste (that is, soiled or damaged merchandise) more accurately, which, in turn, reduces the level of its unknown loss or shrinkage.

A criminologist considering the cost of crime might also look beyond immediate costs and consider increased insurance premiums, higher costs for additional security and internal controls, decreased employee activity, lowered morale, decreased service quality and damage to the company image. Additional costs and problems can be generated when staff members are dismissed as a result of their deviance — the cost of replacing them if they were highly trained (which can be up to one third of their annual salaries), increased workloads for other workers until the replacement worker starts, lowered morale from unsettled employees when staff turnover is high and possible adverse publicity. All of these can interfere with efficiency, worker morale and, ultimately, profits.

There are, of course, also costs to the community that flow from crime against business. For government, there are losses in taxes and the costs involved in the criminal justice system dealing with business crime. For the public, there are higher prices and possibly fewer employment opportunities because of business failures and the lack of investment in future business.

FOCUSING BUSINESS ATTENTION ON CRIME PROBLEMS

The difficulty in quantifying the losses suffered by any company from any particular crime makes life most difficult for the crime prevention practitioner. This is primarily because business will only consider a crime prevention initiative if its cost-benefit ratio can be clearly demonstrated. From experience, I have discovered that taking the high moral ground is not sufficient. At the end of the day, if it costs more to implement a crime prevention initiative than the costs of losses resulting from the crime in question, the initiative will simply not be considered.

In general, if the costs of any crime against the business are demonstrably huge, even though their exact quantum cannot be agreed, a crime prevention initiative may be considered. Other factors that may cause business to decide to tackle a crime problem include visibility, economic indicators, negative consumer reaction, customer safety and staff morale, each of which is discussed below.

Visibility

Some business crime problems become so evident to the world at large that they simply cannot be ignored. As an example, vandalized and unusable street pay phones were a highly visible problem in Australia in the 1980s. Apart from the negative and critical publicity this attracted, the levels of customer service were poor and repair costs had soared to over

$18 million (in Australian dollars) annually. The problem was substantially addressed by forming a dedicated unit within Telecom with the sole responsibility for the pay phone business that included initiating measures to prevent criminal damage to street pay phones (see Challinger, 1991; Bridgeman, this volume). Not only were maintenance and repair costs reduced to around 20% of the previous figure, but increased use of the pay phones -because they were now operational, clean and intact — generated a significant increase in revenue.

Sometimes the visibility of crimes suffered by some business is enough to cause other businesses to take preventive action. For instance, a retailer may learn through the media of an increase in ram raiding, where offenders crash vehicles through display windows of stores, load up goods and quickly speed off. That may lead the retailer to install protective bollards outside its own stores to prevent their falling victim to ram raiding in the future. The role that the media plays in making crime problems visible to the public and, therefore, to business is obviously most valuable.

Economic Indicators

The economic indicators by which businesses are usually assessed include their profits, sales or revenue figures and their share price. Diminishing profits are arguably the greatest concern to a business, and criminologists have enthusiastically drawn attention to the positive impact on profit that can flow from reducing losses. For example, D'Addario (1989:2) commented that "crime prevention is rapidly becoming a priority in the private sector...[with] businesses increasingly rely on loss control to protect profit margins." The same sentiment has been expressed about internal crime: "economics seems to have forced the issue. Management is simply demanding that internal thievery be reduced...[I]t has become a huge issue because of deteriorating profit margins" (Sympson, 1995:76).

In practice, many businesses have yet to appreciate the benefits of managing their losses down. That will change with the implementation of more crime prevention initiatives that can be shown to bring a financial gain. The introduction in 1994 of a new Coles Myer policy to address their refund-fraud problem is a case in point. All cash refunds constitute negative sales, and fraudulent refunds constitute real loss. When it became plain that those losses were significant, even though the quantum of losses from those frauds could only be estimated, an initiative to prevent the frauds occurring was obviously needed. So the company introduced a new policy allowing cash refunds to be given only when a receipt for the goods was provided (see Challinger, 1996). Over the next year, both the number of fraudulent refunds and the amounts refunded dropped to about 22% of their previous levels. After a further year, the number of reported refund frauds had stabilized at about the 23% level, but the total value of the frauds had dropped further to about 17% of the pre-policy level. So, apart from there being fewer fraudulent refunds, they were also of a much lower average value. In addition, more of the legitimate refunds were concluding with an exchange of merchandise, meaning the sales revenue remained within the business.

No company likes to see a decline in its share price — a critical measure of a company's well-being — and some business people fear that publicity about crime or misconduct will adversely affect it. The research suggests otherwise. For instance, Lukawitz and Steinbart (1995) found no evidence that investors reacted negatively to hearing about employee fraud that became public. I believe this may be because the public, or at least investors, may actually be pleased if a company is known to be actively dealing with employee deviance. However, when the company itself has engaged in some misconduct that has become publicly known, a fall in share price may occur. This may occur primarily because of lost reputation, not because of perceived incompetent management, increased future criminal penalties, or possible loss of future profits (Karpoff and Lott, 1993).

Negative Customer Reaction

Customer reaction strongly influences service industries, such as retailing and telecommunications. Yet many business executives believe that focusing on crime may upset customers. The telephone application fraud described earlier was not immediately addressed after it was identified as a source of loss because the company suggested that legitimate customers would find a more rigorous application procedure off-putting. It was also argued that considerable negative customer reaction would arise if the costs of the preventive procedures were passed on to them and, if those costs were greater than the total losses, it would be bad business anyway.

It is easy to attribute views to customers that they may not have. For instance, some merchants believe that retail customers are, or would be, put off by security equipment in stores to prevent shoplifting. The research suggests otherwise (see, for instance, Hastings, 1981; Dawson, 1993; Dougherty, 1993). An excellent recent example of customer acceptance of crime prevention initiatives is provided by Gorman (1996), who describes how proactive patrolling of American retailer WalMart's parking lots has not only met with positive customer approval, but that approval has translated into a 12% increase in night-time patronage and an increase of 13% in night-time profits. These patrols also achieved the intended decrease in recorded offenses in those locations.

There are, of course, a number of possible negative responses by customers to a focus on crime and its prevention. They could see it as harsh, as casting aspersions on honest customers, or as illustrating a company's previous incompetence at dealing with its crime problems, especially internal crime. My view is that customers are more likely to react negatively to a retailer who has little security in place and to object to paying more for merchandise to cover losses they believe the retailer is actively allowing. Establishing customers' views will be a necessary part of retail crime prevention work in the future.

Customer Fear and Safety

A particular issue for the retailing industry is the safety of customers. Most retailers will react quickly to situations where shoppers may feel unsafe and will work towards increasing customer perception of safety in their stores. A good example of this is the "Police Beat" program in the Australian State of Queensland. It involved opening fully operational police stations in shopfronts within shopping centers (malls), aimed precisely at improving the community feeling about personal safety and reducing community fear.

The "Police Beat" initiative followed research (Research and Evaluation Branch/Community Development and Crime Prevention Unit, 1993) showing over 60% of respondents were afraid of crime while in shopping centers and 90% thought a police presence in shopping centers was either essential or positive. The Police Beat program has achieved considerable success. A 1994 evaluation (Queensland Police Service, 1994) showed a decrease from 175 reported thefts, 50 vandalism offenses and five assaults in a three-month period for a number of malls prior to the initiative to 34, 22 and zero, respectively, twelve months later.

In the 1994 survey by America's Research Group, 14% of the surveyed Americans reported they were likely to shop less in shopping centers in the future because of fear of crime (Longo, 1994). Whether those fears were justified is not the issue. If shoppers stay away, retailers make fewer sales and less profit. Some time ago, market research by 7-Eleven stores found that women shoppers avoided their stores because they found them "dingy and unsafe" (Levy and Weitz, 1995:109). This led to the company promptly changing their store layouts at some cost, but the patronage they were seeking increased.

Customer safety is always taken into account in retailers' construction and refurbishment programs for shopping centers. While they would probably not recognize the phrase Crime Prevention Through Environmental Design (CPTED), they invariably adopt that approach. Thus, they provide well lit and open parking lots, sturdy but attractive store fixtures and focused activities, such as parking lot patrols. Retailers hope that, because customers feel safe at their shopping center, they will be encouraged to return and shop there again and that this will enhance sales and profits. That feeling of safety is every bit as important to employees in the retail workplace as it is to customers.

Staff Morale

The morale of its work force is a major concern for any business. Low morale is also associated with higher losses from crime (see Hollinger and Dabney, 1994). This is true not only because employees in a low-morale environment are more likely to engage in deviance themselves, but because they may also be less motivated to engage in a guardianship role and protect their employer's assets from external offenders.

Low morale can arise for a number of reasons, including what employees may see as unfair management practices or industrial insensitivity. On this point, Berlin (1993) reported that a major U.S. retailer experienced an increase of over 33% in its losses over a two-year period primarily because of a sharp decline in employee morale following changes made in response to the sluggish economy. Those changes included below-normal pay increases, cuts in hours of work and reductions in the size of the work force, which led to employees feeling overworked, unfairly paid and not appreciated.

Low morale can also arise when employees are themselves victims of crime at work (e.g., armed robbery or assault) or see such crimes occur. Employees' morale may also decline from seeing crimes committed against the company after poor management decisions (e.g., watching thieves stealing merchandise from a display that the manager insisted should be placed outside a retail store). Or it can arise from watching fellow employees engaging in misconduct without any apparent management concern.

Numerous studies demonstrate that internal crime has a pronounced negative impact on employee morale. For instance, one national survey of American security professionals' perceptions of workplace crime found that respondents saw the most significant and damaging indirect cost of petty theft and fraud at work to be the negative effect on staff morale (Baker and Westin, 1987). Lowered employee morale was seen as the most significant indirect cost of internal crime by 40% and 25% of respondents in two other similar studies (*Security*, 1989). And one of America's foremost researchers in this area pointed out the reality of internal crime is that "most thieves who are caught go unpunished, the problem goes unsolved, consumers pay higher prices than are necessary and businesses suffer serious morale problems" (Snyder, 1992:A22).

WHAT CAN BE DONE? CRIME PREVENTION BY ANY OTHER NAME

Business does not ignore its crime problems. However, it tackles only some of them and, then, in an unscientific way. Criminology needs to demonstrate to business its ability to reduce crime in an orderly fashion that will reduce loss and enhance profit. This will require criminologists making two immediate adjustments to contribute to the business world. First, they need to be concise. It is not possible to demonstrate how comprehensively you have researched a problem, or to argue the merits of various solutions, in a one-page document. That is often all the business decision maker has time to read.

Second, the pace of business is very fast. Seldom is there enough time to allow Clarke's (1992) five stages of a situational crime prevention project to be completed. Indeed, time may not permit completing the first three steps before the fourth (implementation) must be taken, and, then, quick adjustments or changes to the initiative may be required. In retailing, for example, sales are monitored daily and, if they drop or market share is lost, changes have to be made right away to avoid losing customers who, once gone, are hard to win back. Such changes of plan or practice may make experimentation impossible and interfere with Clarke's fifth step (monitoring).

Criminologists can, however, make contributions to business. I see the following three areas as being the most useful.

Reducing Opportunities

It is obvious to both business people and criminologists that the best way to reduce losses is to make it more difficult for them to occur. Business people call this good business. Criminologists call it situational crime prevention. But at least they have a common aim.

From Coles Myer's point of view, all of Clarke's (1992) techniques of situational prevention are appropriate. Unfortunately, any that are pressed into action will not usually be rigorously evaluated. Consider the introduction of electronic article surveillance (EAS) in some stores. Data from a number of the company's supermarkets showed grocery losses reduced from around $750,000 annually to $250,000 after EAS had been operational for a year. And we have anecdotal evidence from nearby competitors' stores that their thefts increased in that period. Respectively, these show a reduction in losses and displacement of theft, but they are not tight data that could be published in support of EAS as a proven crime prevention approach.

Crime prevention measures in business will not generally be subject to a standard of evaluation that an academic criminologist requires. Yet, the business will be happy that a source of loss has apparently been prevented...until the next time. It is obvious that criminologists can make a contribution here, in large part because they are aware of relevant research that has been rigorously carried out elsewhere. This is invaluable for identifying crime prevention responses more likely to be useful in any situation, including physical crime prevention measures (such as target hardening). These openly confirm to employees and the public that a business views crime seriously and treats protection of all of its assets as a major issue.

A Clear Position on Crime

Businesses must make clear to their employees what it is they expect of them. Coles Myer has a policy on criminal conduct that, in part, states "it is each (employee's) responsibility to assist in preventing and detecting criminal activity."[4] The positive results that can flow from such a requirement have been highlighted by Trevino and Victor's (1993) research. It showed that when fast-food restaurant employees were specifically required to report any internal thefts that they witnessed, then internal theft dropped. Indeed, after the fast-food chain acted on the findings from that research, and increased enforcement, thefts of food fell 80% (Schellhardt, 1993).

Further, it is necessary for a company to have firm procedures in place for dealing with all those they find offending against them. Many businesses, including Coles Myer, have a policy of referring all thieves to the police whether they are external or internal. Thus, in-store posters proclaim that all detected thieves will be handed to the police, and, internally, the Coles Myer prosecution policy says, in part, that "we will pursue prosecution" (see note 4).

The value of this approach has been confirmed by Shepard and Durston (1988:9) who stated that "companies with the lowest incidence of employee theft are those with a clear commitment from top executives to line supervisors that theft will not be tolerated." That theft is not tolerated by employees themselves is evidenced from a number of sources. For instance, Trevino and Ball (1992) found that work-group members who accepted the rules expected rule violators to be punished, and punished harshly. A recent American survey showed that 40% of employee dishonesty came to be noticed through co-worker tip-offs, more than through any other single source (*Security*, 1995).

An in-house survey of 1,264 Coles Myer store-based staff established that Australian employees also had similar firm views towards internal thieves. Some of their typical comments appear below.

If you are tempted to steal once then you'll do it again. If someone does steal it means they cannot be trusted.

If staff member is caught once, how many times have they stolen and not been caught?

If they steal once — more than likely they will steal again. Stealing is an offence. They deserve to be punished.

Staff members are fully aware of the effect stealing has upon the business. They therefore have no excuse and any event should be treated severely — dismissal immediately.

To discourage any one else from trying. It is breaking the law and should, therefore, be prosecuted like any other crime — it's twice as bad because it's against the company they work for.

I believe a staff member should be dismissed and other staff be made aware of the dismissal in the hope that this would deter anyone else.

...when you are employed you are told policy.... Why should we have employees working for us who are crims?

If they are going to steal they should pay the price. They know the rules.

If someone was caught stealing at another store they would face prosecution so why should they get away with it in their own store? Besides if they have been caught once, they have probably gotten away with it before.[5]

Such sentiments form a strong base for enlisting employees to participate in a crime prevention push. They also indicate that there is a firm basis for the company's firm policy on crime and misconduct. The Coles Myer Code of Conduct (of which I was one of the authors) provides guidance for the directors and all employees. It has also been distributed to major suppliers with whom the company does business. Subsequent research has established that the Code has assisted employees with ethical dilemmas and assisted them in giving advice to others about appropriate behavior.

Having clear standards of behavior does not mean that more direct approaches may not be necessary from time to time, and criminologists can assist in developing them. As an example, consider the subtle approach described by McNees et al. (1979) in an initiative aimed at encouraging employees to desist from misconduct. It involved signs being placed near the time clock in a diner drawing attention to particular merchandise that was being stolen during the two hours late at night after the diner was closed but before staff had left. That approach eliminated nearly all of the theft of the specified items, but whether that was because the signs suggested increased risk of apprehension and dismissal, or whether the signs were interpreted as an indicator of management's concern, is not known.

Workplace Culture

A positive and caring corporate culture will lead to highly motivated, loyal and well-informed employees and they are the greatest resource available to business to fight both external and internal crime. As "gatekeepers" they can provide a first line of defense against crime from the outside, especially when they are made aware of the problems of external crime and asked for their assistance in dealing with them. And, as indicated above, they are invaluable in tackling internal crime.

A strong workplace culture will not develop from words alone. It is essential that management's own attitudes and behavior reflect the desired culture. Negative behavior by management or those in supervisory roles has a particularly damaging effect on the workplace culture. As an example, an Australian convenience store franchisee approached his franchiser, a multinational oil company, because he was disenchanted with the level of losses of grocery items from his store. He explained that the losses were much greater than just those items that he had taken for his own consumption! It is reasonable to suggest that his employees were taking his lead and also were supplying themselves from the store shelves.

Criminologists can actively assist in creating a strong workplace culture. At Coles Myer I have produced a handbook and video on loss prevention for employees that assists a common awareness of our problems and indicates how they can help tackle them. We have also introduced mechanisms to keep employees aware of losses in their particular workplaces, inviting their suggestions about reducing those losses.

Criminologists can also work usefully with human resources people to ensure that those recruited to the company are going to be compatible with the culture. The documented success of pre-employment screening programs for job applicants indicates that they can have a marked impact on losses. Consider, for instance, The American Payless ShoeSource retail chain that found in a one-year test of its pre-employment testing program that its inventory shortage decreased by about 20% (*Security Management*, 1996).

CONCLUSION

So where does this leave us? Will crime prevention ever become a business priority? The short answer is that for some businesses it already is although they may not describe it as such. For instance, some retailers who establish that they lose more of a certain merchandise line than they actually sell will cease to stock it. This is a pragmatic (if not brave) business decision, but one that comprehensively removes the opportunity for thieves. This puts other parts of the business world on notice. If manufacturers want their products stocked and sold in retail stores, they may have to make them less easy crime targets. For instance, they may need to make their packaging tamper-proof or electronically tagged. Clearly, then, the layers of the business community need to cooperate to protect each other from losses resulting from crime. Criminologists can play a most useful role in that process.

* * *

Acknowledgments: The views expressed in this paper are the author's alone. They cannot be attributed to, and do not reflect upon, Coles Myer Ltd.

NOTES

1. "Business" in this paper refers to larger public companies and corporations and excludes smaller businesses that, as Barlow (1993) pointed out, may have different agendas and priorities.

2. In practice, manipulating billing data is a more likely way of doing a friend a "favor."

3. This is a particularly severe loss because not only does the retailer suffer the monetary loss, but inventory records would show additional merchandise of the same value that would not be found at stocktake.

4. The Coles Myer policy document, entitled *Policy Statement — Criminal Conduct, Investigation and Prosecution,* is an internal company document. The policy was broadcast throughout the company by memos, circulars and newsletters.

5. These quotations were taken from an internal survey completed by Coles Myer staff. No public document was produced.

REFERENCES

Altheide, D.L., P.A. Adler, P. Adler and D.A. Altheide (1978). "The Social Meanings Of Employee Theft." In: J.M. Johnson and J.D. Douglas (eds.), *Crime At The Top.* Philadelphia, PA: Lippincott.

Analoui, F. and A. Kakabadse (1991). *Sabotage: How To Recognise And Manage Employee Defiance.* London, UK: Mercury.

Baker, M. and A. Westin (1987). *Employer Perceptions of Workplace Crime.* Washington, DC: Bureau of Justice Statistics.

Barlow, H.D. (1993). "From Fiddle Factors To Networks of Collusion: Charting The Waters of Small Business Crime." *Crime, Law and Social Change* 20:319-337.

Berlin, P. (1993). "When Employee Morale Goes Down, Shrinkage Goes Up!" *The Peter Berlin Report on Shrinkage Control,* Store Managers' Edition. June:1-2

Boye, M.W., J.W. Jones, S.L. Martin and R.P. Beck (1995). *Fifth Annual Report of Supermarket Employee Behavior.* Rosemont, IL: London House and Food Marketing Institute.

Buckle, A., D.P. Farrington, J. Burrows, M. Speed and T. Burns-Howell (1992). "Measuring Shoplifting by Repeated Systematic Counting." *Security Journal* 3(3):137-146.

Carter, N., A. Kindstedt and L. Melin (1995). "Increased Sales and Thefts of Candy as a Function of Sales Promotion Activities: Preliminary Findings." *Journal of Applied Behavior Analysis* 28:81-82.

Challinger, D. (1991). "Less Telephone Vandalism: How Did It Happen?" *Security Journal* 2:111-119.

—— (1996). "Refund Fraud in Retail Stores." *Security Journal* 7:27-35.

Clarke, R. (ed.) (1992). *Situational Crime Prevention: Successful Case Studies*. Albany, NY: Harrow and Heston.

D'Addario, F. J. (1989). *Loss Prevention Through Crime Analysis*. Boston, MA: Butterworths.

Dawson, S. (1993). "Consumer Responses to Electronic Article Surveillance Alarms." *Journal of Retailing* 69(3):353-362.

Dougherty, T. (1993). "Loss Prevention: Winning the War Against Theft." *Visual Merchandising And Store Design* 124(10):44-49.

Gorman, D. (1996). "Loss Prevention Racks up Success." *Security Management* 40(3):55,56,58,61.

Hastings, G.B. (1981). "Customer Attitudes towards Security Devices in Shops and Preparedness to Report Shoplifting." *Criminology and Penology Abstracts* 20:639-642.

Hogan, J. and R. Hogan (1989). "How to Measure Employee Reliability." *Journal of Applied Psychology* 74:273-279.

Hollinger, R. and J.P. Clark (1983). *Theft By Employees*. Lexington, MA: Lexington Books.

—— and D. Dabney (1994). "Reducing Shrinkage in the Retail Store: It's Not Just a Job for the Loss Prevention Department." *Security Journal* 5:2-10.

Karpoff, J.M. and J.R. Lott (1993). "The Reputational Penalty Firms Bear from Committing Criminal Fraud." *Journal of Law and Economics* 36:757-802.

Levy, M. and B.A. Weitz (1995). *Retailing Management*. (2nd ed.) Chicago IL: Irwin.

Longo, D. (1994). "Crime Changes Shoppers' Habits." *Discount Store News* 33(10): 45.

Lukawitz, J.M. and P.J. Steinbart (1995). "Investor Reaction to Disclosures of Employee Fraud." *Journal of Managerial Issues* 7(3):358-367.

McNees, P., S.W. Gilliam, J.F. Schnelle and T. Risley (1979). "Controlling Employee Theft through Time and Product Identification." *Journal of Organisational Behavior Management* 2:113-119.

Masuda, B. (1992). "Displacement vs. Diffusion of Benefits and the Reduction of Inventory Losses in a Retail Environment." *Security Journal* 3(3):131-136.

Queensland Police Service (1994). *Shopping Centre Security Project*. n.p.: author.

Research and Evaluation Branch, Queensland Police Service/Community Development and Crime Prevention Unit, Queensland University of Technology (1992). *Report on an Evaluation of POLICE BEAT*. n.p.: author.

Schellardt, T.D. (1993). "To Prevent Theft, Make Ratting Part of the Job." *Wall Street Journal* April 2nd:B1.

Security (1995). "Retail Theft a Staggering $10 Billion a Year." September:73.

Security (1989). "Employee Crime: Lower Employee Morale, Productivity Top Employee Crime Pricetag." 26:10.

Security Management (1996). "If the Shoe Fits..." 40(2):11.

Shapland, J. (1995). "Preventing Retail-Sector Crimes." In: M. Tonry and D. Farrington (eds.), *Building a Safer Society: Strategic Approaches to Crime Prevention. Crime and Justice: A Review of Research.* Chicago, IL: University of Chicago Press.

Shepard, I.M. and R. Durston (1988). *Thieves at Work: An Employer's Guide to Combating Workplace Dishonesty.* Washington, DC: The Bureau of National Affairs.

Snyder, N.H. (1992). "Prosecute Employee Theft." *The Washington Post,* November 28th:A22.

Sympson, R. (1995). "To Catch A Thief." *Restaurant Business* 94(13):72,76,80,82.

Trevino, L.K. and G.A. Ball (1992). The Social Implications of Punishing Unethical Behavior: Observers' Cognitive and Affective Reactions." *Journal of Management* 18:751-769.

—— and B. Victor (1993). "Peer Reporting of Unethical Behavior: A Social Context Perspective" *Academy of Management Journal* 35:38-64.

MEASURING CRIME AND ITS IMPACT IN THE BUSINESS ENVIRONMENT

by Richard C. Hollinger
University of Florida

Abstract: *Individuals are not the only victims of crime in our society. In fact, the financial impact of crimes committed against business organizations constitute a larger annual financial impact. Analyzing the prevalence and impact of crime within the business environment creates an entirely new set of special problems for the researcher. Using experiences generated from conducting the annual National Retail Security Survey, the author details the special methodological and logistical challenges entailed in measuring the scope of crimes committed against retail stores.*

CRIMES AGAINST BUSINESS ORGANIZATIONS

The occurrence of both violent and non-violent crimes against business establishments has long been considered a critically important threat to the stability of our capitalist economic system (Lipman, 1973). Throughout the 19th and 20th centuries numerous laws were enacted and criminal justice resources were mobilized to protect an assortment of commercial interests from predatory crime, as well as violent labor unrest. Examples include protection provided to the railroads, banks, automakers, telecommunications providers and defense contractors against various real and perceived criminal threats. In fact, the historical origins of both the FBI and the Secret Service can be traced to the protection of the banking industry against the interstate bank robber and the counterfeiter, respectively (U.S. Law Enforcement Assistance Administration, 1976).

The last 20 years, however, has witnessed vacillating support for the business community in their efforts to protect themselves against crime. In fact, many business leaders feel that the criminal justice system has abandoned them in a politically expedient effort to control only those crimes that more directly affect the general public (that is, voters), such as street violence and drugs. Even as we cautiously note signs of improvement in the war against both street violence and drugs, the crimes committed against the business community continue to increase in prevalence and to become much more violent in nature.

Workplace Crime and Theft

One of the most recent estimates of the prevalence of crime in the workplace was taken from the 1987-92 National Crime Survey data, suggesting that, of the over 6.5 million acts of violence experienced by U.S. residents age 12 or older, 15% take place while at work — including 8% of rapes, 7% of robberies, and 16% of all assaults (Bachman, 1994). Characteristic of many crimes, over half of all workplace victimizations were not reported to police. Even though violence was common, the most widespread crime in the workplace was theft, as nearly one quarter of all personal larceny victimizations happen while at work. It is obvious from these findings that the workplace is a surprisingly crime-filled environment and that official police incidence data are not likely to accurately reflect the true level of criminal involvement. Moreover, it should be noted that these National Crime Survey data do not include any of the victimizations in which the business itself, not an individual employee, is the entity harmed by the criminality.

Levels of Crime Loss Against Business

The annual financial impact of the crimes that directly victimize the business community has always been known by insiders to be enormous but has generally been unappreciated by those on the outside (U.S. Department of Commerce, 1976). Of all the commercial segments of the U.S. economy, the retail industry has assembled the best data on how much crime affects the profitability of these firms. For example, using data gathered in the *1995 National Retail Security Survey*, an annual study conducted by the University of Florida, 341 major retailing corporations estimated that they lost an average of 1.835% of their annual sales volume to a combination of shoplifting (that is, shop theft), employee theft, vendor theft and fraud, in addition to various bookkeeping and accounting errors (Hollinger and Dabney, 1995). This percentage is what retailers call their "inventory shrinkage" (or "shortage"). In the same survey, retailers estimated that employee theft and shoplifting were the two largest components of the inventory shrinkage total, comprising 39% and 35% of their annual losses, respectively. Thus, assuming a $1.4 trillion U.S. retail marketplace, these two crimes alone take $10 billion and $8.5 billion out of the pockets of retail businesses annually. As large as these dollar impacts are, they do not include many of the other crime losses, such as the theft of cash, that are not even reflected in this "inventory shrinkage" statistic. A recently published book by the Bureau of National Affairs reported that the range from $15 billion to $25 billion per year represents a conservative estimate of annual economic losses to U.S. business from employee theft (Shepard and Duston, 1988).

Quite simply, there are no other conventional property crimes that come anywhere close to costing as much money annually as business crime (Lary, 1988). The cost of all auto theft combined only annually averages slightly under $1 billion each year. In 1992, the Justice Department estimated the direct cost to citizens of *all* reported property crimes to total no more than $17.5 billion. The multi-billion dollar shoplifting and employee theft losses experienced by American businesses are so large that they cannot be tolerated by firms that expect to remain profitable. The net result is that hundreds of businesses go bankrupt each year, many the direct or indirect consequence of employee theft, embezzlement, or other forms of workplace deviance. In fact, the Chamber of Commerce has long estimated that at least 30% of business failures are directly or indirectly precipitated by internal crime and fraud (Chamber of Commerce of the United States, 1974). In every segment of the economy in which it occurs — manufacturing, health care, restaurants, hotels, service, wholesale, or retail — the cost of crime against business is causing increasing levels of financial difficulty. Marginal or nonexistent profit margins in a climate of greater international and domestic competition do not permit the toleration of any significant losses due to crime. Instead, the cost of crime against business ultimately must be passed on to the consumer as a "crime tax." Both the cost to recover the loss and the price of increased security must be included. In addition, some of these costs are insured so that we all will pay higher insurance premiums as a result (Bacas, 1987). Furthermore, uninsured financial losses due to crime are tax deductible thereby increasing the national debt. Unfortunately, all consumers are forced to pay this tax regardless of their social status or economic resources (*Canadian Business*, 1976).

Other Nonviolent Crimes Against Business

Thus far in this paper, I have focused on the "big two" crimes committed against businesses, shoplifting and employee theft. However, these are not the only crimes that produce a substantial financial drain on the profits and public image of the business corporation. Twenty years ago the U.S. Department of Justice asked the prestigious American Management Associations (AMA) to compile a "best estimate" derived from interviews with security experts regarding the annual financial impact of "nonviolent crimes against business" for the calendar year 1975 (AMA, 1977). The yearly dollar losses to business that were attributable to various forms of nonviolent criminal behavior were staggering to those who knew little about the scope of the problem — which was generally everyone since this type of study had never before been conducted. The AMA study dramatically confirmed that the vast majority of the crime-related financial loss experienced by business were caused by the firm's own employees. For example, employee pilferage, kickbacks and bribery, securities theft and fraud, as well as embezzlement were the four highest impact crimes, resulting in a minimum of $17.5 billion to a maximum of $29 billion per year (in 1975 dollars) in direct financial losses. Alternatively, the more familiar crimes, such as arson, burglary, vandalism, shoplifting, insurance and check and credit card fraud, all constitute a much lower financial impact on the victimized organizations and are all usually committed by outsiders or customers (Hollinger, 1989). The above facts constitute the paradox of the crime problem that plagues the business community. Namely, the crimes that the public and the criminal justice system find most costly and alarming are not the same set of crimes that have the most significant impact on the business community. Therefore, it is difficult to get the attention of non-business interests, especially the criminal justice system, to appreciate the nature and scope of the problem.

There is a single historical exception to the above observation, however. During President Carter's administration, the American Management Associations study served as a antecedent to a small group of subsequently funded National Institute of Justice studies, all of which were focused on the more significant internal employee threat. For example, John Clark and Richard Hollinger (1983) conducted a three-industry, three-city study to examine the prevalence and correlates of employee theft. Terry Baumer and Dennis Rosenbaum (1984) assembled information on the various programs being used successfully across the country to combat workplace crime. Additionally, Allen Baker and Martin Westin (1988) conducted a study of employer perceptions of the workplace crime problem. Since this flurry of academic interest in the 1980s, however, little subsequent federally funded research has been initiated in the U.S. to help us understand the scope, impact, or the causal nature of crime against business. Interestingly, the climate has been far more supportive in the U.K. where the Home Office recently has supported a series of research studies attempting to estimate the scope of business premise victimization (Mirrlees-Black and Ross, 1995a; 1995b).

Why Do We Not Know More about the Nature of Crime Against Business?

We cannot blame our ignorance entirely on the lack of government funding interest in the problem. Like many other white-collar offense categories, crimes against business are very difficult to research for a number of reasons. Occupationally related crimes are hard to detect and oftentimes are only discovered by accident since they are committed by perpetrators who are generally brighter than the average criminal. Moreover, many offenses are committed alone and in secret, carefully hidden from both in-house security and the police. For example, professional shoplifters are the masters of deception, concealing their actions from video cameras, in-store security and electronic article surveillance. Employee thieves and embezzlers are referred to as "trust violators" (Cressey, 1953) because they surreptitiously violate the trust placed in them by their bosses. Moreover, perpetrators of various frauds and scams are involved in offenses with very complicated *modus operandi*. Fellow employees who may know of their co-worker's criminal involvement oftentimes observe an unspoken code of silence. In short, with crimes against business, there is very seldom the obvious "dead body" or "smoking gun" that a signals that a crime has even taken place.

Even if we know that a crime has occurred against the business, usually there is no audit trail to determine whether the crime has been perpetrated by an insider or an outsider. Accurately determining the source of a property or cash-asset loss can be quite difficult or impossible (Bamfield and Hollinger, 1996). In the *1995 National Retail Security Survey*, we asked retailers to tell us where their losses are coming from. While they make an estimate for our survey, we all know that this is an educated guess. Last year, for example, retailers "guesstimated" that 39% of their inventory shrinkage was due to employee theft, 35% attributable to shoplifters, 20% bookkeeping errors and 6% due to vendor fraud. Over the past five years that we have been collecting these data, however, this percentage has varied significantly, especially between retail market segments (Hollinger and Dabney, 1995).

The most common ways that businesses discover how much they are losing to crime and who is responsible comes from the following: (1) accidental discoveries; (2) confessions by apprehended thieves; (3) co-worker informants; (4) proactive investigations; and (5) electronic or closed-circuit TV (CCTV) surveillance. None of the above happen naturally as a part of the process of doing business. Confessions are the result of a pro-active security presence within the formal organization. Co-worker information is oftentimes not forthcoming without monetary incentives. The heavy use of proactive investigations, especially those employing electronic or CCTV monitoring, can create a draconian work environment that may negatively affect levels of job satisfaction and morale. Moreover, instituting a strong security presence in the workplace is a costly financial investment that will not provide a total return on investment in the very first year of utilization.

COLLECTING DATA ON CRIMES AGAINST BUSINESS

Three types of crime measurement are traditionally employed in the study of criminal behavior, namely, crimes known to the police, victimization surveys and self-report indices. As applied to the problem of crime against business, comparable data sources would include: (1) those offenses against businesses and their employees that are officially reported to the police; (2) anonymous self-report surveys of crimes and deviant acts committed within the workplace; and (3) victimization studies of crimes committed against the corporate entity, the premises and its individual employees. Official reporting of business crime is available, but suffers even more than individual data from massive underreporting problems (U.S. Federal Bureau of Investigation, 1995). Collecting self-report data on offenses committed against business has been attempted by this author and others but is also fraught with methodological difficulties (Clark and Hollinger, 1983). However, of these three data sources, victimization surveys conducted in the workplace continue to be the most underutilized as a valid and reliable source of information on crime against business.

Victimization studies of businesses are somewhat different from traditional crime surveys, as we can survey either the "natural" person (the employee) (for example, Bachman, 1994) or the "juristic" person (the corporation), or both. Victim surveys of juristic persons benefit from the impartial collective memory of the bureaucratic record-keeping system. As we already know from years of National Crime Surveys, one's recall of criminal acts is greatly affected by the temporal proximity of the most recent victimization incident and the overall levels of criminality to which the respondent has been exposed. Unlike individual actors, businesses that regularly collect data on crime victimizations should not be affected by variable memory recall. The quality of victimization data available from businesses range from extremely detailed to completely nonexistent. Larger organizations generally have the most detailed statistical records on crime. Driven by the demands of their insurers and accounting systems, many medium-to-large business organizations keep very detailed records regarding the specific criminal victimization events that occur during the course of the year. However, very small firms often keep incomplete data or no data whatsoever.

National Retail Security Survey

The National Retail Security Survey (NRSS) (Hollinger and Dabney, 1995) is the most widely disseminated and most representative survey of crime victimizations of U.S. retail firms conducted at the present time. The NRSS is a four-page, self-administered, anonymous questionnaire survey. It is annually mailed to the major retail chains doing business in the United States and in Canada (using a slightly different instrument). The questionnaire asks retail loss-prevention executives (who have the required data) to report on their company's: (1) most recent levels of inventory shrinkage; (2) perceptions of the sources of loss; (3) loss-prevention department budgets and personnel; (4) use of pre-employment screening; (5) use of awareness programs; (6) asset control policies; and (7) deployment of loss-prevention security systems. The NRSS also asks retailers to provide victimization incidence data on over twenty different types of retail-specific and conventional crime offenses that regularly occur within the retail environment. The data are analyzed using descriptive statistical techniques to provide managers with up-to-date nationwide information.

The survey population for the NRSS is generated using a proprietary mailing list developed over the past five years by combining the names and addresses of previous respondents to the last five National Retail Security Surveys in addition to lists provided by several other sources. For example, we have collected the names and addresses of large retailers from comprehensive commercially available mailing lists, such as Dunn & Bradstreet's *Million Dollar Directory* and *Chain Store Guide Information Services*. We have also incorporated the current membership lists from several retail trade associations and security-service providers, such as the National Retail Federation, the National Association of Chain Drug Stores, the Jewelers Security Alliance, the National Association of Recording Merchandisers, and Loss Prevention Specialists, Inc. The end result is a mailing list encompassing over 3,000 separate firms providing a broad representation of the very largest retail chains among the 27 largest vertical market segments within the retailing industry. The mailing list is purposely biased toward larger retailers since we have learned from past experience that they are more likely to have both separate loss-prevention departments and access to the information required to answer the questions posed.

NRSS survey materials are distributed by U.S. mail to loss-prevention and security executives using a two-stage mailing process. Each potential respondent on the list was mailed, via first-class mail, a packet containing the following materials: an explanatory cover letter; a questionnaire; a business-reply envelope; and a business-reply postcard. Respondents were asked to complete the questionnaire and return it anonymously in the business reply envelope. Those interested in obtaining a copy of the final report were instructed to provide their names and addresses on the business reply postcard and return it separately. Approximately two weeks later, the second phase of the mailing was conducted in which each potential respondent was sent another postcard thanking those who had already completed the instrument and encouraging the participation of those who had not.

Data from the returned questionnaire instruments are tabulated and reported via a shorter (four-to-five page) executive summary and a full detailed report (over 80 pages). Copies of both are provided without charge to all respondents and supporters of the University of Florida's Security Research Project. All others can receive a copy for a nominal charge to cover printing, postage and handling. Complimentary copies are also provided to professional journalists who are working on articles about retail security. Funding for this research project is provided jointly by the Sensormatic Electronics Corporation and the twenty-five other Supporting Partners of the University of Florida's Security Research Project.

The NRSS *Final Report* is primarily used by three groups of people. First, as mentioned above, journalists writing in both the popular and trade press about the scope of the retail crime and loss-prevention issues use the report regularly. Second, security equipment and services vendors use the NRSS to gauge current and predict future interest in their various products. The single largest group of users of the report, however, are retail loss-prevention managers or directors. Those who are most directly responsible for preventing losses in small, medium and large retail chains use the NRSS *Final Report* to assess how well (or not) they are doing in the continuing battle against crimes against business. Specifically, medium and large retailers regularly employ both the overall and market-specific averages to compare against their own firm's current level of loss and security countermeasure deployment. Small retailers use the report to evaluate the conventional wisdom about those countermeasures that are thought to yield the most significant return-on-investment (ROI). Interestingly, few other academic scholars have requested access to these data for further analysis. An exception to this is that interest has been expressed by a number of foreign scholars (for example, Bamfield and Hollinger, 1996). This lack of interest by U.S. scholars no doubt reflects the paucity of interest in business-related crime analysis and prevention research by most North American criminologists at the present time.

Inventory Shrinkage

Because proactively detecting crimes in the workplace is a costly venture, most businesses rely almost totally on more passive, reactive mechanisms for detecting violations and violators. As mentioned earlier, the most common indirect measure of crime used by retailers is their "inventory shrinkage" statistic. This percentage is generated as a by-product of the traditional inventory auditing process necessary to replenish merchandise and determine periodic sales figures. Unfortunately, as a measure of criminality, inventory shrinkage statistics are fraught with inaccuracy (Shapland, 1995). As mentioned earlier, shrinkage is a composite measure combining a number of disparate crime types. Second, it is not an offense-driven statistic, but one that merely indicates the total level of financial cost to the victimized company attributable to these crimes and other non-criminal sources of loss. A significant portion of the shrinkage statistic is not even larceny, but rather, is due to bookkeeping and accounting errors in the inventory-control system. For example, if a retailer fails to inform corporate accounting that a particular item has been sold at a reduced (marked-down) price, the difference between the sale price and the normal retail price will also show up as "shrinkage."

To make matters even more complicated, retailers use a variety of methods to calculate their shrinkage statistics. Some compute their losses as a percentage of the original retail asking price that they would have received from the unaccounted-for merchandise. Other retailers maintain that this "retail" method of calculation inflates the real loss to the company because it includes a "markup" for lost profit and overhead expenses. As such, these retailers calculate their shrinkage as a percentage of their wholesale "cost" paid for the merchandise - specifically excluding their markup for profit and overhead. And, to make matters even more confusing, some retailers calculate their shrinkage losses at both "retail" and "cost." Needless to say this results in a serious data contamination effect that compromises the comparability of these statistics.

A final problem with using inventory shrinkage as an indirect measure of crime in the retail industry concerns the secretive status of financial information. Since retailers, like other business persons, are in constant competition with each other, they usually treat any information that relates to their profitability as proprietary information. This means that some security directors are not willing to release publicly their shrinkage data. Others release a "sanitized" version of their shrinkage to the public, the press and the financial market analysts that is significantly lower than their real level of loss. Some retail industry experts argue that the number of companies reporting "politically acceptable" shrinkage percentages has become so numerous as to permit using "inventory shrinkage" figures for nothing more than gross comparisons.

The current situation is quite understandable as high levels of financial loss due to criminality are personally and corporately embarrassing. Documenting high rates of crime in the workplace, just like in the larger society, is a two-edged sword. While significant levels of crime can be utilized to secure additional security resources, too much loss will eventually become a serious career-threatening liability to the same loss-prevention executive. In fact, some directors of loss prevention in retail chains do not even want their own corporate executives to know the firm's actual level of loss because a high number might reflect badly on their management effectiveness. The excessive level of turnover among loss-prevention executives is evidence of this fact. Just as we have many times discovered with the reporting of official police crime data, it is always problematic when those who are expected to control crime are also involved in counting it. There is a natural tendency to exaggerate to get resources or to minimize levels to protect one's job. Furthermore, it is especially embarrassing to admit that one of your own is deviant. And, even if the security staff is capable of acknowledging high levels of workplace crime to itself, it is even harder to get a company that is very concerned with its public image to admit to being victimized.

Using economic indicators like inventory shrinkage as a proxy measure of crime is problematic for other reasons. One of the most serious issues is precipitated by the impossibility of determining the frequency or prevalence of crimes like employee theft or shoplifting by using only the net monetary loss experienced. For example, is a $1000 loss due to one serious professional shoplifter "boosting" two $500 suits or 100 teenagers each stealing a $10 compact disk? Without knowing the nature of the loss, reconstructing and determining the causal linkage is next to impossible. In response, the *1995 National Retail Security Survey* recently has incorporated a series of specific questions relating to the incidence counts for a number of criminal categories for each retail chain. Hopefully, we can avoid some of these difficulties brought about by these measurement issues in future studies (Hollinger and Dabney, 1995).

The "inventory shrinkage" statistic is a seriously compromised measure of criminal activity within the typical retail business. However, until greater interest in the problem is observed, we are not likely to see much improvement in the validity of these data. Most retail firms would rather ignore the problem by selling enough merchandise to preclude the need for security and loss prevention. The same can probably be said for many other sectors of the business economy as well. For if the profit margin is large enough, they can afford to absorb significant losses, or the cost can be easily passed on to their customers or insurers (for example, defense contractors or health care providers). In fact, if profit margins are acceptable, most businesses view the only other "down sides" of crime to be a public relations or legal liability problem. After all, effective loss-prevention and security systems are costly, personally invasive, technically complex, prone to breakdowns, and are overly relied upon. Moreover, they can create an atmosphere of distrust between management and workers, aggravating already tenuous worker-management relations (for example, the case of the Austin, Minnesota, Hormel plant) or creating a public relations nightmare (for example, Hudson Bay Company's use of civil recovery for shoplifters) (Hollinger and Dabney, 1994).

OTHER METHODOLOGICAL AND ANALYSIS PROBLEMS

In addition to the veracity of the "inventory shrinkage" percentage (discussed above), there are a number of other methodological and analysis problems that continue to challenge criminological research conducted among retail business organizations.

Determining the Sampling Universe of the Retail Business Community

Unlike that which is easily available for individuals, there is no definitive annual census of the retail business community. While many lists of corporate business entities exist, such as Dunn & Bradstreet's *Million Dollar Directory*, a significant number of addresses from these commercially available mailing lists are filled with inaccuracies and redundancies. These inaccuracies are primarily due to the constantly changing nature of the retailing industry. Each year a surprisingly high number of retail firms start up, go out of business, change their corporate addresses, are sold to new owners, divide corporate assets, or merge together. This is especially true in mediocre economic conditions, such as the present.

Even if we know the corporate address, obtaining the name of the most senior loss-prevention executive is another major difficulty. We have noted that sending these questionnaires to no specific occupant (a "dear occupant" salutation) is detrimental to questionnaire response rates. As such, we try to identify the most appropriate recipient by title and actual name, if possible. The problem is that some firms have no specific person in charge of loss prevention. Oftentimes, loss prevention can be the responsibility of the owner, president, senior vice-president, or vice-president for operations, finance, operations, or distribution. Some small firms even delegate security to individual store managers. Among those firms with a specific person in charge of loss prevention and security, this person could be variously entitled a manager, a director, or even a vice-president.

Alternatively, sending a crime victimization questionnaire to a specific person also has its dangers, especially if that person has retired, quit, been promoted, demoted, re-assigned, or has been "downsized" and is no longer employed by the firm. As a result of the above plethora of problems, using inaccurate addresses and names is the "Achilles' heel" of research with the business community. In response, we have employed a part-time staff member to do nothing but verify the accuracy of these lists in the few months immediately prior to sending the NRSS questionnaires.

Response Rates

Over the five years of conducting the National Retail Security Survey, our response rate has not come close to equaling the level achieved by many other mailed, self-report social science surveys. Return rates of ten to 20% have been the norm. We believe that our response rates are depressed for a number of reasons. First, even if we do have a correct address to which we can send the questionnaire, a number of firms do not know what to do with the NRSS instrument after they receive it. Most smaller, one-to-two store retail operations, do not have a loss-prevention manager, a security department, or even someone who tabulates the data that we are interested in. Second, for many firms, even if we are lucky enough to get the questionnaire into the hands of the person knowledgeable about loss prevention, some view the completion of a detailed, four-page questionnaire as requiring too much of their time and energy to warrant participation. In sum, the hard reality is that there are only a limited number of retail corporations that have the loss-prevention resources available to provide the data requested by our questionnaire. In fact, regardless of the number of questionnaires that we send out, no business crime victimization survey that I am aware of has ever received completed questionnaires from more than 400 retail corporations.

Comparing Apples and Oranges: Accurately Depicting the Retailing Respondent

Categorizing retail chains into unique market segment groups to make equivalent comparisons among them is also very difficult. Early mercantile stores sold virtually everything that their customers wanted. After World War II, retailers increasingly began to specialize by type of product. Now with the advent of the retail "superstore," grocery stores sell drugs, drug stores sell hardware and home center or hardware stores sell stereo equipment and appliances. Finding a prototypical retail store within many current market segments is next to impossible. This mega- or super-store trend makes inter-firm comparisons problematic. Real questions now exist, in particular, regarding the actual differentiation between grocery stores or supermarkets, department stores and discount stores.

Another serious analysis problem involves how one counts organizations in business crime studies? In traditional victimization studies of "natural" persons, the victim is a single person. Business corporations vary greatly in size. Some of the respondents to the NRSS are single store, "mom and pop" retailers with less than one million dollars in annual sales. Other respondents are huge international retail chains with thousands of store locations and many billions in annual sales revenues. Do we count these business as two equal victims? Or do we "weight" the "juristic" victim according to the magnitude of its corporate size or business activity? And, if we do, what should be the appropriate denominator: store locations, store physical size, sales, or number of employees; to name just a few possibilities? Counting them equally clearly biases the overall results toward the smaller firm; however, weighting by a size-related variable converts the study into effectively a study of huge multi-national corporations. In essence, this question revolves around what should be the "unit of analysis" in the business crime survey. Should the most appropriate unit of analysis be the individual employee, single-store premises, the regional or division unit, or the entire corporation? While there are no definitive answers to these questions, in the NRSS we have operationally defined the corporation as the unit of analysis, however, often standardizing the responses by annual sales volume and number of store units. Alternatively, in recent research surveys conducted in the U.K. by the British Home Office, the unit of analysis has been the randomly selected business premises - a sampling design that uses street addresses, not the corporate parent (Mirrlees-Black and Ross, 1995a; 1995b).

Data Contamination, Interpretation and Utilization Problems

Over the years of doing research on business crime, we have recognized a number of other problems that involve the integrity of the data and findings. One of the most disturbing involves concerns of data contamination. Since we provide a very detailed report of the findings from our study to the respondents, we are concerned that eventually responses will regress to the mean. This concern is especially true for the questions like "source of shrinkage loss" that we know are based more on opinion than fact. Each year it appears that the results more and more conform to the results of the previous year's survey. Perhaps this is due to a normalization of the phenomenon under study. However, we worry greatly that, with each report, we are directly influencing the results of the succeeding year's study.

Despite our best efforts in achieving an even and widespread representation of the major categories of retailers across the country, we still have problems with over- and under-representation of some market segments. For example, due to the zealous support of a single trade association (that is, National Association of Recording Merchandisers), we received an over-representation of music and video stores, especially small store locations. While this enlarged our N and improved the response rate, it inadvertently biased our results toward this particular market segment. Alternatively, we have had a hard time getting enough respondents in some markets to be able to calculate meaningful statistics for the category of stores. For example, the aggressive marketing growth of a few national "superstore" office-supply chains (for example, Office Depot and Office Max) has literally "killed off" hundreds of small, locally owned and operated office-supply companies. During the past five years, we have seen a precipitous drop in response due to this and other similar retail market changes.

Another problem involves the interpretation of responses from business corporations. Many of the questions incorporated in the NRSS involve polling the organization as to whether it utilizes a particular countermeasure or program. The response choices are generally dichotomous. What if the chain employs electronic article surveillance (EAS) systems, but only in 20% of their "problem" stores? Currently our instrument cannot differentiate between a "partial use" response and a firm that uses a loss-prevention or security procedure, policy, program, or system in all of its stores. Response weighting is an even more complicated problem to resolve than the related "unit of analysis" problem discussed above.

Finally, despite our best efforts to improve speed of data collection, analysis and report preparation, every report that we have issued on retail loss prevention is "old information" by the time that it appears in print. We send out questionnaires in early April to tap data that has just been tabulated for the preceding fiscal year (usually ending January 30th for most retailers). Questionnaires trickle in during the months of April, May and early June. By the time that we release the preliminary results at the National Retail Federation Loss Prevention Meetings held in June of every year, our data are at least six months old. Moreover, by the time we finish the writing of the final report, get it printed and sent out by mail to the respondents, the NRSS findings are almost nine months old. While even longer data reporting lags are quite commonly found in the criminal justice reporting system (for example, Uniform Crime Reports, National Crime Survey, Bureau of Justice Statistics), this is an unacceptable delay to the retailer who must quickly respond to the dynamic changes occurring in the both the criminal community and among his or her competitors in the industry. Retail loss-prevention decision makers need and deserve more timely and accurate information to construct their responses to the threat. They cannot afford to be tardy, as this may be too late to protect valuable assets or restore profitability to the firm.

WHAT IS THE RESPONSE OF THE CRIMINAL JUSTICE SYSTEM TO BUSINESS CRIME?

Unfortunately, the modal response to crime in the business setting is to ignore it, hoping that it will just go away. Maybe this is why, when managers catch someone involved in dishonesty, the cheapest and simplest option is to do nothing if they are an outsider (for example, shoplifter) or dismiss them (that is, transportation model of punishment) if they are an employee. In fact, often the most attractive solution seems to involve passing one's crime problems on to someone else, maybe even a competitor!

Many companies publicly state that they will prosecute all discovered cases of crime and dishonesty to the fullest extent allowed by the law. But, good intentions and deterrence notwithstanding, very few criminal prosecutions of larceny in the business setting are successful (Robin, 1970). Recent National Retail Security Survey results have shown a steady drop in the proportion of shoplifters and employee theft cases prosecuted (Hollinger and Dabney, 1995). Prosecution success rates for violent crime are not much better. In fact, in many urban jurisdictions, retailers tell me that, when they call the police to take a shoplifter or dishonest employee into custody, which the company has apprehended using its own security personnel, they are often told to wait until later when officers are done dealing with "real crime." Moreover, even if the dishonest employee or shoplifter is formally charged, various pre-trial intervention and diversion programs almost ensure that the non-violent property offender will serve no jail time nor receive any significant fines. In fact, many times professional shoplifters are back on the street victimizing other businesses the very same afternoon. In short, there is very little objective criminal deterrence currently offered by our criminal justice system for the two most frequently committed and costly of all larceny offense categories.

Civil Recovery in Lieu of (or in Addition to) Criminal Prosecution

In response to the actual and perceived ineffectiveness of the criminal prosecution option, many retailers have chosen to use "civil recovery" as the preferred sanction for shoplifting and dishonest employees. At first glance, the benefits to all concerned appear numerous. First, the victimized business can encourage a confession from the accused more easily without the threat of criminal punishment hanging over the head of those accused. And, if the retailer agrees not to prosecute, the offender will have no permanent criminal record. All the guilty party pays is restitution for the items taken, plus possible treble damages or a minimum of about $200 (Florida). The retailer saves testimony time of his staff, attorney fees, adverse public relations damage, plus they recover enough money in many cases to help defray the operational costs of catching other dishonest people. Forty-nine states now have "civil recovery" statutes in place. On the down side, there is no criminal conviction for the offense that will show up in the record of the individual. This translates into minimal shaming or stigma consequences for the offender (Braithwaite, 1989). Many are afraid that civil recovery trivializes the significance of this normative violation by treating it as a civil tort. Others worry that this non-punitive option will be more likely offered to middle- and upper-class white offenders and denied to lower-class blacks, it will intensify the social-class bias plaguing the criminal justice system (Davis et al., 1991). Moreover, because there are really no negative consequences in the threat by retailers to take unresponsive shoplifters to civil court if they do not pay up, the majority of these cases are ignored and generate no revenue. Retailers will tolerate this for a while, but if the non-response percentage gets worse, it will effectively spell the end of the civil-recovery option - since businesses do not have the resources or the will to take all of these torts to court.

Crime Prevention

Most of the energy expended by loss prevention and security in a typical business is reactively directed toward detecting those persons responsible for the losses of assets, recovering any available restitution and then taking steps to incapacitate the offender from future violations. Much less attention has been placed on proactively preventing crime from occurring in the first place. Assuming that only a handful of offenders are actually detected, a reactive strategy will never be as effective as a preventive one.

Although the trend has been changing recently, very little scholarly research has been conducted on determining which of the various programs, policies and countermeasures have the greatest impact on crime in the business sector. Of the extant literature, perhaps the largest body of research to date has been focused on preventing armed robbery in the convenience store (see Bellamy, 1996, for a recent literature review). A number of other recent studies have been focused on such retail crime prevention technologies as closed-circuit TV cameras (Poyner, 1988; Chatterton and Frenz, 1994), outdoor public lighting (Ditton and Nair, 1994; Painter, 1994), electronic article surveillance (DiLonardo, 1996), and benefit-denial devices (such as ink tags) (DiLonardo and Clarke, 1996). While this recent research is encouraging, much more needs to be done, as most security deployments are made without valid evidence of effectiveness. From the results of the National Retail Security Survey, it is clear that very large companies are investing millions in crime prevention and deterrence technologies with only the vendor's word that these countermeasures actually work as advertised. On the other end of the continuum, small businesses are doing without simple and effective crime prevention tools, only because they cannot independently evaluate their suitability.

CONCLUSION

The significant negative impact of crime against business is clearly a major problem affecting the continued viability of our nation's economic health. As we move into a business world with increasing international and domestic competition, crime becomes a much more important problem. Toward this end, a number of changes need to occur.

First, businesses need to do a better job of assessing the prevalence and detecting the crimes committed against them. As the principal victims of the offense, they are also the most capable of both detecting and immediately responding when these offenses occur. Private corporate security operations should be given substantial legal responsibility and logistical support in this effort. Public law enforcement cannot be expected to finance, take over, or even coordinate this effort. Instead, this should be done privately with the assistance and active cooperation of local law enforcement. Proportionately more support should be afforded to smaller businesses who do not have a separate security department.

Second, monies should be expended at the national level to help business tabulate the crimes and losses discovered. Just as official crime statistics and victimization data are assembled for crimes against the public, business crime should be elevated to a major research focus as well. Along with the Uniform Crime Reports and the National Crime Victimization Survey, an annual survey of business crime should be initiated.

Third, controlled research studies need to be funded and conducted that allow for an impartial scientific evaluation of the various loss-prevention programs, policies and systems that are contemplated or currently in use. Clear evidence of actual effectiveness needs to be documented before money is wasted on crime prevention countermeasures that do not work or actually make the problem worse.

Finally, resources need to be provided at the national and state level to enhance the training of private security and loss-prevention personnel. Just as local, state and federal police are trained at various academies, private security should also be assisted in these efforts to improve educational standards. Given the scope of this crime problem, the effect on our economy and the numerous interrelationships between those crimes committed against business and conventional criminality, we must do a better job of improving the training standards of this, the most-numerous, category of law enforcement personnel. While the various trade and professional associations have taken significant steps toward improving the level of security and loss-prevention training in this country (for example, American Society for Industrial Security, Association of Certified Fraud Examiners, the International Association of Hospital Security, the National Retail Federation, and the International Mass Retailers Association), a much more coordinated effort needs to be made in our battle with crime against business. Every recent study conducted on the state of the art in the area of private security has come to this very same conclusion (see Kakalik and Wildhorn, 1971; Van Meter, 1976; Cunningham and Taylor, 1985; and Cunningham et al., 1990). The need was most clearly stated, as follows, in the first *Hallcrest Report*:

> Citizen fear of crime and awareness that criminal justice resources alone cannot effectively control crime has lead to a growing use of individual and corporate protective measures, including private security products and services and neighborhood based crime prevention. Law enforcement resources have stabilized and in some cases are declining. This mandates greater cooperation with the private sector

and its private security resources to jointly forge a partnership on an equal basis for crime prevention and reduction. Law enforcement can ill afford to continue isolating and, in some cases, ignoring this important resource. The creative use of private security human resources and technology may be the one viable option left to control crime in our communities [Cunningham and Taylor, 1985:275].

REFERENCES

American Management Associations (AMA) (1977). *Summary Overview of the "State of the Art" Regarding Information Gathering Techniques and Level of Knowledge in Three Areas Concerning Crimes against Business.* (Draft Report). Washington, DC: U.S. National Institute of Law Enforcement and Criminal Justice.

Bacas, H. (1987). "To Stop a Thief." *Nation's Business* June:16-23.

Bachman, R. (1994). *Violence and Theft in the Workplace.* Washington, DC: Bureau of Justice Statistics, U.S. Department of Justice.

Baker, M. and A. Westin (1988). *Employer Perceptions of Workplace Crime.* Washington, DC: Bureau of Justice Statistics, U.S. Department of Justice.

Bamfield, J. and R. Hollinger (1996). "Managing Losses in the Retail Store: A Comparison of Loss Prevention Activity in the United States and Great Britain." *Security Journal* 7:61-70.

Baumer, T. and D. Rosenbaum (1984). *Combating Retail Theft: Programs and Strategies.* Boston, MA: Butterworth.

Bellamy, L. (1996). "Situational Crime Prevention and Convenience Store Robbery." *Security Journal* 7:41-52.

Braithwaite, J. (1989). *Crime, Shame and Reintegration.* New York, NY: Cambridge University Press.

Canadian Business (1976). "Crime in Business: Stop Employee Theft, It's Money Down the Drain." 49: 12,14,16.

Chamber of Commerce of the United States (1974). *A Handbook of White Collar Crime.* Washington, DC: Chamber of Commerce.

Chatterton, M. and S. Frenz (1994). "Closed-circuit Television: Its Role in Reducing Burglaries and Fear of Crime in Sheltered Accommodations for the Elderly." *Security Journal* 5:133-139.

Clark, J. and R. Hollinger (1983). *Theft By Employees in Work Organizations. Executive Summary.* Washington, DC: U.S. Government Printing Office.

Cressey, D. (1953). *Other People's Money.* New York, NY: Free Press.

Cunningham, W., J. Strauchs and C. Van Meter (1990). *Private Security Trends 1970-2000: The Hallcrest II Report.* Boston, MA: Butterworth-Heinemann.

—— and T. Taylor (1985). *Private Security and Police in America: The Hallcrest Report.* Portland, OR: Chancellor Press.

Davis, M.G., R. Lundman and R. Martinez (1991). "Private Corporate Justice: Store Police, Shoplifters, and Civil Recovery." *Social Problems* 38:395-413.

DiLonardo, R. (1996). "Defining and Measuring the Economic Benefit of Electronic Article Surveillance." *Security Journal* 7:3-9.

—— and R.V. Clarke (1996). "Reducing the Rewards of Shoplifting: An Evaluation of Ink Tags." *Security Journal* 7:11-14.

Ditton, J. and G. Nair (1994). "Throwing Light on Crime: A Case Study of the Relationship Between Street Lighting and Crime Prevention." *Security Journal* 5:125-132.

Hollinger, R. (1989). *Dishonesty in the Workplace: A Manager's Guide to Preventing Employee Theft.* Rosemount, IL: McGraw-Hill/London House.

—— and D. Dabney (1994). "Reducing Shrinkage in the Retail Store: It's Not Just a Job for the Loss Prevention Department." *Security Journal* 5 (1):2-10.

—— and D. Dabney (1995). *1995 National Retail Security Survey. Final Report* with *Executive Summary.* Gainesville, FL: University of Florida.

Kakalik, J. and S. Wildhorn (1971). *The Private Police in the United States: Findings and Recommendations.* Santa Monica, CA: The Rand Corporation.

Lary, B. (1988). "Thievery on the Inside." *Security Management* 32:79-84.

Lipman, M. (1973). *Stealing: How America's Employees are Stealing Their Companies Blind.* New York, NY: Harper's Magazine Press.

Mirrlees-Black, C. and A. Ross (1995a). *Crime Against Manufacturing Premises in 1993.* Home Office Research Findings No. 27. London, UK: Home Office Research and Statistics Department.

—— and A. Ross (1995b). *Crime Against Retail Premises in 1993.* Home Office Research Findings No. 26. London, UK: Home Office Research and Statistics Department.

Painter, K. (1994). "The Impact of Street Lighting on Crime, Fear, and Pedestrian Street Use." *Security Journal* 4:116-124.

Poyner, B. (1988). "Video Cameras and Bus Vandalism." *Journal of Security Administration* 11(2):44-51.

Robin, G. (1970). "The Corporate and Judicial Disposition of Employee Thieves." In: E. Smigel and H. Ross (eds.), *Crimes Against Bureaucracy.* New York, NY: Van Nostrand Reinhold.

Shapland, J. (1995). "Preventing Retail-Sector Crimes." In: M. Tonry and D.P. Farrington (eds.), *Building a Safer Society: Strategic Approaches to Crime Prevention.* Crime and Justice. Vol. 19. Chicago, IL: University of Chicago Press.

Shepard, I. and R. Duston (1988). *Thieves At Work: An Employer's Guide to Combating Workplace Dishonesty.* Washington, DC: The Bureau of National Affairs.

U.S. Department of Commerce (1976). *The Cost of Crimes Against Business.* Bureau of Domestic Commerce, Domestic and International Business Administration. Washington, DC: Superintendent of Documents.

U.S. Federal Bureau of Investigation (FBI) (1995). *Crime in the United States, 1994. Uniform Crime Reports.* Washington, DC: Federal Bureau of Investigation.

U.S. Law Enforcement Assistance Administration (1976). *Two Hundred Years of American Criminal Justice.* Washington, DC: U.S. Government Printing Office.

Van Meter, C. (1976). *Private Security.* Report of the Task Force on Private Security. Washington, DC: National Advisory Committee on Criminal Justice Standards and Goals.

TECHNOLOGY, BUSINESS, AND CRIME

by Marcus Felson
Rutgers, The State University of New Jersey

Abstract: *Technology involves a human touch. Business and industry are the driving forces of technological innovation. They produce crime opportunities as well as crime prevention. Inadvertent examples are probably more important than those in which business and industry prevent crime intentionally. Such obnoxious examples as the auto alarm tell little about the broad role of technology in crime prevention. In this chapter, we take a look at human ecological theory and the theory of inventions, as well as incremental changes in technology that can assist in crime prevention. These changes depend greatly on human growth, organization and usage.*

Technology and crime are related. Yet to understand their relationship, we need to get beyond public knowledge. Public experience with technology, and even the public meaning of the word, is terribly misleading. Technology in 1996 implies the "World Wide Web," advanced computers, robotics, heavy technical education, nerds, complex microcircuitry, bioengineering, Hubbell telescopes with computer enhancements, positron microscopes and whatever complex scientific gains get on the list by the time this paper is published.

Unfortunately, the word "technology" has been hijacked to represent only a small share of what actually happens in business and industry, and in society itself. Some scholars of technology offer us a theory for analyzing and describing it and how it influences society. I review their main points. Then I apply these points to help analyze how technological changes have consequences for crime and crime prevention. In the process, I emphasize how business and industry make technology work for practical purposes. That means making money. It also means making jobs easier. Yet, there are bad side effects sometimes, with business and industry helping to expand crime opportunities. These same actors in society also help to improve crime prevention. They do so best in areas that get the least publicity.

The words "technology and crime" bring to mind the example of a sophisticated hacker. The words "technology and crime prevention" bring to mind the image of a complex household security system or a noisy car alarm waking up the neighborhood. No examples could be less representative of what is important. It is easy to recognize this with a little information from the sociology of technology, a field to which I now turn.

Reviewing the Theory of Technology

William F. Ogburn (1964) is perhaps the leading sociologist ever to have studied technology. Emerging from the "Chicago School" at the University of Chicago Department of Sociology, Ogburn's essays and books examined how specific technologies changed society. He was very critical of the more remote theories of "social structure." In particular, he doubted that social norms and social inequality were the driving forces of social change. His punishment was to be removed from the standard lists of theorists by sociologists and criminologists. Indeed, the Chicago School is generally described with Ogburn's name left out.

Ogburn thought that changes in technology tend to drive changes in society. He also coined the term "cultural lag." The idea was simple: technology changed first and culture changed later; but culture took a while to catch up. Any element of culture that is not very practical for the current state of technology is a cultural lag. Thus, a business person in Paris who still goes home for a heavy midday meal with wine represents a cultural lag; traffic is too heavy for this to be practical, but many people do it anyway. Yet fast food grows, even in Paris. Traffic paralysis forces behavior to change and overwhelms culture itself. This does not deny that culture exists, or that it hangs on, or that it is an intervening variable; but technology is ultimately the stronger force. This offers a lesson for criminology: we must stop assuming that changes in crime must be driven by changing culture. Most likely, changing technology forces crime to change, with culture trailing along in the background distracting the analyst.

For Ogburn, some of the most important technology was far from complicated. Indeed, very basic items could change everyday life. A favorite example is barbed wire. It is made by sharpening ends of wire and twisting wires in opposite directions — simpler than building space capsules. Yet it served to settle the American West by making it possible to privatize stretches of the range, keeping one owner's cattle away from the neighbor's land. The history of technology is replete with examples of *small* inventions with major significance.

S.C. Gilfillan (1970) developed this important point in a 1935 classic entitled, *Sociology of Invention*. Among the questions Gilfillan asks is: Who invented the ship? The answer is that no single person did so. The ship was invented in small increments over thousands of years. Gilfillan points out that most technology develops incrementally. Moreover, a single clever improvement will be largely ignored for years until the other pieces are in place. Gilfillan's perspective on inventions closely resembles the general theory of science offered later by Thomas Kuhn (1970).

Another principle emerges from Ogburn: technology is not just gadgets, but also requires that people know how to use them. Norman (1988) has written of making gadgets easy for people to use. Ideally, this involves one easy step, like pushing a button. But when many steps are required, they need to be organized. Thus, a complex organization may be designed so that everyone within it has a clear and easy task, a point well recognized from the work of Max Weber (1922). In addition, teaching individuals the complexities of their responsibilities at work or the gadgets they use in leisure time depends upon simplifying steps, even for a complex gadget. The more complicated the gadget, the more necessary it is to simplify how people use it and learn to use it.

These various points are summarized in the following six principles of technological innovation, which together tell us much about how technology grows and serves people and society:

(1) the Small is Big Principle — small inventions have major consequences;

(2) the Little Steps Principle — complex technology grows in small increments;

(3) the Not Yet Principle — a technological gain is not used right away because a larger system must be ready for it;

(4) the People Do It Principle — people and human organization make gadgets work;

(5) the Easy Use Principle — the easier it is to use, the more impact it will have; and

(6) the Break it Down Principle — complexity is a lot of simple little steps; teaching technology and organizing people to use it require dividing it up.

These six principles of technological innovation are better understood not as fragments but as part of a more general theory. Ogburn's technological theory of society does part of the job but not all of it.

Human Ecology as a Larger Framework

The theory of human ecology helps us to organize information about how technology relates to crime. Toxic waste dumps or polluted water are a tiny corner of human ecology, and certainly do not define the field. Amos Hawley (1950) systematized human ecology and made it part of a larger ecological theory of living things. Its basic principle is adaptation to the environment. This includes business, making money, saving money, going to college, buying a home, keeping the home safe — anything that helps people survive and prosper. Human needs and wants are defined broadly. Interdependence among people serves adaptation to the environment. Symbiosis, cooperation, competition, predation — each of these processes helps us to understand human adaptation. Technology is a major tool for adapting to the larger environment. Thus, Ogburn's theory fits neatly within Hawley's theory, which gives technology itself a driving force.

The combination of technology and human ecology has been summed up by O.D. Duncan (1959), who offers us the acronym, P.O.E.T., for Population, Organization, Environment and Technology. The population (P) adapts to the environment (E). It uses technology (T) and organization (O) to make that adaptation.[1] In practice, it is often difficult to slice technology and organization into two distinct parts. (The current paper does not worry about this.) Yet these analytical distinctions, along with the six principles of technological innovation, help us understand the role of technology in crime production and crime prevention. These principles also help us to understand why business is at the core of technology.

Business and the Six Principles

High school history books tend to pick a famous individual who invented something important and complex. This "great man theory" raises two problems. First, it neglects the significance for the growth of technology of many people. Second, it forgets that most improvements in technology are small and incremental. We quickly see that business is the instrument for incremental innovation. Business develops small inventions that may have major consequences. Business takes the small steps to make something practical, usable, easy to mass produce and marketable. Business figures out which bits of technology can be put to quick use and when to wait. Business trains people to use gadgets. Business makes things easier to use and spreads it so more people can use it. Business evaluates the human use of gadgets, dividing it into slices and steps. In the process, business produces opportunities for people; sometimes offenders take advantage. Thus, if we want to understand how the six principles relate to crime production and prevention, we need to consider business. I shall come back to this point later. Next I discuss the three minimal elements of predatory crime that help us analyze its change.

Minimal Elements of Crime

A direct-contact predatory crime requires direct physical contact among these three elements: a likely offender, a suitable target, and the absence of capable guardians against a crime. A likely offender may be a young male or anybody else so inclined, but we should assume that virtually the whole population has the ability to be tempted if the opportunity is right. A suitable target against a crime is determined by four elements summed by the acronym VIVA: value, inertia, visibility, and access. When something is highly valuable *to the likely offender*, that makes it a more suitable target for crime. Thus, invention and mass production of goods appealing to youths make more targets. Inertia refers to the difficulty in moving a target. Lightweight targets make for more crime. Goods that are very high in value per pound, or are on wheels, are excellent targets. Any inventions that reduce inertia of valuable goods make them more suitable targets for crime. Visibility includes placement of targets where they can be seen by likely offenders. Access refers to the offender's opportunities to get to the crime target and to make his exit. The diffusion of goods to a large population, the production of accessories to be placed in cars, the use of one-story buildings to store valuable goods, the spread of self-service stores, the construction of boulevards and straight streets with easy access, the development of transit systems taking people around more quickly — all of these contribute to the visibility and access of crime targets.

The third minimal element of a predatory crime is the absence of a capable guardian against it. In non-business crime, the guardian is most likely a friend or family member or you looking after yourself or your property. Guardianship seldom involves police. It is mostly inadvertent, occurring in the context of normal life. Indeed, the third minimal element is defined by absence rather than presence. In a business setting, one naturally thinks of private guards as guardians against crime. However, guardianship is more complicated than that (see Felson, 1995b). Store clerks, customers, drivers, dock foremen, receptionists — all of these serve a guardianship function in business settings. They may be assigned the job of checking entry, of having responsibility for an area, or checking goods and equipment in and out. In the process, they are very important for crime prevention, even if they have no uniform or if the word "crime" is never mentioned in their job titles. As with non-business settings, absences are as important as presences in making crime easy to do. Given the high cost of hiring guards, it may make more sense to build guardianship into larger job responsibilities and to organize business areas so that it is feasible to put such guardianship into action. Thus, an office suite organized so the receptionist can see who enters and then offer assistance is less likely to suffer from thefts and need not hire a guard doing no other productive work.

These minimal elements have an important implication: we can have a crime wave without necessarily having more offenders. Such a wave may result from an increase in suitable targets or absences of capable guardians. Most important, we need to think in terms of convergences among the minimal elements. If a likely offender finds a suitable target in the absence of a capable guardian, that convergence has occurred and so can a criminal act.

We now seek to explain America's major 20th century crime rate in terms of the minimal elements, plus the six principles mentioned earlier.

Technology of a Crime Wave

From 1963 to 1975, the United States experienced a massive crime wave. The wave has only receded partly since; even some noteworthy reductions have not put crime rates back at the 1960 level. This historic crime wave hit all modern nations except Japan.

Prior research on the American increase (Cohen and Felson, 1979; Felson and Cohen, 1981) concluded that it has two major sources: a diffusion of lightweight durable goods and the dispersion of activities away from family and household. The diffusion of lightweight durable goods in the American population during those years produced many more targets for crime. It was made possible by technology: plastics and transistors. Both had been around for a while but were not immediately ready for cheap mass production. There were plastic transistor radios made in the 1950s, but these were mere curiosities. During the 1960s, the baby boom reached its teenage years to find a vast increment in things easy to steal. Lightweight television sets, radios, stereo components, combined with an expanding economy to feed crime. (Note that the old saw that bad economic times are the source of crime does not hold in a modern industrial economy.) One study (Felson and Cohen, 1981) found that the best predictor of the burglary rate in any particular year was the weight of the lightest television in the Sears catalogue for that year.

A dispersion of activities away from family and household settings was even more important. There were many more people living in single-adult households, with young adults moving out to their own apartments sooner and with those widowed and divorced not moving in with other adult family members. Intact husband-wife households more often had the wife working. Around 1950, about two-thirds of households fit the traditional pattern: husband and wife living together with the wife not working. By 1975, only a third of the households fit that traditional pattern. This left most households empty during the day when people went to work or when single adults left to do any other business. Not only one's own household, but neighboring households, were empty. This meant the guardians were absent.

Technology also helped disperse activities away from households. As less brawn was required to do work, women could do it as readily as men. As automobiles became more accessible, the two-car family became commonplace and women were freed from the neighborhood. Society's leading guardians against crime had other fish to fry. Friendships for men or women no longer were confined locally, and work choices no longer structured by mass transit lines or walking distance. Thus, work, social life and even shopping were dispersed over more space, leaving one's own block relatively unsupervised. This is why there was a crime wave: more offenders (baby boomers getting old enough) found more targets (lightweight durables) in the absence of guardians (household members at home and people one knows well right there).

Note that the six principles of technological innovation apply readily. Tiny transistors contributing to a massive crime wave offer an excellent illustration of the Small is Big Principle. The Little Steps Principle applies as these transistors were perfected and used to create a new consumer electronics industry. The Not Yet Principle applies well to plastics, which had been around for decades but for which the other parts of the stereo system and its marketing were not yet ready. The People Do It Principle is important because the organizational structure of work and job location took time to adjust to the automobile's potential to deliver a labor force. As work, job and shopping spread, guardianship of property was diluted and crime made easier (see Felson, 1994a). The Easy Use Principle was applied by those producing and marketing stereo sets beyond aficionados; as the general market was found, there were more targets to steal and more demand for a hot stereo set. The Break It Down Principle applied to the development of the entire home entertainment industry, including television, stereo, car tape players, compact disk players, and video cassette recorders. Each of these industries began with entrepreneurs and innovative technical people; even their customers worked by trial and error. The industries in time broke the parts down, taught the technology, divided up the labor, made things easy for the public and spread their goods everywhere. Hundreds of millions of people could own and use these electronic products, which were now worth stealing.

Will the March of Technology Solve Its Own Problem?

In time, certain goods became so widespread and low in cost that they were not worth stealing. For example, the electronic calculator was once a high-priced item, often stolen. In time, the plain calculator became under five dollars in value; few people would bother to steal it any more. As prices for the basic model fell, the industry followed a standard pattern: it added new features and complexities in order to have something to sell at a higher price. These new calculators then became the target of theft. However, a smaller segment of the population was interested in the new complexities or could even use them. Meanwhile, even scientific calculators fell enough in value that there was no reason to steal them anymore. Computers took over much of their market and themselves went through the same growth cycle, with costs for old features declining while capacities and features expanded to keep the prices from falling. As computers have packed more value into less weight, the resulting laptop computers created another family of crime targets. Their high value per pound makes laptop computers excellent for crime, but they, as yet, are far less widespread than portable television sets or radios.

Some developments in technology, following the Little Steps Principle, make non-targeted items of the past more interesting to offenders of the present. For example, thieves in the past stole the computer but left the laser printer alone. As laser printers are becoming much lighter, they too are prime targets for theft. In short, sometimes products change and sometimes their functions change within a larger system. In either case, the suitability for theft shifts over time.

We face, here, a theoretical question: is there any limit on the capacity of the electronics industry to invent valuable lightweight goods with mass appeal? Will new goods appear at high cost and others replace them when the price has to fall? Will old goods that were too heavy for theft finally be changed so they are no longer unattractive?

Certainly, industry has incentives to make things lighter, more convenient, suitable for more customers and, thus, more amenable to theft. Perhaps there is no long-run prospect for technology to solve its own problem. On the other hand, four factors do give us a prospect that technology can reduce the targets for crime. First, goods tend to get less expensive over time and eventually not worth stealing. Second, to add value they must become more esoteric, narrowing their market for sales and for fencing stolen goods. Third, an aging population may be less interested in the sort of consumer durables that are most easily stolen, especially those in the car. This could be the strongest explanation for any recent declines in crime rates from their peak. Fourth, home electronics producers may be reluctant to make goods too light and small since customers might not be willing to buy expensive items whose small size makes them hardly seem to be worth the price. Unlike electronic goods in cars, whose compactness is justifiable due to limited space in which to place them, home electronics products usually need not be so compact. This is consistent with the growth in marketing of very large and heavy television sets — a reversal of the long-term trends toward lighter television sets. Having tried to carry a newer model, even with the help of a very large friend, I will never do so again. There is every reason to expect that burglars have discovered this same point. Thus, there remains some room to argue that the technologies that fostered crime-rate increases may contribute to their reductions.

Even if a "natural" solution is not forthcoming, we can foresee cycles in the value of goods and lapses in time before new high-priced items are widespread enough to influence the national crime rates. Crime-rate cycles may reflect product changes: when old products are fading in value or their markets are saturated, crime rates should fall; as new products come in, the rates may begin to rise, especially as they become mass-market items.

Designing Out Crime

The term "designing out crime" (Clarke and Mayhew, 1980) covers several categories of crime prevention. They may roughly be divided further according to "people," "places" and "things." "Designing people" means, in effect, designing business management systems so as to reduce crime. "Designing places" is often called "crime prevention through environmental design" or CPTED (see Jeffery, 1971; Brantingham and Brantingham, 1991; Felson, 1995a). "Designing things" is an often-neglected category (Felson, 1987). Products can be designed to be difficult to steal or to self-destruct if removed illegally. Clarke's 12 categories of situational crime prevention (see Clarke, 1995; 1992; 1983) include many examples of redesigning things. Most often, efforts to redesign things to prevent crime occur within business locations. For example, retailers add ink tags to make their clothing not worth stealing, since attempts to remove the tags spoil the target of crime.

Often neglected is a special subcategory of redesigning things (see Felson, 1987). I call this "intrinsic prevention." By this, I mean the design and production of goods in the factory itself to make them difficult to steal or to use for crime. For example, many auto electronic products are now designed so the faceplate can be removed by the car owner. What is left is not worth stealing. Thus, the product intrinsically prevents crime, as long as the owner removes the faceplate. This is an improvement on the products that slid out because owners typically failed to slide them out or stored them in the trunk or under the seat. Offenders figured this out and broke in anyway. The faceplate is light enough that it is quite easy to take with you. Unfortunately, some owners still forget to do that.

It is quite easy to design products that require a four- or five-digit activation code. Just as each of us memorizes a bank code number, we can we use the same or a different code to render our car tape player, television, video cassette recorder (VCR), compact disk player, or other goods unusable to the thief or his customers. This makes these goods intrinsically unsuitable for theft. However, it does not suffice if only a few people have such goods. A burglar is very likely not to know that your VCR is intrinsically unusable; he may steal it anyway and dump it somewhere when he finds it does not work. Until it becomes widely known which goods have this property, the incentive to steal VCRs remains. Ideally, all or most VCRs should require an activation code, and all or most owners should avoid using 000 or some obvious code.

The issue is not the small cost of making intrinsically unstealable products but getting the system to change. The industry has little incentive to make that change. If someone has trouble getting the code to work or forgets the code, he or she may come back to the merchant or service company. The merchant wants the customer to pay, leave and not return. Keeping a national registry of product numbers and secret codes is not desirable. Having customers complain when they cannot get the product activated is not desirable. Perhaps the organizations will sort all this out in time.

Designing out crime at automatic teller machines (ATMs or ATM machines) involves many of Clarke's categories. Management systems can be put into place to close these machines at dangerous hours. Redesigning places can include locating ATMs for more safety, while removing hedges and other obstructions and making it difficult to enter ATM areas without a card. Intrinsic prevention can also apply to ATMs, as manufacturers have already proven. Some ATMs beep to get the customer to take the card back right away. Keyboards are tilted so someone behind you cannot pick up your number easily for illegal use later. Machines can be designed to release less cash in a short period from the same account, or even from different locations. Some ATMs require re-entry of the code number when new tasks are requested. Many ATMs are also designed to get the customer to sign off so no one waiting in the wings can come back and get money from that account.

These intrinsic prevention examples closely fit under the rubric of situational prevention and designing out crime. It is especially interesting because it extends technology to reduce the crime that technology may have created in the first place.

The six principles of technological innovation apply clearly. The simple tilting of the screen is a Small is Big example. The Little Steps principle applies to many of these incremental improvements in ATMs. The Not Yet Principle is exemplified by the touch screen, which was developed over 25 years ago, but was not widely applied for public use until the ATM made that possible. The touch screen also makes it easy to give people who cannot type an easy way to choose among several selections and to enter codes quickly. This helps expand the potential for the machine while keeping controls working. The People Do It Principle corresponds to the growth of experience that banks have in making ATMs work for customers while reducing some of the crime potential. The Easy to Use Principle is relevant since an easy and quick use of the machine helps the customer avoid getting mugged or tricked by people pretending to help. Finally, the Break it Down Principle is increasingly evident in the ATM software, easing the customer's movement through the tasks, getting money and getting out without making mistakes. This helps reduce ATM-related crime.

Intrinsic prevention applies most directly to reducing property crime by making products difficult to steal or not worth stealing. However, products can be programmed to thwart violent crime, too. To discourage forced withdrawals from ATMs, they can be programmed to recognize strange withdrawal patterns or to recognize emergency codes. Then they would notify authorities, freeze up, or release only small amounts of money. To limit carjackings, automobiles can be programmed to require periodic entry of personal code numbers, without which they would cease operations. In short, technology can bring with it some potential reductions in crime opportunity.

Not only can one design out violent crime, but it is also possible to design out certain types of fraud. Many contemporary automobiles include computers that allow mechanics to analyze repair problems. All one has to do is plug in a line from the repair shop's computer to the auto computer. This produces a printout of the problem. Not only can the customer have a look at the printout, but he or she can purchase (for about $40) a kit to do a repair analysis independent of the mechanic. To be sure, a dishonest repair service can still recommend inappropriate solutions or claim problems in systems not computerized (such as the suspension, shock absorbers, steering and tires). Even so, computerized repair analysis can reduce the range of possibilities for repair fraud.

Welfare fraud can be reduced by improved computer scanning and comparisons of welfare lists. Design of auditing and accounting systems — taking into account computers, physical files and human checking — can contribute significantly in limiting fraud and malfeasance. In short, technology plays a role not only in contributing to crime problems but also to solutions. However, this is not accomplished without taking people into account when designing technology and when applying it to real-life situations. Nowhere is this more significant than with alarm systems.

Security Hardware — Putting People Back In

Unfortunately, the word "security" has come to refer to guards, locks, alarms and closed-circuit television (CCTV) — perhaps the least-effective instruments of crime prevention. Alarms and CCTV are the most widespread. Each has its limitations in reality, unless combined with strategic thinking and consideration of people.

Alarms are so commonplace that they tend to be ignored by citizens, police and private security personnel. They cry wolf electronically. The owner of something is often at some distance and unable to respond to the alarm. A remote alarm in a dispersed area gives the offender time to leave before security or police arrive. A home alarm in a neighborhood where not many people know one another is unlikely to be effective. The key to an effective alarm is a social structure to back it up. People have to know who belongs there and feel a responsibility to assist them. This is why I suggest a new form of alarm, linking human organization to technology. Let us suppose that three friendly neighbors with rather different schedules agree to set up a mutual car alarm system such that an incursion into any of their three cars will ring inside all three homes. They agree to look outside and see if something is really wrong with any of the cars and call the police or call out to the offender to stop the crime. Their mutual assistance makes use of technology, but it also uses social structure. They do not pretend that technology can substitute for neighborliness; they merely use it as an extra tool. This is quite consistent with Clarke and Mayhew (1980), who suggested that car alarms should ring only in the owner's home. It is also consistent with the British findings that neighborhood watch succeeds mainly when it is highly focused upon very close neighbors (Pease, 1992; Farrell, 1995).

Bringing the Public In

I have proposed (Felson, 1994b) a "crime prevention extension service" to help bring crime prevention ideas from criminology and get them into practice. Like the agricultural extension services, the information flow from lab to field is a two-way street. However, trying to reach everyone in the public through information campaigns is a difficult task, given the vast information overload in the mass media. Therefore, it makes more sense to work with business as purveyors of technology. It is easier to reach 100 business people than their 100,000 customers.

It is important to distinguish business crime prevention that is oriented toward the public from that which is detached from the public. Beginning with public-oriented business prevention, we cite Barry Poyner's (1996) important point that the goal of crime prevention is to help people to help themselves. For example, an alarm that is directed toward those who can do something about it is essentially public oriented. This is quite consistent with the concept of "routine precaution" (see Felson and Clarke, 1995), which states that people engage in crime prevention every day, but that crime prevention specialists can help them do so more intelligently. Business can contribute to this improvement in prevention by providing technology and tools that make people more effective. This does not mean that elaborate instructions need to be conveyed. Indeed, the greatest impact is probably achieved when very simple designs help people, for example, to find a safe parking spot, to make a car alarm work reasonably and directly (without driving the neighborhood crazy) and to make a car less amenable to theft.

This means that some prevention will be carried out without involving the public at all. For example, designing larger packages for compact disks helps reduce the ability to steal them. Such prevention is initiated by industrial designers and produced in the factory, without bringing the larger population into it. Nonetheless, these packages reflect a sense of how people behave and how to change it; how people are tempted and how to reduce such temptation while increasing the effort and risk for the potential offender. Similarly, the design of offices to make them less amenable to theft, or of ATMs to reduce their contribution to robbery, involves more than physical design. They are examples of *human* design. The general principle for business to learn in seeking to prevent crime is that technology, no matter how sophisticated, requires a human touch.

* * *

NOTES

1. The six principles above can be interpreted accordingly. Small technological changes may assist environmental adaptation (Principle 1). Technological steps are incremental as other parts of society and technology adapt (Principles 2 and 3). Human organization is an essential part of adaptation, combining with technology (Principles 4, 5 and 6). Note that Duncan not only makes more of organization but defines it distinctly from technology itself. We may think of Principles 4, 5, and 6 as included within O, while 1, 2, and 3 are part of T. However, the Easy Use Principle (Principle 5) and the Not Yet Principle (Principle 3) each touch upon both T and O.

REFERENCES

Brantingham, P.J. and P.L. Brantingham (1991). *Environmental Criminology*. Prospect Heights, IL: Waveland Press.

Clarke, R.V. (1983). "Situational Crime Prevention: Its Theoretical Basis and Practical Scope." In: M. Tonry and N. Morris (eds.), *Crime and Justice: A Review of Research*, vol. 4. Chicago, IL: University of Chicago Press.

—— (ed.) (1992). *Situational Crime Prevention: Successful Case Studies*. Albany, NY: Harrow and Heston.

—— (1995). "Situational Crime Prevention." In: M. Tonry and D.P. Farrington (eds.), *Building a Safer Society: Strategic Approaches to Crime Prevention. Crime and Justice: A Review of Research*, vol. 19. Chicago, IL: University of Chicago Press.

Clarke, R.V. and P.M. Mayhew (1980). *Designing out Crime*. London, UK: Her Majesty's Stationery Office.

Cohen, L.E. and Felson, M. (1979). "Social Change and Crime Rate Trends: A Routine Activity Approach." *American Sociological Review* 44:588-608.

Duncan, O.D. (1959). "Human Ecology and Population Studies." In: P.M. Hauser and O.D. Duncan (eds.), *The Study of Population: An Inventory and Appraisal*. Chicago, IL: University of Chicago Press.

Farrell, G. (1995). "Preventing Repeat Victimization." In: M. Tonry and D.P. Farrington (eds.), *Building a Safer Society: Strategic Approaches to Crime Prevention. Crime and Justice: A Review of Research*, vol. 19. Chicago, IL: University of Chicago Press.

Felson, M. (1987) "Products Which Go Kaputt When Stolen." Paper presented at the annual meeting of the American Society of Criminology, Montreal, CAN, November.

—— (1994a). *Crime and Everyday Life: Insights and Implications for Society.* Thousand Oaks, CA: Pine Forge Press.

—— (1994b). "A Crime Prevention Extension Service." In: R.V. Clarke (ed.), *Crime Prevention Studies*, vol. 3. Monsey: NY: Criminal Justice Press.

—— (1995a) "How Buildings Can Protect Themselves Against Crime." *Lusk Review for Real Estate Development and Urban Transformation* 1(1):1-7.

—— (1995b). "Those Who Discourage Crime." In: J.E. Eck and D. Weisburd (eds.), *Crime and Place. Crime Prevention Studies*, vol. 4. Monsey, NY: Criminal Justice Press.

—— and R.V. Clarke (1995). "Routine Precautions, Criminology, and Crime Prevention." In: H.D. Barlow (ed.), *Crime and Public Policy: Putting Theory to Work.* Boulder, CO: Westview Press.

—— and L.E. Cohen (1981). "Modeling Crime Rate Trends — A Criminal Opportunity Perspective." *Journal of Research in Crime and Delinquency* 18:138-164 (as corrected (1982) 19:1).

Gilfillan, S.C. (1970). *The Sociology of Invention.* Cambridge, MA: MIT Press. [originally published in 1935]

Hawley, A.H. (1950). *Human Ecology: A Theory of Community Structure.* New York, NY: Ronald Press.

Jeffery, C.R. (1971). *Crime Prevention through Environmental Design.* Beverly Hills, CA: Sage.

Kuhn, T.S. (1970). *The Structure of Scientific Revolutions.* (2nd ed.) Chicago, IL: University of Chicago Press.

Norman, D.A. (1988). *The Psychology of Everyday Things.* New York, NY: Basic Books.

Ogburn, W.F. (1964). *On Culture and Social Change: Selected Papers.* Edited by O.D. Duncan. Chicago, IL: University of Chicago Press.

Pease, K. (1992). "The Kirkholt Project: Preventing Burglary on a British Public Housing Estate. In: R.V. Clarke (eds.), *Situational Crime Prevention: Successful Case Studies.* Albany, NY: Harrow and Heston.

Poyner, B. (1996). "Keynote Speech." In: *Policy Forum on Crime Prevention through Real Estate Development and Management, June, 1995.* Washington, DC: Urban Land Institute.

Weber, M. (1922). *Wirtschaft und Gesellschaft.* Tubingen: J.C.B. Mohr. [Translation (1946) as "Bureaucracy." In: H. Gerth and C.W. Mills (eds.), *From Max Weber: Essays in Sociology.* New York, NY: Oxford University Press.]

TOWARDS EFFECTIVE PUBLIC-PRIVATE PARTNERSHIPS IN CRIME CONTROL: EXPERIENCES IN THE NETHERLANDS

by Jan J.M. van Dijk

Netherlands Ministry of Justice and University of Leiden

Abstract: *This paper describes recent developments in public-private cooperation in the area of crime prevention in the Netherlands. These developments were carried out in the context of a Dutch society in which there were rising crime rates, fear of crime and a generally non-punitive attitude. Successful crime prevention measures from the 1980s, combining service-oriented surveillance and social crime prevention-with-a-bite, are described. In the 1990s, commercial crime victimization studies were conducted and a National Platform for Crime Control (The Platform), including participants from both the business sphere and governmental agencies, was set up. This paper describes several initiatives supported by the Platform, including the International Crimes against Business Survey (ICBS).*

INTRODUCTION

Recent developments in public-private cooperation in the control of crime in the Netherlands must be seen against the background of overall trends in crime prevention and control in that country. In the first twenty years after the Second World War, the Netherlands was still relatively little touched by crime: it had one of the lowest recorded crime rates of Europe. The imprisonment rate declined to a mere 20 per 100,000, an international record.

Up to the mid-1960s, Dutch society enjoyed a high level of social integration. Existing class differences were mitigated by the welfare state and powerful religious denominations. But, as elsewhere in the Western world, the joint processes of modernization, urbanization and secularization brought about a more individualistic and hedonistic lifestyle in the 1960s. The increased economic wealth also created more opportunities to commit crimes, such as shoplifting, car vandalism and bicycle theft. As a consequence, a sustained increase in petty crime was set in motion. This trend was reinforced by the growing number of hard-drug addicts and unemployed youngsters. For those who thought that the rising crime rates were due to improved reporting, police recording of crime, or both, the results of the first two International Crime Surveys (van Dijk et al., 1990; van Dijk and Mayhew, 1992) were disappointing. The overall victimization rate, including bicycle theft and car vandalism, stood at the level of that in the U.S.A. The Netherlands together with the U.K. ranked the highest in Western Europe. Although it can be noted that the murder rate in the Netherlands is still fairly low (about one per 100,000 inhabitants), crime definitely had become a serious social problem in the larger Dutch towns.

The combination of rising crime rates and fear of crime and a generally non-punitive attitude posed a particular problem for Dutch policy makers. Expansion of the prison capacity, although inescapable with a view to international sentencing tariffs for drugs dealers, was seen by only a few as a cure for the problem. Treatment in prisons had lost much of its credibility as a realistic aim of criminal justice. The deterrent value of more punitive policies was also regarded as doubtful. Further expansions of the welfare state with the aim to address social root causes of crime did not seem realistic either. In many respects, the welfare state in the Netherlands was and is among the most generous and comprehensive in the world. In the context of a fiscal crisis, globalization of the economy and the deepening of European economic integration further expansions seemed unlikely.

In response to the growing concerns about crime, the prison capacity was expanded, but serious investments were also made into an underdeveloped, but promising, new policy — crime prevention. The main thrust behind the new policy came from a committee of experts, set up in 1983 by the government, to reassess crime control policies (the Roethof Committee). The committee was critical of tendencies to belittle the seriousness of crime. It also criticized over-idealistic approaches by street-corner workers. The committee of representatives of all major political parties recommended a strengthening of the government's commitment to crime prevention, the involvement of the private sector and the encouragement of interagency cooperation at the local level.

The government presented in 1985 a policy plan to combat crime that announced an expansion of the prison system, as well as a new, full-fledged crime prevention policy. The philosophy behind the crime prevention policy was both pragmatic and eclectic. The policy was given three practical aims:

(1) crime prevention through environmental design;

(2) strengthening of surveillance in high-risk environments by service personnel such as conductors in public transport, concierges in public housing, janitors in schools and park wardens; and

(3) better social integration of high-risk youngsters through, for instance, truancy control in the school system, supervised leisure activities and job-guarantee programs for young people leaving school.

To implement the policy, a fund was set up of $30 million (in U.S. dollars) to subsidize promising projects by local government. Ten percent of the budget was set aside for evaluation purposes.

A meta-evaluation of 30 carefully evaluated projects concluded that crime prevention projects can indeed be effective (Polder and Van Vlaardingen, 1992). The most successful projects introduced employee surveillance in public housing (Hesseling, 1992), shopping centers and public transport (van Andel, 1989; Hauber, 1987) and community service to benefit the victimized party, as a diversionary option for juvenile vandals and shoplifters (Kruissink, 1989) and a better control over truancy and dropping out (Willemse, 1994).

The concept of employing the long-term unemployed as surveillance and service personnel — first pioneered in public transport — was extended to other areas. In the inner cities of several towns, teams of *city guards* were introduced. City guards are uniformed functionaries who patrol public areas without police authority. They give advice to tourists and intervene if people litter the street, drive a bicycle on the pavement, or otherwise cause problems. They also report on irregularities to the parking police and other municipal agencies. If necessary, the police provide a back-up service. The city guards are recruited from the long-term unemployed and largely paid for by the Ministry of Employment. They are given a three-week initial training by the police and are supposed to pass an examination for private security guard after a year or so.

The city guard projects were evaluated positively by the University of Leiden (Hauber et al., 1994). Feelings of insecurity and some forms of crime were reduced. Most city guards find secure employment with private security firms within two years. At present, city guards are operational in more than 40 towns. City guards were also introduced in residential areas, parking lots and recreational parks, among other places.

In general, success in crime prevention was related to three factors. First, the preventive effort needs to be strong and intensive (one concierge or janitor in a large housing block has no measurable effect). Second, the more serious the crime problem, the more difficult it is to get results with prevention (the behavior of people with a history of serious crimes is not easily changed by simple interventions outside the criminal justice system). Third, increasing the perceived effort needed to commit crimes and the perceived likelihood of punishment seem to be important elements of successful prevention projects. Neighborhood projects must be geared toward higher perceived probabilities of receiving some formal or informal sanction — for instance, through reduced accessibility, neighborhood watch and target hardening, combined with the presence of neighborhood police or city guards. Projects that supplied only information to the public or just some extra facilities for youngsters at risk (such as graffiti zones, leisure centers, or the assistance of detached workers) nearly always produced negligible results. In short, crime prevention must not be seen as a free lunch for the groups at issue, but as a mixture of carrots (new opportunities) and sticks (the threat of punishment).

In sum, the Dutch experience in the late 1980s provides evidence that situational crime prevention, through service-oriented surveillance and social crime prevention-with-a-bite, holds great potential as an answer to present or future crime problems and is a cost- effective crime-reduction strategy. In the 1990s, the crime prevention policy of the Netherlands government was pursued with new extended funding and a stronger infrastructure. At the municipal level, crime prevention is promoted as part of a more general policy drive to improve living conditions in deteriorated areas. The larger towns in particular were given substantial funding (over $100 million, in U.S. dollars) to address the marginalization of young people and the improvement of the quality of life in bad neighborhoods. Youth probation services and involuntary vocational training programs for hard-drug addicts will be strengthened as well. The sale of cannabis in so-called "coffee shops" will continue to be tolerated as a means to separate the consumers' markets for soft and hard drugs, but the rules will be more strictly enforced (The Netherlands' Drugs Policy, 1995).

The present government has also pledged to make funds available for the employment, by the municipalities, of another 10,000 long-term unemployed in surveillance-type jobs, such as city guards or "neighborhood concierges."

Nationally, the infrastructure consists of special policy units in the Ministries of Justice and the Interior and three national agencies with special responsibilities. One of the latter agencies oversees 50 local bureaus for community service orders for juveniles (the "HALT bureaus"). The second supports and coordinates 60 local bureaus for victim assistance. The third promotes and supports 50 or more municipal city-guard projects.

REACHING OUT TO THE BUSINESS SECTOR

The Roethof Committee did not recommend closer cooperation with the business community but emphasized cooperation with municipal agencies and the voluntary sector. Over the years the Ministry of Justice collaborated occasionally with the business community in particular prevention projects. This collaboration was never put on a more permanent footing. Examples include the prevention of crime in shopping centers and on industrial sites. Cooperation was sometimes hindered by mutual distrust and rivalries between police officers and in-house security officers.

The outcomes of the first victim survey conducted among a random sampling of businesses in the Netherlands were published in 1990 (van Dijk and Van Soomeren, 1990). The first commercial crime surveys were conducted in the United States in the early 1970s. These surveys were carried out at the national and city levels. They covered burglary and robbery incidents only. The U.S. commercial surveys were suspended in 1977. The Dutch survey was the first survey into criminal damage suffered by businesses that was carried out at a national scale. The survey showed that the business community in the Netherlands suffered an estimated $2 billion (in U.S. dollars) in losses from crime annually, which made up some 50% of the total damages resulting from conventional crime. The results of this survey helped to raise the awareness of the business community about its stake in crime control.

Apart from this, the business community became increasingly concerned about special crime problems. Major concerns at one point were the threats posed by political terrorism — for example, by groups condemning investments in South Africa. Armed robbery became a major concern of the banks. Against this background, the National Federation of Employers approached the government in the early 1990s with the proposal to set up a council on crime control. This proposal was initially met with reservations by the Ministers of Justice and the Interior. It was felt that the business community unduly claimed VIP treatment by the criminal justice system. It was also felt that security officers sought access to qualified and legally protected government information about criminal activities. Reservations were strongest among the directorates for police and prosecution. The proposals fell more favorably with the newly founded directorate for crime prevention of the Ministry of Justice, which saw interesting opportunities for cooperation with powerful strategic partners. In the ensuing negotiations, more emphasis was put on the actual and potential contributions of the business community to crime control through their own security efforts. Consensus was reached about the need for a real, non-exploitive partnership and the challenge to generate synergy between business security and law enforcement.

Goals and Structure of the National Platform for Crime Control

Eventually, the decision was made to set up a National Platform for Crime Control (The Platform) to address crime problems hurting the interests of the business sector. The goals of the Platform included:

(1) the analysis of crime trends;

(2) the setting of joint policy priorities;

(3) the improvement of security and law enforcement in relation to crimes against business; and

(4) the initiation of joint programs to tackle priority concerns.

It was decided that the Platform would be *action-oriented* and not pursue the tradition of conventional advisory councils of publishing lengthy reports on what the government ought to do. To ensure real commitment and decision-making power, both the government and the business community were to be represented at the highest level. The Platform is chaired by the Minister of Justice and co-chaired by the National Employers Federation's president and the Secretary of State of the Ministry of the Interior responsible for security. Representatives of the business sector are members of the executive boards of leading companies in retailing (AHOLD), industry (UNILEVER), transportation and communication (SCHIPHOL AIRPORT/KPN), banking (ABN/AMRO), insurance (ING), as well as high-ranking representatives of four ministries (Justice, Interior, Transport, and Economic Affairs), local government, prosecution, police and the security industry. The daily management is the responsibility of a small executive board, chaired by the author.

The Platform determines which crime problems will be addressed during the upcoming year. The most important criterion for selecting a subject is that joint action is desirable and cannot be secured by following standard procedures (such as reporting crimes to the police). The formal list of criteria is as follows:

(1) the business sector can be seen as a victim of the problem;

(2) the problem constitutes a threat to the health or welfare of employees, to the integrity, continuity, or profitability of the companies involved, or to both;

(3) the threat must be lasting (not an incident);

(4) collaboration between government and businesses is required;

(5) the project implies that there will be research on crime-control measures, the tackling of a crime problem and the promotion of security;

(6) there must be a transfer of knowledge or skills; and

(7) the results must be measurable.

Most activities are executed by special task forces that address priority concerns. In the first years of its existence, the Platform set up task forces on armed robbery, motorcar theft, information technology and crime, security and safety on industrial estates, financial institutions and crime, and ethical codes of conduct. The first two subjects were chosen at the request of the business sector. The subject of information technology and crime was proposed by the Ministry of Justice, which felt that computer-related frauds remained all too often unreported and that computer security among smaller businesses urgently needed improvement. Security on industrial sites was selected as a topic after the completion of a series of successful pilot projects with collective security arrangements that were based on collaboration between the police and private security firms. Improved collaboration in this area was seen as beneficial to all parties concerned. The choice of financial transactions and business ethics as special topics reflects the growing concern in the Netherlands about the economic activities of criminal organizations such as drug syndicates. The overall strategy of the Platform is determined by pragmatic considerations.

All task forces are supervised by steering committees representing the key partners at management level. In most cases, the steering committees are chaired by representatives of the business sectors that are primary stakeholders in the solution of the problems at hand. All activities of the task forces are, as a matter of principle, co-financed by the main partners. The steering committees present yearly action plans to the Platform that determines the available budgets and sets clear targets for the task forces in terms of output and external effects.

In the following paragraphs, we will discuss the main activities of the Platform. Also discussed will be the key findings of the international crimes against businesses survey, sponsored by the Platform. Finally, we will look at the future prospects for this new type public-private partnership.

Armed Robbery

The first priority concern of the Platform was armed robbery. The Platform decided to set up a steering committee in June 1992. The committee's chairman serves on the executive board of a Dutch multinational in retailing (AHOLD). Members include the Chief Executive Officer (CEO) of the Dutch post offices, the director of the national association of banks, a chief prosecutor, a chief of police and a mayor. The committee decided to form a task force of five full-time experts, comprising a senior inspector of the Amsterdam police, a security officer of the national association of banks, a security officer of the retailers association and a crime prevention expert from the Ministry of Justice. At its disposal for special projects is an annual budget of $1,000,000 (in U.S. dollars).

The task force on armed robberies has been instrumental in forming special robbery investigation units in a dozen regional police forces. Due to improved information sharing and extra efforts, the overall clearance rates have gone up by 50%. The security levels of all banks and post offices have been systematically upgraded through better access control and training of personnel. Four recommendations have been stressed in particular:

1) keep the contents of the cash register low;

2) use safes with time delay in combination with a robbery alarm button;

3) hand over the loot without offering resistance; and

(4) install video cameras in such a way that the face of the offender is clearly visible.

Evidence for the effectiveness of these measures is the reduced average amount of money lost per robbery. For the first time in many years, the total number of armed robberies went down across the board in 1994 and 1995 (see Table 1).

From 1993 to 1995, the robbery rate for financial institutions went down by more than 50%. In other European countries, the robbery rates are declining too but the reduction is much stronger in the Netherlands than elsewhere. There are no indications of displacement to other (commercial) targets, as is often assumed by outside commentators. Clarke, Field and McGrath (1991) also found no evidence of displacement to other commercial targets when bank robberies were reduced. The numbers of attacks on houses went up, but detailed analyses showed that these were committed by different groups of perpetrators and were often linked to drug dealing. There are indications that some robbers are now involved in organized car theft and the drug trade.

Table 1: Number of Armed Robberies Recorded by Dutch Police Forces

OBJECT	1990	1991	1992	1993	1994	1995
Shops	409	403	583	698	761	534
Financial institutions (including banks)	376	530	612	540	348	206
Restaurants	204	263	416	518	483	374
Gas stations	189	175	208	226	191	115
Private money transport services	104	107	124	205	151	151
Miscellaneous private offices	44	54	67	66	51	58
Taxicabs	17	29	28	76	91	53
Subtotal	1,343	1,561	2,038	2,329	2,076	1,491
Private Homes	174	191	174	278	313	409
Miscellaneous	116	95	79	118	113	107
Total	1,633	1,847	2,291	2,725	2,502	2,007

Source: Jammers, V. (1996) *Commercial Robbery in the Netherlands*. Vancouver, April 2, Ministry of Justice, the Netherlands.

Prevention of Crime on Industrial Sites: Public-Private Partnerships

As is true for many countries (compare, for England, Shapland and Wiles, 1993), Dutch industrial sites and parks are highly vulnerable to crimes like burglary, theft and vandalism. The concentration of valuable goods, the abandonment of the buildings after working hours and the isolated location (uninhabited areas and near getaway motorways) make industrial sites attractive for offenders. As was shown by the results of the

International Business Victim Surveys (see below and Appendix), business establishments have much higher victimization risks than private homes. Police forces spent valuable time on following up false alarms in industrial areas. To curb these problems, the Dutch Directorate of Crime Prevention supported a number of field experiments.

One of these experiments was initiated in the city of Vianen. On the main industrial site of Vianen, the transfer point of all telecommunication lines between the companies and the alarm centers of the police and several security firms were sabotaged by a criminal gang. This incident increased the awareness that security could perhaps be a joint effort of all companies together. A group, consisting of three representatives of the business community, two police officials and the mayor (chairman), analyzed the security risks and possible measures. They advised them to increase preventive surveillance as the shared responsibility of the companies and of the police: surveillance of the whole site by a private security firm should supplement police surveillance.

So the concept of public-private partnership was applied to enhance crime prevention. The companies — that is, 40 out of 190 — joined forces with the mayor and the police in a business partnership to improve the security of the Vianen Industrial Site. This partnership, funded by the participating companies, made a master contract with a private security firm. Agreements were made about responsibilities and the division of work by the police and the security firm. The extra, private surveillance during the night and (part of) the evening during working days (and all of the time during weekends) started on April 1, 1992. The effect was impressive: while daytime crime did not change (no extra surveillance), nighttime crime dropped by nearly 50%. This positive effect could be assessed for all of the target crimes, except for petty crimes like vandalism and small theft (see Table 2).

As a valuable side-effect, the police were no longer bothered by false alarms because the private security employee checked these out. By April 1994, 66 companies were participating in the project.

In a similar public-private partnership to improve security on an industrial site in the city of Enschede, the offense rate was reduced by 50% (Bergh and Jacobs, 1991). Encouraged by these successes, the National Crime Platform decided to extend this approach to other locations: a Task Force Collective Protection of Industrial Sites was set up to promote the original concept and to enlarge it with, for example, fire prevention. The directorate of crime prevention supports the further expansion of these projects by supplying subsidies. At the moment, more than 40 industrial sites have introduced similar protection measures. In several cases, the partnerships received financial support from the National Association of Insurers. This association offered this support as part of an agreement with the labor unions to create new jobs at the lower end of the job market. At the end of June 1996, due to this agreement, 800 jobs had been created in the field of security and surveillance.

Table 2: Crime Incidents on Industrial Site, City of Vianen, the Netherlands: In the Years Before and After Introduction of Extra Security Surveillance, April 1992

Offense Type	Before Extra Surveillance	After Extra Surveillance	Change
Theft of car/trailer	18	11	-39%
Theft from car	22	11	-50%
Commercial burglary	75	36	-52%
Misc. prop. crime	18	20	+11%
Total	133	78	-41%

Source: Van den Berg, E.M.C. (1995). "Crime Prevention on Industrial Sites: Security through Public-Private Partnerships." *Security Journal* 6 (1):27-35.

The future of this approach is promising: public-private partnership in the field of security has proven to be feasible, for the profit of all parties involved. The concept could possibly be applied to other security risks — like fire — and to other locations, like shopping centers, hospitals, or nature reserves.

A basic problem is the "free rider" phenomenon (Miethe, 1991): as the cooperation between the partners is voluntary, enjoying more security without participating — that is, without paying — is tempting. As mentioned in the Vianen project, not all companies could be persuaded to participate. A related problem is the well-known prevention paradox: effective prevention can nourish the impression that the problems are over, so that prevention can be abolished.

To solve the free-rider problem, it may prove necessary, in time, to develop stronger incentives. Differentiated insurance premiums or variable priorities in police reactions are examples of such measures. An important breakthrough was the decision of leading insurance companies and brokers to offer premium discounts to companies that participate in certified security arrangements. The issue of premium discounts was repeatedly raised during meetings of the Platform by representatives of both the government and industry.

Business Ethics

In May 1994, the Prime Minister of the Netherlands, the president of the Employers Federation and the president of the largest labor union federation publicly signed a national manifesto on professional ethics for public officials, company employees, members of the bar, public accountants and others. The publication of this manifesto, which lays down basic principles, was followed up by an intense information campaign. Information packages, including a videotape to raise consciousness among employees, were widely distributed. As a result, several companies and public agencies have introduced or updated codes of ethics. A special aim of this initiative is the prevention of corruption by and cooperation with organized crime in both the public and private sector. The National Center for Business Ethics and Crime Prevention was established by the Platform in 1995.

The task force was instrumental in persuading the Bar Association, the Association of Public Notaries and the Association of Chartered Accountants — which were all participating at the highest level — to introduce more stringent regulations for their dealings with suspicious clients (for example, not accepting payment in cash above certain levels and, under certain conditions, reporting suspicious activities to the police).

In compliance with the new anti-money laundering law of 1994, financial institutions sent in 16,215 reports on suspicious transactions in 1995. Of these reports, 14% were referred to criminal investigation departments for further screening. The banking world is not fully satisfied with the follow-up given to its information and would like to receive more feedback.

In the task forces on business ethics and financial institutions, one of the recurrent themes is the exchange of information about suspicious activities between the police and prosecutors and the business community. Solutions that satisfy both parties have not yet been found and will probably require changes in data-protection legislation.

Car Theft

The number of stolen cars has gone up sharply in most European countries during the 1990s. This rise is partly caused by increased demand for second-hand cars in the ex- communist countries. Insurance companies, in particular, expressed an interest in addressing this problem and a task force was set up in 1994.

The first priority of the task force was to develop an integrated computerized databank for stolen cars, to be fed and consulted by all interested parties — that is, the police, the insurance companies and the Ministry of Transport. The question of ownership proved to be a major bone of contention between the government agencies involved. Particularly contentious were the activities of car-hunting agencies working for insurance companies. Eventually all parties concerned agreed to build an integrated databank that is owned by the Ministry of Transport.

Another priority of the task force was the development of standards for tracing and tracking devices and immobilizers. Although the rates of car theft have been decreasing since 1995, the platform has decided to continue the activities of the task force.

The International Crimes Against Businesses Survey (ICBS)

The Platform was involved in the initiative to carry out an international victimization survey among businesses. The objective of the International Crimes against Business Survey (ICBS) is to arrive at an international comparative overview of the business communities' experiences with crime and fraud and the costs entailed, including preventive measures such as the screening of personnel prior to hiring.

The first round of the survey of businesses focused on the experiences of the retail trade. In a number of countries, including the Netherlands, businesses in other sectors were also included in the survey. To date, the survey has been conducted in Australia (Walker, 1994), the United Kingdom, the Netherlands, France, the former West Germany, Italy, Switzerland, the Czech Republic, Hungary (Budapest) and South Africa (Naudé et al., 1994).

The ICBS confirmed that public-private partnerships in crime control have great potential. Annually, a large number of businesses in the Netherlands and elsewhere were victims of crime. National rates of household victimization were strongly related to rates of victimization of businesses. Where households rates were high, such as in South Africa and the Czech Republic, commercial victimizations rates tended to be high as well. Low-crime countries, such as Switzerland, showed low victimization rates across the board. In the U.K. and the Netherlands, both household and business victimization rates were moderately high. The survey clearly showed that, for several types of crime, individual businesses were at much greater risk than households. The chance of being burgled, for instance, was, in most countries, ten times greater for businesses in retailing than for private households. Cases of fraud by personnel or corruption occurred relatively infrequently. However, 20% of entrepreneurs were of the opinion that corruption in one form or another occurs often or very often in their sector. This percentage was particularly high in the catering (restaurant) sector (45%).

The business community invests considerable amounts in security equipment. In general, the national level of security measures follows the level of criminal damage. In line with this, Dutch businesses have an average security level. In all countries, it appeared that many of the security measures were taken after the business in question had been victimized. This indicates that the security measures were taken reactively and not on the basis of objective security standards.

Twenty percent (20%) of Dutch businesses participated in some or other form of collective security, such as the partnerships on the industrial sites in Vianen and Enschede. More than 40% indicated their interest in such an arrangement. Therefore, there is a market in the Netherlands for more public-private partnerships in security.

All in all, the survey demonstrated that the Dutch business community was at an average European level in terms of both crime and security levels. In view of the high percentage of repeat victimization, it is therefore not surprising that some Dutch entrepreneurs in the retail and catering sectors perceived crime as being a (very) big problem. There appears to be leeway for growth in certain forms of prevention.

In a discussion of the results, the Platform concluded that investments in security should be stepped up. Smaller companies, in particular, must be given financial incentives to improve their security. Incentives should come from (local) government and insurance companies, working together in the promotion of collective security arrangements for industrial sites and shopping malls.

DISCUSSION AND OUTLOOK

Judging from both police recorded crime and victimization survey results, the overall level of crime in the Netherlands has stabilized during the 1990s. The two-track policy of strengthening and expanding certain parts of the criminal justice system, as well as introducing crime prevention measures on a large scale, is being pursued. The commitment of the Netherlands government toward crime prevention is still strong, as evidenced by recent additional investments in juvenile delinquency prevention amounting to $100 million (in U.S. dollars) per year.

An important supplement to the crime prevention policies by local government is the newly established partnership with the business sector. The National Platform on Crime Control (Platform) has been successful in several of its undertakings. Most notable is the achievement of the task force on armed robbery, reducing the numbers of armed robberies by using a comprehensive package of preventive and law enforcement measures. The participating parties from the business sector are concerned that this achievement will not be lasting if the special efforts are not continued. The financial commitments for continuation of the task force for another three years have been made. One of the new challenges for the task force is to develop and promote best-practice standards for both security measures and law enforcement activities. The Minister of Justice has agreed to keep armed robbery on the list of law enforcement priorities in the coming years.

The results of other task forces are somewhat less concrete. Discussions in the steering committees have often helped to prevent antagonism and stalemates in areas where the government and the business sector have conflicting interests (for example, regulations on encryption). In many cases, even-handed solutions could be found by the steering committees that were fine-tuned and implemented by specialists afterwards.

A new development is the establishment of *local crime-control platforms*. It was felt that some forms of cooperation can better be organized at the local level. The involvement of smaller companies can more easily be secured locally. Also, exchange of information on current crime threats can be more focused. In Rotterdam, Amsterdam and four other large towns, platforms were already set up. In Rotterdam, loss prevention and professional integrity in the port area are of paramount interest. In Amsterdam, tourist safety is a major issue. Several other regions are likely to follow with their own platforms. The platforms are legally independent from the national Platform and determine their own agendas, but they are supported by the various national task forces (for example, the task force on professional ethics).

The Executive Board of the Platform is presently reassessing the organizational structure of the Platform. Some concern is felt about the span of control of the board. Representatives of government have also expressed concern about the loss of democratic control over certain activities. Business representatives have expressed their disappointment with the progress made with the exchange of information on criminal groups.

As may well be true for most public-private partnerships, the success of the Platform seems to hinge to a large extent on the commitment and mutual trust of the key persons involved. Business representatives in the Platform seem not to be exclusively motivated by commercial interests in loss prevention. They have often expressed their willingness to collaborate with the government to serve national interests. Their commitment seems to derive in part from a sense of responsibility toward the society at large. The consensus seems, at any rate, to be that the Platform is an example of successful public-private partnership and fully deserves to be continued.

***

REFERENCES

Bergh, G.J. and J.C.M. Jacobs (1991). *Eindverslag van Het Project Reductie Criminaliteit Industriepark Enschede-Haven*. Enschede, The Netherlands: Stichting Publick Private Veiligheidszorg Twente.

Central Bureau of Statistics (1995). *Statistical Yearbook 1995*. The Hague: Government Printing Office.

Clarke, R.V., S. Field and G. McGrath (1991). "Target Hardening of Banks in Australia and Displacement of Robberies." *Security Journal* 2:84-90.

Hauber, A.R. (1987). *Delinquency and Vandalism in Public Transport: The Netherlands*. Leiden: State University of Leiden, Criminological Institute.

Hauber, A.R., L.J. Hofstra, L.G. Toornvliet and J.G.A. Zandbergen (1994). *Stadswachten: Effectiviteit, Draagvlak en Organisatorische Aspecten*. Den Haag: Ministerie van Justitie, Directie Criminaliteitspreventie.

Hesseling, R.B.P. (1992). "Social Caretakers and Preventing Crime on Public Housing Estates." In: *Dutch Penal Law and Policy*, vol. 6. The Hague: Research and Documentation Centre, Netherlands Ministry of Justice..

Kruissink, M. (1989). *Diversion of Vandals in the Netherlands (HALT-Projects): Results of an Evaluation Study*. The Hague: Ministry of Justice, Research and Documentation Centre.

Miethe, T.D. (1991). "Citizen-based Crime Control Activity and Victimization Risks: An Examination of Displacement and Free-Rider Effects." *Criminology* 29(3):419-440.

Mirrlees-Black, C. and A. Ross (1995). *Crimes against Retail and Manufacturing Premises: Findings from the 1994 Commercial Victimisation Survey*. London: Home Office, Research and Planning Unit (Draft, March 23, 1995).

Naudé, C.B.M. et al. (1994) *South African Businesses as Victims of Crime: Summary of Research Findings*. Pretoria: University of South Africa, Department of Criminology.

Polder, W. and F.J.C. Van Vlaardingen (1992). *Preventiestrategieën in de Praktijk: Een Meta-evaluatie van Criminaliteitsprojecten*. Arnhem: Gouda Quint.

Shapland, J. and P. Wiles (1993). *Crime against Business*. Sheffield, UK: University of Sheffield, Centre for Criminological and Sociological Studies.

The Netherlands' Drugs Policy: Continuity and Change (1995). Hageman, Zoetermeer: Netherlands Ministry of Foreign Affairs, Staatsuitgevery.

van Andel, H. (1989). "Crime Prevention that Works: The Care of Public Transport in the Netherlands." *British Journal of Criminology* 29(1):47-56.

Van den Berg, E. (1995). "Crime Prevention on Industrial Sites: Security through Public- Private Partnerships." *Security Journal* 6(1):27-35.

—— P. Mayhew (1992). *Criminal Victimization in the Industrialized World: Key Findings of the 1989 and 1992 International Crime Surveys*. The Hague: Ministry of Justice, Department of Crime Prevention.

―― P. Mayhew and M. Killias (1990). *Experiences of Crime across the World: Key Findings from the 1989 International Crime Survey*. Deventer/Boston: Kluwer Law and Taxation.

―― and G.J. Terlouw (1995) "Fraude en criminaliteit Tegen het Bedrijfsleven in Internationaal Perspectief." *Justitiële Verkenningen* 4:119-142.

―― Van Soomeren and Partners (1990). *Bedrijfsleven en Criminaliteit: Kengetallen uit de eerste Nederlandse Slachtofferenquête onder Bedrijven, 1988*. Den Haag: Ministerie van Justitie, Directie Criminaliteitspreventie.

Walker, J. (1994) *The First Australian National Survey of Crimes against Businesses*. Canberra: Australian Institute of Criminology.

Willemse, H.W.M. (1994). "Developments in Dutch Crime Prevention." In: R.V. Clarke (ed.), *Crime Prevention Studies*, Vol. 2. Monsey, NY: Criminal Justice Press.

APPENDIX

SOME RESULTS OF THE INTERNATIONAL CRIME AGAINST BUSINESS SURVEY (ICBS)

The survey contained questions on victimization for burglary and attempted burglary, vandalism, theft from or of company vehicles, thefts by customers, personnel, outsiders or persons unknown, fraud by personnel or outsider, (attempted) robbery, assault and corruption (van Dijk and Terlouw, 1995). Table 3 gives the percentages of victims in the retail trade of the different crimes in the various European countries (data from all countries are only available on the retail trade). The results of the Australian survey (Walker, 1994) have been included to serve as a comparison. First, Table 3 shows that most companies regularly encounter crimes such as theft and burglary. The victimization percentages are many times higher than those of private citizens.

In all participating countries, the risk of burglary for retailing outfits is about ten times higher than that for households. Warehouses and shop windows make attractive targets. The attraction of such premises is enhanced by the fact that they are not inhabited at night.

In an international context, the Netherlands can be set in the middle bracket. Fraud by outsiders occurred relatively rarely in Dutch retail stores — in eighth position with 12.6% victims in 1993. Corruption — that is, bribed or blackmailed personnel — was also infrequent in the Netherlands.

In comparison, retail stores in the Czech Republic were found to have a remarkably high victimization percentage. This country headed the list in four of the ten types of crimes, and came second three times. Italy was at the other extreme of the victim spectrum, occupying the lowest position four times.

Table 3: Percentages of Victimization of Retail Businesses for Nine Countries

	Hungary	Czech. Rep.	Netherlands	Germany	UK	Australia	France	Switz.	Italy
Total theft by persons[1]	83.0	72.3	66.4	63.5	61.7		61.3	60.5	44.5
Burglary[2]	35.9	40.0	34.7	28.7	36.9	29.4	31.6	24.9	14.4
Vandalism	17.6	23.1	18.1	9.6	22.0	23.0	8.9	7.6	2.5
Theft of company vehicles	1.5	4.7	3.0	3.1	10.0	3.2	9.4	1.5	9.1
Theft from company vehicles	18.3	19.4	17.7	12.7	23.2	6.1	14.3	9.1	8.0
Robbery	4.2	5.6	4.4	4.6	4.0	2.2	5.2	1.5	1.4
Assault	22.6	10.3	11.0	5.7	17.6	13.6	7.3	3.4	1.0
Fraud by personnel	2.9	6.0	3.0	3.1	2.5	1.7	1.3	1.3	1.6
Fraud by outsiders	11.2	21.2	12.6	27.6	21.0	19.7	42.3	13.6	24.7
Corruption	3.0	4.7	2.4	3.2	1.8	1.0	4.8	3.6	1.5

[1] Total theft by persons comprises theft by customers, personnel, outsiders, and persons unknown.
[2] Including attempts.

Source: van Dijk, J.J.M. en G.J. Terlouw (1995). "Fraude en Criminaliteit Tegen het Bedrijfsleven in Internationaal Perspectief." *Justitiele Verkenningen* 4.

Table 4: Victimization for the Netherlands
(Weighted According to Business Size)

	Retail trade %	Industry %	Catering %	Total %
Burglary	34.7	21.8	38.5	32.3
Vandalism	18.1	14.8	21.6	17.9
Theft of company vehicles	3.0	3.2	2.6	3.0
Theft from company vehicles	17.7	16.9	11.0	16.6
Robbery	4.4	1.1	3.1	3.4
Assault	11.0	5.1	10.4	9.5
Theft by persons	66.4	48.1	37.3	58.5
Fraud by personnel	3.0	2.8	2.6	2.9
Fraud by outsiders	12.6	10.1	8.0	11.3
Corruption	2.4	5.2	1.6	2.9

In addition to information pertaining to the retail trade, victimization data are also available for the Dutch catering (restaurant) sector and industry (Table 4). When looking at a combination of the three sectors, the highest victimization percentage is due to theft by persons (for instance, by personnel or outsiders). More than half of the interviewed businesses stated that they had been victims of theft in 1993 (58.5%). One in three businesses suffered (attempted) burglary (32.3%), while approximately one in six businesses had to deal with theft from company vehicles (16.6%). The same was true for vandalism (17.9%). Attempted robbery, theft of company vehicles, corruption and fraud by employees were relatively rare (all approximately 3%).

When looking at the extent to which the various sectors reported having been victims of the various forms of crime, it becomes clear that, in general, the retail trade accounted for the most victims (Table 4). The catering sector, however, was first when it came to being victims of burglary and vandalism. Businesses in the industrial sector encountered most cases of corruption and theft of company vehicles.

In addition to being questioned on their own experiences as victims of corruption, the respondents were asked whether crimes, such as extortion by government officials or others — demands for "protection money," blackmailing and the like — occurred in their sector. According to 16% of the interviewed Dutch entrepreneurs, practices such as these occur often or rather often in their sectors. Forty-five percent (45%) of those in the catering sector shared this opinion. Table 5 provides an overview of the retail traders' responses per country. This table also shows that retailers in the Czech Republic, Hungary, and Italy were of the opinion that a reasonable amount of corruption occurred in their sector. What is interesting is that very few French retailers shared this opinion, even though the victimization percentage in their country was fairly high (see Table 3).

Table 5: Perception of the Incidence of Corruption in the Respondent's Own Sector in Eight European Countries (%) for the Retail Trade
(Weighted According to Business Size)

	Rarely	Not often	Rather often	Often
Czech Rep.	34.4	31.4	24.1	10.0
Netherlands	58.3	30.8	8.8	2.1
Italy	62.9	21.6	14.1	1.3
Hungary	64.0	19.5	15.2	1.2
Germany	65.7	19.6	11.8	2.9
UK	71.1	21.5	6.4	1.0
Switzerland	87.5	9.8	2.8	0.0
France	95.8	2.8	0.9	0.5

Risk Features

When classified per sector, it appears that a link between the surface area of the business and the extent of victimization (in terms of frequency) only exists in the retail sector (figures not shown). In the small retail businesses (one-to-ten employees), positive correlations were found in terms of theft of vehicles and fraud by outsiders. In larger retail businesses, the following applied to shoplifting by customers and fraud by employees: the larger the surface area, the higher the number of crimes.

There was little difference in victimization between businesses trading in various wares (figures not shown). In the non-food sector (electronics, furniture, clothing, jewelry and the like), a relatively large number of companies were victimized by shoplifting by customers compared to businesses in other sectors, such as foodstuffs (roughly 56% versus 29%). Non-food businesses also reported more incidents of fraud by outsiders than other sectors (approximately 17% against 9%). Jewelers and dealers in precious metals suffered the largest percentages of robberies and attempted robberies (11.7%).

Looking at these figures per sector, it appears that mainly tobacconists (26%), software (39%) and electronics retailers (25.9%) were burgled. Electronics dealers and furniture and clothing shops suffered multiple thefts from company vehicles (32.4% and 23.5%, respectively). Often, they were also the victims of shoplifting (60.9%), as were jewelers (65.9%) and tobacconists (59.7%). This last group reported relatively many cases of theft by staff members, outsiders, or persons unknown. Cases of fraud by employees were mainly reported by tobacconists and off-sales (9.6% on average). On the other hand, fraud by outsiders occurred mainly at jewelry shops, with 26.7% reporting such cases. Corruption was not a crime that occurs often in the retail sectors (see Table 4).

A very different picture emerged when it came to fraud and corruption at industrial companies. Cases of fraud were reported exclusively by software and electronics companies (approximately 5.3%) and clothing and furniture traders (4.2%). These businesses also experienced fraud by outsiders and corruption. In this sector, the figures for corruption were 8.8% and 78.4%, respectively, and 21.3% and 10.4%, respectively, for fraud by outsiders.

Financial Damages

Victims of crime in the Netherlands in 1993 were asked to estimate the damages as an immediate result of incident(s) of a certain type (such as burglary). It appeared that, in general, damages did not exceed NLG 7,500 ($4,700, in U.S. dollars). Of course, this does not imply that certain victims did not suffer higher damages: they were, however, in the minority and were mainly the victims of burglaries (37.4%) and fraud by outsiders (40%).

When grouped according to crime figures for burglary, the data show that the highest damages (that is, NLG 7,500 and over) occurred in the retail sector and industry (46.2% and 46.4%, respectively) in 1993. As a comparison, only 22% of companies in the catering sector reported similar damages. This picture is not much different when it comes to fraud committed by outsiders. The damages suffered as a result of this type of crime were also high (in excess of NLG 7,500) for industrial companies (55.7%) and retailers (40.5%). In a financial sense, the catering sector suffered less from fraud by outsiders: only 12.3% of victims reported damages higher than NLG 7,500.

The total damages suffered by the retail trade in the Netherlands amounted to 1,455 million guilders ($910 million, in U.S. dollars); in the United Kingdom, this figure was 2,424 million guilders ($1,515 million, in U.S. dollars) (Mirrlees-Black and Ross, 1995). Therefore, the amount of damages per retail business was considerably higher in the Netherlands.

Crime Reporting Behavior

A previous survey (van Dijk, Van Soomeren and Partners, 1990) showed that by far the most businesses reported burglaries and car thefts to the police. The reason for this is that almost all businesses are insured against such crimes. This survey also showed that, in the Netherlands, almost all companies (91.4%) were insured against burglary. When classified according to sector, it appeared that in the catering sector, as well as in industry and the retail trade, at least 90% of businesses were insured against burglary. In general, more than 90% of retail businesses in other countries were also insured against burglary. The percentage of insured companies was comparatively low only in the Czech Republic, Hungary and Italy (84.6%, 81.6% and 78.8%, respectively).

In this survey, the victims of shoplifting by customers and by personnel were asked whether they had reported these crimes to the police. The answers showed that in the Netherlands about half of the burglaries committed by customers were always, usually, or sometimes reported to the police while only one third of the burglaries or fraud committed by the companies' own personnel were reported. Apparently, crimes committed by a company's own personnel are solved internally more often. The reason for failing to report a crime is usually the lack of evidence or that the matter is regarded as an internal problem. The latter argument is mainly used in cases of fraud committed by personnel. The reporting percentages did not vary much between the various countries. The highest reporting percentages were noted in West Germany and the lowest in Hungary and Italy.

Preventive Measures

Of course, businesses take all kinds of measures to protect themselves from crime. The measure reported to have been taken most frequently was the installation of a burglar alarm system. Half of the Dutch businesses questioned (49.6%) and 52% of retailers reported having a burglar alarm system. This is a significantly higher percentage than reported by previous surveys of retailers in the Netherlands (van Dijk et al., 1990).

Another frequently taken measure was to protect windows by fitting impact-resistant glass, bars, shutters and the like (44.1%), the installation of security lighting (43.3%) and instructing personnel on ways to act in the event of violence (40.8%). These security measures are the top four in all three sectors surveyed. There is, however, some difference among the sectors in the extent to which security measures are taken. For instance, the most-popular measure taken by the retail trade was to install a burglar alarm system (51.6%), whereas most industrial companies installed security lighting (51.2%), and the catering industry trained their personnel (44.5%). The least-favored measures were access checks during business hours (9.9%), surveillance by security companies or appointing a supervisor after business hours (7.8%) and surveillance by security companies during business hours (3.7%).

Security Measures Taken per Country

Table 6 shows the security measures taken by retail businesses per country. The number of security measures taken by Dutch retail businesses did not generally deviate much from those taken in Europe. However, Dutch companies only made half as much use of a security company after closing time as their European counterparts. This is remarkable in view of the high percentage of burglaries and the fact that burglaries in the Netherlands generally take place after closing time. In the Netherlands, businesses did not screen their new employees as often as was the case in West Germany or the United Kingdom, despite the fact that theft and fraud committed by this category can hardly be said to occur rarely in this country.

Table 6: Security Measures Taken per Country (Multiple Responses) (%) for Retail Businesses
(Weighted According to Business Size)

Measure	SA	UK	I	F	AUS	H	N	G	CR	S
	%	%	%	%	%	%	%	%	%	%
Burglar alarms	80.0	71.4	64.9	59.2	52.6	52.0	61.6	46.3	37.4	24.3
Window protection	59.1	60.1	44.0	56.1	54.9	74.8	49.5	46.8	61.5	31.0
Security lights	59.1	51.2	24.5	33.2	57.5	44.6	42.2	51.2	22.7.	25.3
Personnel instructions	n.a.	57.5	2.5	33.8	n.a.	48.8	48.9	58.6	27.6	46.9
Security company alarm system	33.0	42.1	32.7	29.2	36.4	9.6	25.3	22.9	4.2	11.4
None of these (other)	1.3	5.2	7.3	14.4	7.0	4.4	14.1	9.7	10.2	26.5
Property marking	0.8	21.1	8.1	10.8	35.6	3.2	12.2	14.2	11.9	10.7
Closed-circuit TV	n.a.	20.0	10.0	15.2	n.a.	3.0	11.5	17.3	3.9	19.4
Screening new personnel	n.a.	43.8	8.6	6.4	n.a.	44.4	10.8	32.3	15.3	11.9
Entry check	53.0	12.8	8.7	10.5	31.7	3.8	6.1	14.8	7.5	7.7
Security outside office hours	44.3	12.6	46.7	11.8	48.6	9.8	5.6	13.7	11.9	12.1
Security during office hours	n.a.	8.3	8.1	6.1	n.a.	7.6	4.1	5.0	5.0	4.4

n.a. - not available

The anti-burglary measures taken most in all countries were the installation of burglar alarms with or without follow-up by security companies, lighting and window security. In countries where businesses have to deal with many cases of burglary, more anti-burglary measures were generally taken, although there were many exceptions to this rule. South Africa and the United Kingdom, with relatively high burglary percentages, also had the highest percentage of burglar alarms. The number of private individuals who had installed burglar alarms was highest in the United Kingdom. The number of burglaries in Italy was relatively low, but they had a relatively high percentage of burglar alarms. In Switzerland, both burglaries and victimization percentages were low. It is noteworthy that many burglar alarms have been installed in Hungary and the Czech Republic, albeit without a contract with a security company.

Most of the security measures appear to have been taken by the respondents as a result of becoming victims of a specific form of crime. For the Netherlands, this mainly involved marking valuable objects. This was done by 55-to-57% of Dutch retailers who personally experienced victimization. When this victimization criterion was not specified, only 12.2% of retailers appear to have taken take this particular measure. On the other hand, this measure was reported to have been taken by relatively fewer victims in other countries. Other measures taken by those who had become victims of a crime (both in the Netherlands and other countries) were the installation of burglar alarm systems, burglar proofing on windows and security lighting. These figures indicate that security is improved once someone has become a victim. This also implies that many businesses have an *ad hoc* policy as far as security is concerned instead of applying objective standards.

Interest in Collective Arrangements

Entrepreneurs were asked whether businesses in their neighborhood had taken any joint anti-crime measures, such hiring security teams, company guards, or mutual warning systems. It appeared that 18% of the Dutch companies participated in a collective security arrangement (21% of the retailers and 14% of the others). Once again, the figure for the Netherlands is in line with European averages. Higher percentages were reported in the United Kingdom (31%) and France (26%). When asked whether they would be interested in joining such an arrangement, more than 40% replied positively. This suggests a vast (unutilized) potential for such arrangements in the Netherlands as well.

DO PREMISES LIABILITY SUITS PROMOTE BUSINESS CRIME PREVENTION?

by John E. Eck

University of Maryland, College Park
and Crime Control Research Corporation

Abstract: *It has been alleged that the threat of premises liability cases against business motivates business to invest more in crime prevention, thus increasing public safety. Premises liability suits occur when the victim of a serious personal crime sues the owner of the location where the assault took place on the grounds that the business was able to foresee that such a crime was likely but failed to take adequate security precautions. There is a lack of empirical evidence showing that premise liability suits influence business investment and public safety. Therefore, this paper examines three alternative models of how attorneys and business might make decisions with regard to premises liability and crime prevention. Only one of the models predicts that the threat of premises liability suits improves public safety, though all three models predict some increase in business crime prevention. In two of the models, there is over investment in crime prevention that is designed to forestall suits rather than improve the safety of place users. In one model, places where serious personal crimes are most likely will have the least crime prevention and places where the risk to the public is the least will have the most crime prevention. The paper concludes with recommendations for research to test these models.*

PREMISES LIABILITY AND CRIME PREVENTION

Recently, there has been considerable debate over tort reform. Particular attention has been paid to products liability and medical malpractice. In this paper, we explore a related matter — the possible link between premises liability and business crime prevention. Business owners have a duty to protect people invited on to their property (Calder and Sipes, 1992; Gordon and Brill, 1996). These people can include customers, employees, delivery people and others. If one of them suffers injury from a criminal attack while using a business place, the victim (or the victim's estate) can sue the place owner for failing to protect him or her. If the plaintiff can demonstrate that the attack was foreseeable and that the business owner failed to provide a suitable level of protection, then the court can award damages.

What are the social consequences of premises liability suits? The risk of civil suits may force businesses to provide safe places for their customers, employees and other place users. Bates and Dunnell (1994:5) asserted, for example, that "From the view point of social benefit, premises security liability has been one of the greatest motivators for property owners to improve security." The threat of suits may increase the use of Crime Prevention Through Environmental Design by property managers, according to some (Gordon and Brill, 1996). Are these claims plausible? It is also possible that premises liability suit risks do not improve the safety of business place users. Maybe they simply raise the cost of doing business. Or, possibly, the threat of premises liability suits increases the use of crime prevention in some businesses but not in others.

This paper addresses two questions: (1) does the threat of premises liability promote business crime prevention? and (2) does this investment in crime prevention improve the security of place users? Unfortunately, there is too little empirical evidence to give a definitive answer to these important questions. Therefore, rather than evaluating data on this topic, we examine alternative models of the relationship between suits and prevention and compare their predictions. Each model makes a set of relatively concrete predictions. Though readers may prefer one model or the other, systematic inquiry is required to form a definitive conclusion. Therefore, this paper concludes with a research program to test these models.

It is important to note that there are other possible motivations for businesses to invest in crime prevention, even if the risk of premises liability suits were zero. Businesses that gain a reputation (whether deserved or not) for being unsafe are likely to lose customers. Similarly, if employees feel unsafe, a business may face higher worker turnover along with greater costs in employee replacement, training and lower operating efficiency. Business crime can also disrupt operations. For example, a holdup resulting in an injury may require the suspension of business activity while emergency medical technicians and police do their jobs. So businesses may invest in crime prevention to reduce the chances of crime and to demonstrate that they are safe.

This paper examines only various conjectures about the possible links between premises liability and crime prevention. The first section of the paper connects this discussion to criminological theory and defines key concepts. We begin addressing the main questions in the second section. Here, we examine a model that links personal crime victimization risk to the chances of a suit. In this model, crime prevention helps avoid costly lawsuits by reducing the risk of victimization. In short, suits reduce the risks of serious crime through prevention. The third section describes an alternative model that results in a more complex connection between the chances of suits and the willingness of businesses to engage in crime prevention. The second model predicts that many businesses where place users have the highest risk of a serious personal crime will under invest in crime prevention. Further, those businesses where users have the lowest risk of being a victim of a serious personal crime will over invest in crime prevention. A third model is presented in section four. This model claims that the risk of lawsuits is driven, not by the risk of crime at business places, but by contextual factors. The fifth section compares the implications of these models and makes a series of predictions for each model. The sixth section describes a program of research to test the conflicting models. We close with a brief discussion of the possible implications of alternative models that might be discovered through this research.

PLACE MANAGERS AND CRIME

Crimes occur when offenders meet potential victims at places without capable controllers (Cohen and Felson, 1979; Brantingham and Brantingham, 1995; Eck, 1995; Felson, 1994; 1995). Most attention has been paid to offenders, victims, guardians (people who watch out for victims) and handlers (intimates of offenders who try to keep them from offending) (Felson, 1994). Though increasing attention is being paid to the places where offenders and victims meet (Sherman et al., 1989; Brantingham and Brantingham, 1995), until recently virtually no attention has been paid to the people who control behavior at these places (that is, place managers) (Eck, 1995; Felson, 1995).

Place managers are concerned about the functioning of places (Eck, 1995). They regulate who has access to places and the behaviors that are permissible there. Place managers include place owners, their employees and, sometimes, contractors. Other place managers include janitors, store clerks, lifeguards, restaurant hosts, parking lot attendants, train conductors, park rangers, bartenders, store clerks, apartment managers, and others who assist people using places and who enforce place rules. The absence of place managers, or the presence of managers who do not control the behaviors of place users, increases the chances of a location becoming a "hot spot" of crime.

We will be concerned with place managers, particularly place owners. These are the people who are sued and these are the people who decide whether to use crime prevention, what types of crime prevention to use and how much crime prevention to use. Place owners have a legal obligation to protect the safety to people who use their place. They are required to protect place users from crimes that are foreseeable and to employ reasonable prevention measures. These obligations are not absolute. Place owners are not required to guarantee absolute safety or employ every possible prevention measure.

What is and is not foreseeable and what are and are not a reasonable prevention measures have been defined in different ways by different state courts. Prior crimes, similar to the event at the center of the suit, can be used as evidence that the crime in question was foreseeable (Calder and Sipes, 1992). Nevertheless, in some states the absence of prior similar events is not conclusive evidence that the crime in question was not foreseeable. Under the "totality of circumstances" test, foreseeability can be demonstrated by establishing a variety of states of affairs, including prior dissimilar crimes at the business being sued, prior similar crimes at other similar businesses, similar and dissimilar crimes in the area surrounding the business, place users' fear of crime when at the business, the use or absence of standard crime prevention procedures and a variety of other factors that may lead someone to believe a serious crime is likely (Calder and Sipes, 1992; Bates and Dunnell, 1994; Gordon and Brill, 1996).

If civil suits promote crime prevention, then there may be two advantages to using premises liability to encourage crime prevention. First, it might encourage place owners to incorporate the expected costs of crime in the price of their goods and services. Place owners balance the expected costs of a suit with the costs and expected benefits of prevention. Some of these costs are passed on to place users as higher prices and access fees. In this way, place users pay for the enhanced security they receive. If these benefits are to be realized, place owners, the plaintiffs' bar and civil courts must use estimates of the crime risk, such as those suggested by Sherman

(1989). Place owners can then balance the cost of reducing these risks with the expected benefits.

A second possible advantage, of using premises liability to promote crime prevention is that it allows prevention to be tailored to the specific needs of the place rather than having a "one-size-fits-all" standard. The security precautions needed for a hotel are different from those of a parking lot. And the prevention measures needed for parking areas around shopping malls are different from those needed for parking lots in apartment complexes. If security precautions are to be tailored to places, then there should be a body of scientific studies that give precise estimates of the benefits of varying crime prevention strategies under a variety of circumstances. Absent such a body of knowledge, businesses will have to rely on experience and anecdotal information. Under these circumstances, this second benefit may not be forthcoming. Rather than basing the utility of crime prevention measures on the likely reduction in risk, the utility of crime prevention measures may be based on what other similar businesses are using.

For these benefits to be realized, several conditions must be met. First, business place owners must perceive that there is a substantial risk of lawsuits and that investment in crime prevention will reduce this risk. We will address this condition briefly in the next paragraph. The other conditions are the subject of the rest of this paper.

One important fact that we do not know is the risk of a suit, given a serious crime at a business. For example, given a rape of a tenant in an apartment complex, what is the chance that the complex will be sued by the victim? Or, given the shooting of a bar patron in the drinking establishment's parking lot, what is the risk of a lawsuit against the bar? If the risk is very small, then we would expect very little influence of suits on crime prevention and place-user crime risk. If the threat of a suit is large, then there may be a substantial influence on crime prevention and safety. In the absence of reliable estimates of the risk of suits given a serious crime, we will assume that it is at least large enough to be taken into consideration by businesses, even if it is not the largest influence on decisions to invest in crime prevention. The validity of this assumption probably varies by business type, state, crime type and a variety of other factors.

The advantages of lawsuits in promoting safety at business places are only hypothetical. If civil suits do not promote crime prevention, then these advantages will not be realized. We need to examine the mechanisms by which the threat of premises liability litigation influences crime prevention. In doing so, we will restrict our attention to personal crimes that cause death (homicides), serious injury (woundings resulting in long-term or permanent disabilities), serious psychological trauma (such as kidnapping or rape), or some combination of these harms. Few suits result from property crimes in which the offender and victim have no contact (such as shoplifting or car break-ins). In their review of 267 premises liability cases for ten years (1983-1992) throughout the United States and listed in *The Law Reporter* (a monthly publication of the American Trial Lawyers' Association that reports settlements and verdicts favorable to plaintiffs), Bates and Dunnell (1994) found that 96.6% of these cases involved rape, sexual assault, assault and battery, wrongful death, or robbery. Unless otherwise noted, any references to crime in the remainder of this paper will refer to these serious personal crimes.

We will also differentiate between two types of crime risks. The first we will call "individual risk." This is the risk of becoming the victim of a serious personal crime faced by the average place user. The simplest way of calculating individual risk is the number of crimes at the place during a specific time period divided by the number of users of the place during this time period (Clarke, 1984; Sherman, 1989). The second form of risk we will call "place risk." This is the probability that a specific location will have an occurrence of a serious personal crime during a specific time period. We can think of this as the number of places of a specific type with a serious personal crime divided by the total number of places of this type, during a specified time interval. The distinction between individual and place risk will be important when we compare the three models.

Brantingham and Brantingham (1995) distinguished between four types of places: crime generators; crime attractors; crime-neutral locations; and fear generators. Crime generators draw large numbers of people, most of whom come for legitimate reasons. The mixture of a large number of people, a few of whom are offenders, produces many crimes at the location. Thus, crime generators may have high place risks. However, because of the large number of place users, individual risks may be very low at these locations. Sherman (1989) provided a good example of a hotel that served as a crime generator with low individual risk. Crime attractors draw in large numbers of potential offenders who know that they can commit their offenses at these locations. One reason that some locations serve as crime attractors is that they have weak or absent place management (Eck, 1995). We would expect that individual risk and place risk would be relatively high at these locations. Crime-neutral places are neither crime generators nor attractors. Since these places do not attract many people and do not have a reputation among offenders, we would expect them to have low place and individual risks. Fear generators are locations where place users feel they are vulnerable to crime, though their objective risk may be very low. Fear generators will be crime generators, crime attractors or crime neutral. The models we will examine next give different predictions for investment in crime prevention at these four types of places.

These models describe the aggregate decision making of plaintiffs' attorneys and place owners. Though each decision occurs at the level of the individual, these independent decisions have aggregate social consequences. We will see, for example, that the models differ in their descriptions of how plaintiffs' attorneys make individual decisions. The aggregate results of these decisions influences place owners' perceptions of the risks of suits. And the cumulative effect of these individual decisions influences social investment in crime prevention and changes in crime risk. This cascade of decision making and consequences, individual and social, will unfold over time. Though we will not address the speed of this unfolding, we would expect some time lags. The length of these lags is uncertain.

MODEL 1 — INDIVIDUAL RISK AND SUITS

Model 1 describes a non-recursive process. This is shown by the black solid arrows in Figure 1. Places with the greatest individual risk have the greatest risk of a costly lawsuit (arrow A). The costs of a suit may not be straight forward. Even if insurance offsets some costs, it may not cover all of the costs. In addition to the direct costs of fighting and losing a suit, there are many other costs that place managers must take into consideration. These include the lost time of having to find and reproduce documents, engage in discussions with attorneys, give depositions and testify at trials. Insurance premiums can go up if insurance companies perceive that a type of business has increasing risks of suits. Perhaps more importantly, the publicity surrounding suits may increase the perceived risk of potential customers and this will reduce revenues. So whether the costs of a suit are directly born by place owners or whether insurance covers some of the costs, the costs are not trivial. Once the expected costs of a suit begin to exceed the expected costs of prevention, place managers will invest in additional prevention (arrow B). The additional prevention reduces individual risks (arrow D) but also directly reduces the risks of suits (arrow C).

Figure 1: Models of Premises Liability and Crime Prevention

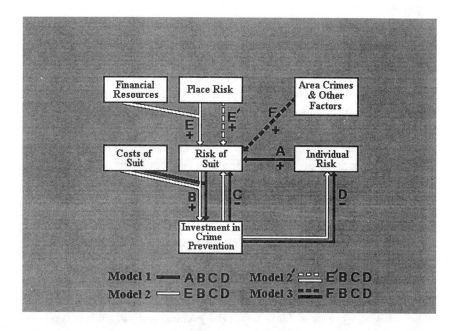

This model suggests that there may be an equilibrium that balances conflicting incentives and delivers an optimal level of prevention (that is, the expected cost of the next serious personal crime is roughly equivalent to the extra safety of the additional prevention). In other words, the costs of crime are successfully internalized by place owners.

Model 1 forms two loops. Arrows B and C form the first loop. As the expected costs of suits increases, so does investment in prevention. We see that investment in crime prevention is a function of the interaction of the risk of a suit and the costs of a suit (arrow B), including attorneys' fees, the chances of monetary settlements, the likely size of settlements and the loss of customers' good will.

Arrows A, B and D form the second loop. As crime prevention increases, individual risk declines (arrow D). We would expect that the first investments in crime prevention would, on average, reduce individual risks more than later additional amounts of prevention. Thus, there are declining marginal returns to crime prevention (like almost everything else), assuming no changes in the social and physical environment surrounding places. The importance of the declining marginal returns to crime prevention cannot be underestimated. This assumption means that, at some level of crime prevention, there will be no improvement in place users' safety by adding more preventive measures. This assumption also implies that investments in crime prevention should also reduce the risk of suits, but at declining rates.

There are a number of problems with this model. A place without any crimes will have zero individual risk of a serious personal crime up until the moment of the crime. But suits are often brought over a single incident without the plaintiff calculating individual risk. So, for the place manager, the individual risk of a serious personal crime may not be as important as the place risk. This can be seen if we note that, by simply increasing the denominator in the risk formula, we can drive down the individual risk. Doubling the number of place users could halve the individual risk but still increase the place risk (see below). Complicating this further is the fact that plaintiffs often argue that other types of crime are indicators of the chances of a serious crime or that people's perceptions of individual risk are accurate measures of individual risk. Thus, the number of thefts from automobiles in the parking area of a shopping mall may be used as evidence that the rape of a patron was foreseeable. Or domestic violence inside apartment units may be used by a plaintiff as evidence that a stranger-to-stranger robbery-homicide in the apartment complex parking lot was foreseeable. Or a resident's concerns about walking from her parked car at night is provided as evidence that parking lot users had a high risk of attack.

A second criticism is that a victim's decision to sue may be only partially linked to being the victim of a serious crime. The victim must also get an attorney to take the case. If attorneys take into consideration the ability of owners to pay, then owners who do not have the financial resources will have a lower risk of suits than those with financial resources, regardless of the individual or place risk.

To address these difficulties with Model 1 we will examine two alternative models.

MODEL 2 — PLACE RISK, ABILITY TO PAY AND SUITS

Model 2 is shown by the solid white arrows in Figure 1. This model asserts that risks of suits is proportional to the interaction of financial resources that could payoff plaintiffs and place risks (arrow E). In other words, place owners who have many financial resources (such as large insurance policies that cover the crime in question) will face large risks of being sued. And places without these resources will face minor risks of being sued. Owners of crime attractors with few financial resources may fall into this second category. Owners of places with extremely low place risks of a serious personal crime also will face only a small chance of being sued. Owners of crime-neutral places may be in this category. Managers of crime-neutral or crime-attractor places will not invest much in prevention, regardless of individual risk.

Place owners who have both the financial resources and at least moderate place risks will face much greater chances of being sued. Owners of crime generators fall into this category. Such place managers will invest a great deal in crime prevention, regardless of individual risk.

Model 2 has no loops between crime risk (individual or place) and crime prevention. This means, that whatever the decreases in individual risk that additional crime prevention measures create, this increased safety has no influence on the risk of suits. The only feedback shown is that increased investment in crime prevention reduces suits. Note that this will occur, according to Model 2, even if this crime prevention is totally ineffective in reducing crime.

Because there is no feedback between suits and individual risk, there is no reason to believe that an optimal level of crime prevention will be used. Some high individual-risk places will have little crime prevention and some low individual-risk places will have more prevention than is needed.

Model 2' is a close relative of the second model. This model asserts that place risk influences the risk of suits, but that the financial resources of the business are not considered by plaintiffs' attorneys. This model is shown by the white arrows, but with arrow E' substituting for arrow E. We would not expect to see differentiation in suit risks by ability to pay. But, because of the absence of a feedback between individual risk and risk of suits, we would expect to see over investment in crime prevention as a way of preventing suits, especially by businesses that can afford to invest heavily in crime prevention. As with Model 2, Model 2' implies that much investment in crime prevention will have a negligible effect on public safety at businesses.

MODEL 3 — TOTALITY OF CIRCUMSTANCES, AREA CRIME AND SUITS

The final model we will consider ignores prior crimes at the site in question. Instead, it is based on the "totality of circumstances." Proponents contend that, if place or individual risk must be high to demonstrate foreseeability and security adequacy, then every business would get at least one "free" serious crime before it could be successfully sued (Gordon and Brill, 1996). They contend that even in the absence of prior crimes at a site, a location can have a high serious-crime risk. Further, proponents of the totality of circumstances argument claim that crime risk can be determined by examining a variety of factors, such as crime in the surrounding area, fear of crime by place users, other non-personal crimes at the site and the lack of use of standard crime prevention measures.

What would we expect to find if the risk of suits were influenced only by the totality of circumstances? Model 3 is shown in Figure 1 by the black arrows F, B, C and D. This model differs from the first model by the absence of arrow A and the inclusion of a cluster of factors that include the amount of crime in the area (dashed arrow F). Unlike the second model, Model 3 does not include place risk or financial resources.

This model implies that businesses in high-crime areas or with many property crimes on the site will face high risks of suits. To the extent that attorneys and courts interpret testimony about fear of crime as evidence of risk of serious personal crime, we would expect fear-generator places to also have high risks of suits. Businesses facing these conditions will invest heavily in crime prevention.

Businesses in high-crime areas or with many property crimes will invest heavily in prevention. However, unless there are large diffusions of benefits (Clarke and Weisburd, 1994), this will have little impact on crime in surrounding areas or on the property crime at the site. This crime prevention investment, therefore, will be designed to help fight possible suits. It will give the business owner the ability to demonstrate in court that it has adequate security though it may not improve individual risk. Fear-generator places will also invest heavily in crime prevention, but unless these crime prevention measures provide psychological assurances to place users, this will not reduce fear. In fact, businesses are consistently warned by legal experts to refrain from giving assurances to place users that might make them feel secure. In a suit, it can be argued that the plaintiff was induced to be less careful by these assurances and that, if the plaintiff had not had such assurances, he or she would have taken greater precautions (Bates and Dunnell, 1994). Consequently, the primary reason for fear-generating businesses to invest in crime prevention will be to help in litigation.

Plaintiffs' attorneys are unlikely to overlook business locations with high individual or place risk and instead focus solely on the totality of circumstances. When there is a history of serious crimes at locations, we would expect either place risk or individual risk to be the center of plaintiffs' cases. One would expect that absent high place or individual risk at sites, plaintiffs' attorneys would use the totality of circumstances argument. Thus, Model 3 might be best viewed as an adjunct to either of the first two models that would apply to locations without any prior serious criminal history, and especially to fear-generator or crime-neutral places.

COMPARISON OF IMPLICATIONS

These models yield very different predictions for investment in crime prevention. In particular, they differ in the expected relationship between the number of place users and suits and the conditions under which place owners will invest in prevention.

Number of Place Users, Individual Risk and Place Risk

Before considering the predictions of the models, we need to examine four possible results from an increase in the number of place users. In the simplest case [a], as the number of place users increases, the number of crimes declines or stays constant. In this case, individual risk declines. This might occur if the additional place users increase guardianship. Alternatively, as the number of new place users increases, so do the number of targets and offenders. If the number of crimes increase as place users increase, but at a slower rate [b], then individual risk would decline. Or, [c], the number of crimes increases at the same rate as the user population, so individual risk remains constant. Finally, [d], the number of crimes increases faster than the number of users, so individual risk increases.

According to Model 1, under cases [a] and [b] an increase in the number of place users will decrease individual risk and this will decrease the risk of a suit. Under condition [c], there will be no change in individual risk or the risk of a suit. However, under condition [d], the risk of suit will increase because of individual risk increases.

Model 2 gives a different set of predictions. First, if the place owner has few resources, changes in the number of place users will have no effect on the risk of a suit. But what happens if the owner has sufficient resources? Then, under condition [a], place risk remains constant or declines so the risk of a suit does not change or goes down. Under conditions [b], [c] and [d], place risk increases so the risk of suits increases. Both models predict that the risk of suit will increase under condition [d].

Model 3 makes no straight forward predictions under any of these circumstances because crime at the place is less important than other factors. If changes in the number of place users increases crime in the surrounding area, property crimes at the business, or place users' fear of crime, then we would expect the risk of suits to increase under conditions [a] through [d].

The implications are straight forward. If businesses have enough resources to make a suit worthwhile, we get the following set of predictions. Businesses that have few place users and small individual risk (crime-neutral locations) will have small chances of suits under Models 1, 2, and 2'. Businesses with high individual risks (crime generators) face high risks of suits according to Model 1, Model 2, and Model 2'. Businesses with many place users, many resources and low individual risk (crime attractors) will have small chances of a suit under Model 1 but high chances of a suit under Model 2 and Model 2'. Regardless of the financial resources available, crime-neutral locations in high-crime neighborhoods, with many property crimes, or that are also fear generators would have high risks of suits according to Model 3.

Investment in Prevention

Model 1 predicts that owners of places that pose the highest risk to place users will have the highest investment in prevention. This investment will bring individual risk down. Model 1 also asserts that owners of places, where individual risk is low, will not invest in prevention. Though the types and amount of prevention deployed at places may be highly variable, depending on the environments within which the places are located, we would not expect to find much variation in individual risk across places. This would occur over time as owners of high individual-risk places invest more in prevention to drive risks down and owners of places with very low individual risk disinvest in expensive prevention measures and allow individual risk to drift up. In a stable environment, we can expect individual risk to become similar for comparable types of commercial places. For example, small convenience grocery stores tend to produce equivalent individual risks, whether they are owed by large corporations, franchise operations, or are independently owned and operated. Large and small apartment complexes should move to similar levels of individual risk. Parking lots and structures should also drift to comparable individual risks, regardless of location, size, or financial well being of the owner. Though there should be variation in individual risk within a homogeneous set of business places across states (due to variation in state court rulings), within a state, we would expect to see little variation in individual risk regardless of business locations. Motels in the inner city should have virtually the same individual risk as motels in suburbs or in rural towns. Gas stations located at highway interchanges should have the same individual risk as gas stations on side streets.

In contrast, Model 2 predicts that owners of places that have a high likelihood of a serious personal crime and have financial resources that could be lost in a suit will invest heavily in prevention. Further, owners with few financial resources to lose in a suit and owners of places with low place risk of a serious crime will not invest in prevention. Rather than heterogeneity in crime prevention measures and relative homogeneity in individual risk, Model 2 implies two types of places for any given business place type. One group of places will have very low risk of a suit. This group of places will display a high degree of homogeneity in their deployment of crime prevention measures; they will have very few. Individual risk, however, will vary a great deal. Some of these places will have extremely low individual risk. They may be located in isolated areas or in communities with strong reputations for guardianship, for example. Other places in this group will have high individual risk.

According to Model 2, a second group of places have a high risk of a suit. This group will display low variation in individual risk and the types of crime prevention measures used. Since the risk of a suit does not depend on individual risk, this may seem to be an odd prediction. Let us examine why this may be the case. First, because place owners with a high risk of a suit cannot eliminate the possibility of a serious personal crime, they will invest in crime prevention measures to assist them in fighting suits. From a strict crime prevention perspective, this implies that they will *overinvest* in crime prevention. That is, the additional level of crime prevention they use will not reduce individual risk any further. Thus, all the places in this group will have low individual risks. What variation in individual risk that can be found will be minor compared to the difference in risk between this group and the first group.

The homogeneity in crime prevention measures stems from the same source. Industry standards for crime prevention are instrumental to a successful legal defense. A defendant in a suit whose place does not have crime prevention measures like most of the similar places in the area is likely to be penalized by the court (Calder and Sipes, 1992). Thus, there is an incentive to use the same prevention measures as other similar commercial places in an area. This incentive will exist regardless of any link between the use of the crime prevention measure and individual risk at the place. For example, police officers may be enticed to live in apartment complexes, not because they improve the safety of residents, but because other complexes in the area give officers reduced rents.

The results predicted by Model 2 are that many places with high individual risks will not have an incentive to invest in crime prevention. In these places, crime prevention could be very effective. In contrast, many low individual-risk places will over invest in crime prevention in order to be able to reduce their losses when they are sued. Model 2 implies that there will be a substantial misallocation of crime prevention across businesses, in large part due to the incentive structure created by premises liability civil suits. If most people spend much of their time in places where there is a high risk of a suit, then, even with the misallocation of crime prevention resources, the aggregate level of serious personal crimes would be lower than it would be otherwise. However, if most people spend a great deal of time in places with low risks of suit, it is possible that the aggregate level of serious personal crime is higher than it would be otherwise. If Model 2 is correct, the misallocation of crime prevention resources will mean that too much is being spent on the wrong places. The users of the businesses that under invest in crime prevention will suffer disproportionate risks of victimization.

Model 2′ predicts the same outcomes for all places as Model 2 does for high financial resource places only. That is, crime attractors and generators will invest heavily in crime prevention to fight suits. It is the absence of a feedback loop that prevents Model 2′ from assuring an optimal level of prevention and it predicts a misallocation of crime prevention resources, like Model 2.

Model 3 gives another set of predictions for variation in investment in crime prevention and individual risk. Some locations will not have a high risk of suits under the totality of circumstances model. These places will vary in individual risk but will have little crime prevention. Those business places with high risks of suits will invest heavily in crime prevention. Much investment in crime prevention will be designed to stave off premises liability suits. This is because the factors that create the totality of circumstances (for example, crime in the area, property crime at the site, or fear of crime at the site) are unlikely to be addressed by crime prevention measures designed to reduce personal crimes at the site. So crime-neutral places that are vulnerable under the totality of circumstances argument will invest in crime prevention that will have little influence on individual risk but satisfy legal expectations for the types of prevention measures that are suitable. Thus, according to Model 3, we should see both high variation in individual risk and crime prevention; similar business places will employ a standard set of crime prevention practices but will have widely varying individual risks.

Table 1 summarizes several important predictions from these models. The first four rows show their predictions for risk of suits when crime levels change following an increase in place users. The next three rows show predictions stemming from several important elements of the totality of circumstances argument. Finally, the last two rows show the predictions for variation in individual risk and investment in crime prevention for similar places in the same state.

Table 1: Summary of Predictions

	MODEL 1	MODEL 2		MODEL 3
		few financial resources	many financial resources, or MODEL 2'	
When Place Users Increase, Crimes ...		**Risk Of Suits Goes...**		
a -- goes down or stays the same	DOWN	SAME	DOWN	
b -- goes up at slower rate	DOWN	SAME	UP	
c -- goes up at same rate	SAME	SAME	UP	
d -- goes up at faster rate	UP	SAME	UP	
		Risk Of Suits		
Business in high crime in area				HIGH
Business has many property crimes				HIGH
Business place users have high fear				HIGH
		Predicted To Be		
Variation in individual risk	LOW	HIGH	LOW	HIGH
Variation in crime prevention	HIGH	LOW	LOW	HIGH
Influence of Suits on Crime Prevention	INCREASES	NONE	INCREASES	INCREASES
Influence of Crime Prevention on Public Safety	IMPROVES	NONE	SLIGHTLY IMPROVES	SLIGHTLY IMPROVES

TESTING THESE MODELS — A PROGRAM FOR RESEARCH

We have examined alternative models of the link between premises liability litigation and crime prevention. We have seen that they have different implications and Model 1 is the only model that yields the desirable outcomes described at the beginning of this paper. We have provided no scientific evidence supporting any one of the models because there are no studies that can provide us with convincing evidence for the supremacy of one model over another (or for the superiority of some combination of these models). Nevertheless, the models are highly testable. They yield relatively precise predictions that can be compared to empirical evidence.

Because these models yield relatively specific predictions, this section proposes a series of studies to determine which, if any, of the predictions are verified empirically. In principle, one could collect the data necessary to estimate the models using standard econometric methods. However, there are a number of possible confounding influences that we only mention in passing. These include incentives and disincentives to invest in crime prevention for reasons unrelated to civil suits. Instead, we will look at studies designed to refute or confirm the models, without directly estimating the relationships (the arrows in Figure 1).

Who Gets Sued?

Model 1 predicts that the businesses that are sued will have high individual risk relative to those that do not get sued. Model 2 predicts that the businesses that get sued will have far more financial resources, on average, than those that do not get sued. Further, Model 2 claims that, under a broad set of conditions, the average individual risk of businesses that get sued may be substantially less than the businesses that do not get sued. Model 3 asserts that the places that get sued will not be distinguished by the risks of crime at the business sites (or by their levels of financial resources). Instead, assorted factors regarding crime in the surrounding area, fear of crime and non-personal property crimes at the site predict suits. There are a number of useful research designs that could determine which model is correct. We will look at three.

First, one could conduct retrospective studies of businesses. Interviews and site visits to a large sample of businesses could be used to determine if their histories of individual risk, financial resources and contextual factors varied with their experiences of being sued for failure to protect place users. Since different types of businesses may have different relationships among these variables, the sample should be stratified by business type. Further, because state laws vary considerably, and this may influence the relationships among these variables, the sample also should be stratified by jurisdiction. Alternatively, a series of smaller case studies of specific business types in specific states could be conducted (for example, small grocery stores in Texas, commercial parking lots in California, restaurants in Florida and apartment buildings in Illinois).

If suits are relatively rare, then sampling businesses by stratifying on the independent variables will be inefficient. A very large sample will be required to assure that a large enough number of sued businesses are included in the study. An alternative approach is to use a case-control study (Schlesselman, 1982). By stratifying on the dependent variable prior to sampling, a larger proportion of sued businesses can be included in the study for any predetermined sample size. This increases the statistical power of the study for the money expended. If a list of businesses that have been sued in a jurisdiction exists, this could be used as a sampling frame to select a sample of cases. The controls would be a sample of similar businesses in the jurisdiction that have not been sued. Care would need to be taken to assure that the two samples are representative of their populations and the two populations are comparable (Wacholder et al., 1992). The only drawbacks are minor; many common statistical methods (for example, correlation and ordinary lease squares regression) give biased results so alternative methods (for example, odds ratios and logistic function analysis) need to be used instead (Loftin and McDowell, 1988).

Retrospective studies, such as those we have been discussing, suffer from two problems. The first is recall. Individual risk can be estimated based on archival records of customers and crime events. Though police records may go back far enough, business records of place user counts may not. Records of individual risk, financial resources, crime prevention procedures and security practice may also be missing. Also, employees leave businesses and those that stay may forget. The second is the problem of establishing temporal order. Since data on the suits (the dependent variable) are being collected at the same time as the data on the independent variable, it may not be possible to be certain that the presumed cause preceded the presumed effect. Publicized suits, for example, could create a decline in the number of place users (thus, increasing individual risk) or a decline in financial resources.

For these reasons, one may prefer to conduct a multi-year prospective study. This would allow careful measurement of the critical independent variables prior to the instigation of civil suits. Like prospective studies, samples of businesses should be stratified by business type and state. The major drawback to this approach is that it is expensive.

Do Attorneys Care about Defendants' Ability to Pay?

All models describe the decision-making processes of plaintiffs and their attorneys. Model 2 asserts that resources of potential defendants are a prime motivator behind suits. Models 1 and 3 are less cynical. Since all three models describe decision making, decision making should be studied. One could examine the decision process of victims of violent crimes at businesses. It seems unlikely that victims will be able or willing to provide frank accounts of any pecuniary interests that motivated their decisions or the decisions of their attorneys.

Examining how attorneys make decisions to accept cases and when to settle cases may be a more productive approach. Attorneys must consider the chances that they can get a settlement that will reimburse them for their expenses and provide some profit. So it seems plausible that the financial resources of a business would enter into the decision calculus of attorneys. Though this is a rather obvious assertion, the less obvious implications of this, suggested by Model 2, force us to study this aspect of decision making.

What do these attorneys consider when deciding to take a case? How much do they know about the financial well being of the possible defendant before making this decision? Do they estimate individual risk? And, if they do, how do they make this estimate? Or do they decide to take a case without regard to the financial resources or individual risk of the defendant but only consider the merits of the case? Since discovery motions and hired experts may reveal new information, research on attorney decision making should also examine how cases are pursued once they have been taken up. Do attorneys attempt to settle cases sooner if their estimates of individual risk, financial resources, or totality of circumstances decline? If their estimates of individual risk, financial resources, or totality of circumstances increase do they invest more in the case? Is the totality of circumstances argument used more frequently when individual- or place-risks arguments are not supported by evidence?

Model 1 would be supported if attorneys consider individual risk and ignore financial resources both at the point of accepting a case and throughout the litigation. Model 2 would be supported by the opposite findings. If neither resources nor individual risk are considered, then this would be evidence for Model 2'. Model 3 would be supported if neither individual nor place risk are considered, but other contextual factors are taken into consideration. A hybrid model would be required if the totality of circumstances is considered only when place risk or individual risk are negligible.

Since attorneys vary in expertise, heterogeneity in the plaintiff's bar may mask important relationships. Model 2 suggests two possibilities with regard to variation in expertise. One possibility is that attorneys with the most expertise routinely turn down cases where the potential defendant has few resources, regardless of the merits of the case, and focus attention on cases in which the potential defendant has deep pockets. This would leave to attorneys with less experience the cases against place owners with few resources. Alternatively, high-quality attorneys may only consider case merit and low-quality attorneys focus more on resources.

Systematic interviews with representative samples of lawyers with experience representing clients in premises liability suits against businesses could address these questions. Care must be taken to be sure that these attorneys have had experience examining cases involving places with varying amounts of resources. It seems plausible that places with few resources are likely to serve clients with few resources. These clients will probably have less access to attorneys with a great deal of expertise in these suits (Black, 1976). The result may be that these cases get settled earlier since neither side can afford a prolonged case. These relationships could confound the relationships we are interested in examining and need to be controlled to provide a good test of the models.

What is the Distribution of Individual Risk?

Model 1 predicts that individual risk should be relatively homogeneous across similar businesses in the same state. Models 2 and 3 claim that the individual risks will be highly heterogeneous. Empirical studies on crime hot spots (Pierce et al., 1986; Sherman et al., 1989) are more consistent with Models 2 and 3 than Model 1. However, since business type was not controlled for in these studies, they are more suggestive than definitive. Sherman and his colleagues (1992) did conduct a study of taverns in Milwaukee that revealed considerable differences in the numbers of violent crimes. Though the authors did not calculate the individual-risk rates, the large number of bars with no violent crimes (individual risks of zero) suggests that there is considerable variation as predicted by Models 2 and 3. The small number of bars with many personal crimes would need to have extraordinarily large numbers of place users for their individual-risk rates to approach zero. Similarly, Bellamy (1996) summarized the voluminous literature on convenience store robbery. She pointed out that a relatively small number of these businesses are the sites of the vast majority of the robberies. This suggests that convenience stores have a heterogeneous risk pattern, as predicted by Models 2 and 3. Unfortunately, we do not have individual risk for these stores so it may be that the variation in crimes is proportional to the number of place users. Overall, the theory and evidence available is more consistent with the heterogeneous risk pattern across places (business and non-business) than a homogeneous risk pattern (Eck and Weisburd, 1995). Still, this evidence is not adequate to form a conclusive opinion as to the relative validity of the models.

These studies do suggest another way to test the two models. One could examine violent personal crime cases from police records over several years and identify business places with varying numbers of violent crime. One could then gather estimates of the number of place users from the businesses to get an estimate of the at-risk population. Again, this sample must be stratified by business type and state to provide meaningful results. If similar businesses in the same state had similar individual risks, then this would be evidence supporting Model 1. If the risks varied considerably, this would be evidence supporting Models 2 and 3.

Throughout this paper we have made predictions for each of Brantingham and Brantingham's (1995) types of places. One could collect information on crime frequency, user frequency, user criminal backgrounds, crime prevention measures, crime in surrounding areas, and prior premises liability suits for a set of places. The information could then be used to classify the places as crime generators, crime attractors, crime-neutral locations, and fear generators. Then one could determine if the predictions for individual risk, place risk, civil suit history and crime prevention investment described above apply to each place type. A more definitive, but more expensive, variant on such a study would be a prospective examination of the distribution of risk, suits and prevention across these place types.

What is the Distribution of Crime Prevention?

Model 1 asserts that, for a given business type in a given jurisdiction, the crime prevention methods used will vary considerably. This occurs because place managers apply the security precautions required to suit the needs of their location, and these needs will vary across a jurisdiction. Model 2 claims that security precautions for high financial resource businesses of a specific type in the same jurisdiction will be very similar. This will occur because these businesses will be investing in security precautions to be able to fight suits. Insurance companies, who would bear the burden of many of these suits, could be a driving force standardizing crime prevention measures and creating an industry standard. Low-resource businesses of the same type in the same jurisdiction will have little crime prevention in place.

Surveys of businesses in a jurisdiction could address this question. As before, care would have to be taken to control for business type. This type of study might be relatively easy to conduct for types of businesses where there is easy public access and security precautions are highly visible.

We have briefly summarized several feasible studies to answer four questions that could directly test these models. There are other questions to which models give contrasting answers, and there are other designs that could be applied to test the models. It is important that multiple studies be conducted addressing many questions and using alternative designs. In this way, strengths of some studies can offset weaknesses in other studies. This will prevent overall conclusions from resting on the particular methodology of a single study. Further, different types of businesses in differing states need to be examined since it is possible that Model 1 applies to some businesses or in some states while Model 2 applies to other businesses or in other states, and Model 3 applied to yet another set of businesses or states.

CONCLUSIONS

The models described here have conflicting implications. Though there are other possible models that describe the link between crime prevention and the risk of civil suits, their implications will follow those of Model 1 or Models 2 and 3. Any non-recursive model that provides negative feedback between individual risk and risk of suits will show that individual risk is kept low by the chance of suits. It should not matter what additional variables are added to Model 1.

Similarly, any alternative recursive model that does not link individual risk back to the chances of a suit (for example, the chance of a suit is proportional to the outrageousness of the crime committed) will yield results that imply that the chances of a suit do not reduce individual risk at many types of business places, like Model 2. We have already seen that Models 2' and 3 have results that are similar to Model 2. Further, models in which the chances of a suit are not linked to individual risk suggest that premises liability suits cannot have the desirable consequences described at the beginning of this paper. Under these conditions, place owners will invest in crime prevention to fight suits, and not reduce individual risk. These suits may provide justice to the victims of crime, but, under these circumstances, they will serve no other public purpose.

After studying how firms respond to products liability litigation, Eads and Reuter (1983:ix) noted that firms learn very little from the outcome of a particular lawsuit and "the connection between the law and product design is sufficiently weak that even major changes in the law would have little effect on the behavior of firms with respect to consumer product safety." If their conclusions about products liability are reliable and apply to premises liability, then we cannot be optimistic about the connections among liability law, crime prevention and individual risk.

We must be cautious in our conclusions, however. We know relatively little about these connections. The questions that motivated this paper cannot be answered with any acceptable level of confidence. Considerable research must be conducted before we can offer reliable conclusions. We can draw one definite conclusion from this discussion. Absent scientific empirical evidence, we cannot assume that the threat of premises liability suits will increase the use of crime prevention, and even if it does, we cannot assume that the investments in more crime prevention lead to greater public safety.

*   *   *

REFERENCES

Bates, N.D. and S.J. Dunnell (1994). "Major Developments in Premises Security Liability." New York, NY: American Insurance Services Group, Inc.

Bellamy, L.C. (1996). "Situational Crime Prevention and Convenience Store Robbery." *Security Journal* 7:41-52.

Black, D. (1976). *The Behavior of the Law.* New York, NY: Academic Press.

Brantingham, P.L. and P.J. Brantingham (1995). "Criminality of Place: Crime Generators and Crime Attractors." *European Journal of Criminal Justice Policy and Research* 3:5-26.

Calder, J.D. and D.D. Sipes (1992). "Crime, Security, and Premises Liability: Toward Precision in Security Expert Testimony." *Security Journal* 3:66-82.

Clarke, R.V. (1984). "Opportunity-based Crime Rates." *British Journal of Criminology* 24:74-83.

—— and D. Weisburd (1994). "Diffusion of Crime Prevention Benefits: Observations on the Reverse of Displacement." In: R.V. Clarke (ed.), *Crime Prevention Studies.* vol. 2. Monsey, NY: Criminal Justice Press.

Cohen, L.E. and M. Felson (1979). "Social Change and Crime Rate Trends: A Routine Activity Approach." *American Sociological Review* 44:588-605.

Eads, G. and P. Reuter (1983). *Designing Safer Products: Corporate Responses to Product Liability Law and Regulation.* Santa Monica, CA: Rand Corporation.

Eck, J.E. (1995). "A General Model of the Geography of Illicit Retail Marketplaces." In: J.E. Eck and D. Weisburd (eds.), *Crime and Place.* Crime Prevention Studies, vol. 4. Monsey, NY: Criminal Justice Press and Police Executive Research Forum.

—— and D. Weisburd (1995). "Crime Places in Crime Theory." In: J.E. Eck and D. Weisburd (eds.), *Crime and Place.* Crime Prevention Studies, vol. 4. Monsey, NY: Criminal Justice Press and Police Executive Research Forum.

Felson, M. (1994). *Crime and Everyday Life: Insight and Implications for Society.* Thousand Oaks, CA: Pine Forge Press.

—— (1995). "Those Who Discourage Crime." In: J.E. Eck and D. Weisburd (eds.), *Crime and Place.* Crime Prevention Studies, vol. 4. Monsey, NY: Criminal Justice Press and Police Executive Research Forum.

Gordon, C.L. and W. Brill (1996). "The Expanded Role of Crime Prevention Through Environmental Design in Premises Liability." Research in Brief series. Washington, DC: National Institute of Justice.

Loftin, C. and D. McDowell (1988). "The Analysis of Case-Control Studies in Criminology." *Journal of Quantitative Criminology* 4:85-98.

Pierce, G.L., S. Spaar and L.R. Briggs (1986). "The Character of Police Work: Strategic and Tactical Implications." Boston, MA: Center for Applied Social Research, Northeastern University.

Schlesselman, J.J. (1982). *Case-Control Studies: Design, Conduct, Analysis.* New York, NY: Oxford.

Sherman, L.W. (1989). "Violent Stranger Crime at a Large Hotel: A Case Study in Risk Assessment." *Security Journal* 1:40-46.

—— P.R. Gartin and M.E. Buerger (1989). "Hot Spots of Predatory Crime: Routine Activities and the Criminology of Place." *Criminology* 27:27-55.

—— J.D. Schmidt and R.J. Velke (1992). "High Crime Taverns: A RECAP Project in Problem-Oriented Policing." Final Report to the U.S. National Institute of Justice. Washington, DC: Crime Control Institute.

Wacholder, S., J.K. McLaughlin, D.T. Silverman and J.S. Mandel (1992). "Selection of Controls in Case-Control Studies: I. Principles." *American Journal of Epidemiology* 135:1019-1050.

CRIME PREVENTION AND THE INSURANCE INDUSTRY

by Roger A. Litton

Smithson Mason Group

Abstract: *Crime prevention can be hampered by a lack of incentives. The insurance industry is uniquely positioned to motivate its policyholders to take crime prevention measures. This paper, which is written from the perspective of a U.K. insurance practitioner, explores the means by which the industry does this and ways in which criminologists can use the provision of property insurance as a means of promulgating good crime prevention practice. The importance for the insurance industry of criminological work in the fields of environmental risk and repeat victimization is identified and a plea is entered for further research that could inform insurers' crime prevention activities. The possible criminogenic aspects of insurance are explored, as are the prevalence and impact of insurance fraud and the measures that the U.K. insurance industry is taking to combat it.*

INTRODUCTION

Insurance and crime interact. At a trivial level, it is obvious that, without crime, there would be no crime insurance. Because insurance is, at least in part, criminogenic, without insurance there would be less crime.

Crime and criminal activities are important to insurers. In some cases, the activities of criminals merely affect insurers' profit and loss accounts; at the other extreme, whole classes of insurance exist only because crime exists (Litton, 1982; 1990). However, not only can crime affect insurance, insurance can affect crime — either accidentally or deliberately. The provision of insurance can constitute a powerful means by which financial incentives or disincentives can be offered for the adoption of crime prevention measures. Both the insurance industry and criminologists have been slow to recognize and use this potential. It is hoped that what follows will demonstrate how insurers can contribute to their own welfare and that of their policyholders and others by helping to reduce crime, without being asked to do anything that would necessarily interfere with their primary objective of writing profitable insurance business. If crime can be reduced, insurance losses should also be reduced. The benefit to insurers will be self-evident to them: with a correct focusing of their efforts in the crime prevention field, their policyholders, as well as wider society, can benefit too. Criminological research can help with that focusing.

This paper will concentrate on the relationships between insurance and property crime. It will explore the ways in which crime affects insurers, including insurance fraud, and how insurers affect crime. Attention will then turn to the manner in which insurers, by influencing their policyholders, can attempt to influence crime, along with the measures available to insurers to exert such pressure. Finally, the paper will identify two areas of research of which at least U.K. insurers appear to be ignorant but which could enable them to focus their crime prevention resources to better effect — the Environmental Risk Index and repeat victimization. It will also explore other areas in which criminological research could assist insurers in their understanding of crime and of the measures they could take, or encourage, to combat it.

CRIME AFFECTS INSURERS

It is easy to forget that insurers are companies just like any other. They suffer burglary, robbery and embezzlement, as other businesses do. Their reactions to these threats are no different from the reactions of a myriad of other businesses. However, what makes the insurance industry special is that part of its *raison d'être* is to stand ready to be affected by crime and its consequences. Perhaps one of the more obvious ways in which insurers are affected by crime is through insurance fraud — on the prevalence of which there is much folklore but little research.

Insurance Fraud

While insurance company claims departments, as part of their daily duties, are conscious of the possibility of insurance fraud, academic research on the subject appears to be limited. Some of the U.K. research will now be reviewed.

Fraud Survey

Litton (1985) reported a small U.K. study that appears to have been the first of its type although several subsequent surveys have adopted a similar format. In summary, 38% of respondents acknowledged that they knew someone who had invented a loss while as many as 54% admitted knowing someone who had exaggerated a loss. While these results are susceptible to various interpretations (Litton, 1990) — with the caveat that the sample is small — they do indicate that a significant amount of insurance fraud appears, or is said, to take place. They are particularly interesting for their suggestion that the invention of losses for the sole purpose of making an insurance claim may be nearly as prevalent as the exaggeration of losses; and they imply that both insurers and the police ought to be re-thinking their investigation strategy. The general consensus within, at least, the U.K. insurance industry is (or perhaps was) that one has to guard against people exaggerating their losses but that the danger of policyholders inventing losses is more remote (see, for example, Duncan, 1982).

Clarke (1989) concluded, from interviews with insurers and loss adjusters, that 50% of claims were exaggerated and between 1% and 5% were invented. Hughes (1995) reported a survey of some 400 insurance claimants. One in ten of the sample admitted committing insurance fraud, an equal number admitted to being dishonest or exaggerating and a minority confessed to inflating their claim to cover the amount of their policy deductible ("excess"). In an interesting parallel with the Litton (1985) study, half of the respondents said that they knew someone who had committed insurance fraud.

CILA Surveys

In 1992, the U.K. Chartered Institute of Loss Adjusters (CILA) surveyed its members on the subject of insurance fraud (Litton, 1995). The results are detailed in Table 1. Loss adjusters perceived the British public as having become less honest over the previous five years. They also suggested that many claims were exaggerated: 95% of loss adjusters felt that a quarter or more of all claims were exaggerated and nearly half suggested that at least 50% of all domestic claims were knowingly inflated. A clear majority (70%) of the loss adjusters felt that the average householder added at least 25% to his or her claim. Around 10% thought that most domestic claims were dishonestly inflated by as much as 50%.

Table 1: Views of Loss Adjusters on the Honesty of Insurance Claimants — 1992

OVER THE LAST 5 YEARS HAS THE BRITISH PUBLIC BECOME MORE OR LESS HONEST IN ITS INSURANCE CLAIMS?	
	Percentage
Much more honest	00
More honest	06
Same	12
Less honest	72
Much less honest	13
Total	100 (N = 547)

IF LESS HONEST, WHAT PERCENTAGE OF DOMESTIC CLAIMS DO YOU THINK ARE EXAGGERATED?	
Less than 10%	03
25%	42
50%	29
More than 50%	21
Nearly all	00
Total	100 (N = 547)

IF LESS HONEST, WHAT PERCENTAGE OF DOMESTIC CLAIMS DO YOU THINK ARE EXAGGERATED?	
Hardly at all	00
Less than 10%	24
25%	78
50%	08
Double	00
Total	100 (N = 547)

Source: Chartered Institute of Loss Adjusters (unpublished, 1992)

The CILA repeated its survey in 1995 and reported that, as in 1992, the average domestic insurance claim was thought to be inflated by at least 25% and that, despite the best efforts of the insurance industry, the British public was becoming more, not less, dishonest in making claims (57% of respondents). In the commercial field, the Institute's members were slightly more optimistic: nearly three quarters felt that "only" 25% or fewer of commercial claims were exaggerated. Table 2 shows why respondents felt that normally honest members of the public were less than honest in their claims.

Table 2: Why Do You Think Some Normally Honest Members of the Public Are Less than Honest with Their Insurance Claims?

They feel everyone is doing it	69%
They see it as a negotiating position	58%
It is a way of making money	46%
Insurance companies have made it easy	42%
Part of the decline in general morals	42%
It is a 'no-victim' crime	35%
There are no punishments	26%
It is a way of getting their own back on insurance companies	25%

Source: Chartered Institute of Loss Adjusters (unpublished, 1995)

ABI Surveys

The Association of British Insurers (ABI), the trade body for British insurers, has conducted two public-opinion research surveys. In 1992, 20% of respondents claimed to know someone who had made an exaggerated insurance claim while 80% of the same sample agreed that fraudulent claims were a serious problem. Again, in 1994, 20% of the 1,000 respondents claimed to have known someone who had recently submitted a bogus or inflated insurance claim. According to ABI estimates, insurance fraud costs insurers in excess of £600 million annually — around 4% of net written annual premiums — with over 500,000 dishonest claims attempted each year (Litton, 1996).

UK Insurance Industry Anti-Fraud Initiatives

After many years of bemoaning the prevalence of insurance fraud (see, for example, Blunt, 1907), the insurance industry has begun, through the ABI and its recently formed Crime and Fraud Prevention Bureau, to take countermeasures. These measures are discussed below.

Motor Insurance Anti-Fraud and Theft Register (MIAFTR)

The Motor Insurance Anti-Fraud and Theft Register (MIAFTR) is a computer database that came into operation in 1987, primarily to identify multiple fraudulent insurance claims and repeated claims for closer investigation. The register derives its data from all motor insurance total loss claims reported to insurers — from unrepairable wrecks to those considered uneconomic to repair, as well as fire and theft claims and claims dealt with under "new for old" cover. There are currently over four million records on the register and each day between 1,000 and 2,000 new cases are added. New claims are checked against the database for:

(1) name of claimant;

(2) vehicle registration number;

(3) vehicle identification or chassis number; and

(4) claimant's postal code.

A listing of matching items is sent to the reporting insurer for further investigation. Every opportunity is being taken to ensure that the register is given the appropriate publicity in the media and a warning about its existence is now included on motor insurance proposal forms.

Within a few weeks of starting, the register matched — by vehicle registration number — reports of two car thefts by two seemingly unconnected people who were later identified as a husband and wife team — the wife using her maiden name and a different address. The subsequent investigation revealed previous fraudulent claims and prevented intended further claims — a saving to insurers of some £30,000. The register subsequently achieved its most spectacular success in terms of a multiple claim — involving 11 different insurers for the total loss of a single vehicle — with a potential gain to the fraudsters of some £65,000 for what was not a great deal of effort. The register has also been successful in less spectacular ways. Many claims have "gone away" after further inquiries prompted by information from the register. By 1994, the register had reported savings of over £9.5 million. During 1995, the register reported two further successes: a major insurance fraud involving classic cars (and a peer of the realm!) estimated at £4.5 million and the jailing of a major gang of car "ringers" with sentences ranging from one to four years (ABI, 1996).

Talks are currently under way with the police with a view to a link-up with the stolen vehicle file of the Police National Computer and with the Vehicle Licencing authorities with the object of combating the serious problem of the "ringing"[1] of motor vehicles. Five police forces currently have on-line access to MIAFTR; they have found that it increases their efficiency by enabling them to interrogate the database directly and they view it as a useful further tool in the fight against crime and fraud.

Claims and Underwriting Exchange (CUE)

In 1994, the major U.K. insurers writing household insurance established a computerized claims database (CUE) to combat fraudulent and multiple claims and to verify claims history. Members provide details of all settled, current and new claims; new claims are "matched" against the database. Members may receive all the details on the system about the relevant claims, including the identities and addresses of the claimant and insurer and the amount of the claim and payment. Members of the Exchange will be giving maximum publicity to its existence. Through CUE, an insurer recently identified an individual who made 25 claims with ten different companies, ranging from the theft of a portable compact disc player to a bicycle reported stolen four times. The police are now involved (ABI, 1996).

It is intended that MIAFTR and CUE will eventually be merged. Further computer registers, starting with travel insurance, are planned for other classes of insurance.

The Equipment Register

The Equipment Register (Register) is a commercial computer database of mobile construction equipment that functions both to combat fraud (a common fraud is to sell, say, an excavator, ship it abroad and then report it as stolen and submit an insurance claim for a replacement) and as a recovery mechanism to combat straightforward theft. It has four means of registration:

(1) negative — stolen items identified by the police, the loser, insurance company, or loss adjuster;

(2) positive — details of owned equipment registered by paying members;

(3) export — details provided by Register contacts in ports around the U.K. enable Register staff to cross-check if they are subsequently notified of the theft of an item; and

(4) manufacturers — major "plant" (mobile construction equipment) manufacturers provide details of all plant sales so that, if an item of plant is discovered in an unlikely place, the registered owner can be contacted for confirmation that the item should be at that location.

Some 180 construction, plant hire (rental) and insurance companies are currently subscribing members. The Register employs full-time investigators who follow up reports of stolen plant, suspicious exports, or reports of plant spotted in odd places. In the last 12 months, the Register has recovered 151 items with a replacement value of £2.2 million. Insurers are increasingly encouraging their clients to become members by:

(1) offering one year's free membership for any item of plant they insure;

(2) reducing deductibles for registered items; and

(3) publicizing the Register to clients and brokers and producing loss-prevention booklets for the police that refer to the Register.

Art Loss Register

This Register, operated by the same commercial organization as the Equipment Register, is not an anti-fraud measure but is included here for completeness. It comprises an international computerized database, operating out of London, New York and Australia, with offices planned in Europe, and was set up originally because of concern among insurers and the art world about escalating thefts of works of art. Stolen items are registered by the police, subscribing insurers, loss adjusters, or individuals; if the item is insured by a subscribing insurer, no charge is made — otherwise the cost is £20. Subscribers include art dealers, auction houses (who are encouraged to check items they handle against the Register) and insurers. Checks by the police are free and Register staff attend "Aladdin's cave" finds of recovered works of art without charge. Since its inception in 1991, the Register has been instrumental in recovering property worth £18.5 million.

Some Thoughts on Insurance Fraud

As will be apparent from the above, what little research there is survey-based — supplemented by anecdotal evidence — and answers to survey questions should be treated with at least some skepticism. There must be considerable data available in the files of insurers and loss adjusters. While insurers' claims departments are well enough aware of the impact of insurance fraud on their own companies, little effort is made either to collate or publicize this information. Only a small proportion of claims where the insurer detects or suspects fraud are reported to the police (Niemi, 1995). Research data on which cases are referred to the police, and the reasons for referral or non-referral, are lacking. Insurance fraud appears to be a field ripe for the attention of criminologists although it has, to date, had little attention from them (but see Litton, 1995, and Niemi, 1995, for reviews of European and Scandinavian research, respectively). Clarke (1989) reported that the United States and France are the most advanced in organizing the prevention of insurance fraud. By contrast, the Israel Insurance Association (personal communication, 1996) reported that "in the libraries of universities of Israel...insurance fraud is not known and there are no articles, Ph.D. theses or other books available."

If insurers can establish that insurance fraud is a significant problem, then they should target more resources at detecting and defeating it. Eriksson and Tham (1982, cited in Niemi, 1995), however, suggested that it is better to concentrate on reducing the number of losses since this should automatically bring with it a reduction in the number of fraudulent claims. Some significant steps have already been taken along this road in the U.K. with the establishment of the fraud registers detailed above. Increasingly, individual insurers are using their rights under the policy to replace stolen items on the assumption that claim invention will often be directed at obtaining a cash settlement rather than a replacement of the "stolen" item. While insurers have always been able to obtain discounts on replacement items, the growth of the equipment-replacement industry in the U.K. has meant that obtaining replacements quickly, but still at discounted prices, has become easier. The extensive databases held by the replacement specialists also make it more difficult for claimants to claim for a higher-specification item than was actually available at the time of the original purchase. If the insurance industry were able to continue this process of targeting fraud successfully, it would save considerable amounts of insurance claim payments and mitigate the premium burden on honest policyholders.

IS INSURANCE CRIMINOGENIC?

Crime has impacts on insurers both in the ways they expect and in other ways (the principal other way being insurance fraud). To what degree does insurance have an impact on crime? Does the very existence of insurance lead to more crime? These questions can perhaps be addressed from several different viewpoints, of which a selection follows.

Insurance Fraud

Insurance fraud is a crime. It is a truism that, without insurance, there could be no insurance fraud so to this degree insurance is undeniably criminogenic. Perhaps one of the more serious manifestations of insurance fraud is arson, which is acknowledged to be a significant problem throughout the developed world. It is estimated that, in the U.K., 20% of all fires are caused by arson and 5,000 of those are started with the intention of enabling an insurance claim. Again in the U.K., arson accounts for many of the biggest fires, with over half the value of big fire claims coming from fires that were started deliberately. Kelly (1993) suggested that fraudulent arson may represent around 20% of all arson. Other examples of insurance fraud abound and it is undeniable that the existence of insurance causes much loss of or damage to property to enable fraudulent insurance claims to be made. By contrast, however, it cannot be denied that the availability of insurance is a social good that must outweigh its negative consequences.

Assuaging Burglars' Consciences?

We do not know to what degree, if at all, criminals are more prepared to pursue their activities because they know, or assume, that their victims will be insured and, therefore, that at least the victim's pecuniary loss will be reduced. If, in the absence of insurance, burglars would commit any fewer crimes because of the sympathy they would feel for the losses their victims would suffer, then, to that degree, insurance could be argued to be criminogenic.

Research bearing on this subject is scarce, but there are indirect indicators. Much property crime is directed toward the poorer members of society, particularly in urban areas (Forrester et al., 1988; Reppetto, 1974; Scarr, 1973; Stockdale and Gresham, 1995; Waller and Okihiro, 1978), often on victims within a short distance of where the perpetrators live (Bennett and Wright, 1984; Davidson, 1984; Maguire, 1982). Frequently, both offender and victim come from the same social class (Forrester et al., 1988; Maguire, 1982). Poorer members of society are less likely to be insured (Litton, 1990; Maguire, 1982). Within this segment of society, therefore, burglars are unlikely to be able to comfort themselves with the thought that insurance will ease the financial burden on their victims — but this does not stop them from committing burglaries on their fellows. We have no similar pointers available for burglars' attitudes to their wealthier victims (although see Maguire [1982] for evidence that burglars rationalize that wealthier victims are better able to afford the loss), but offenders are hardly likely to feel more sympathy for the wealthy than for the poor.

In the absence of persuasive evidence, it is difficult to postulate that, without insurance, crime would be reduced because offenders' better feelings would lead them to desist from burglary. It is difficult to argue that insurance is criminogenic in this way.

Do Burglars Return in the Expectation that Property Will Have Been Replaced by Means of Insurance?

Given the prevalence of repeat victimization (see below), it is interesting to speculate to what extent burglars return in the expectation that the stolen property will have been replaced and to what extent insurance contributes either to this replacement or its expectation. If the presence of insurance enables policyholders to replace stolen items that they would not otherwise be able to afford to replace, or enables them to replace items more quickly (although some critics of the insurance industry suggest that settlements can take an inordinate length of time and that policyholders would replace items more quickly if left to their own devices), *and* if burglars return in the expectation that items will have been replaced, then, to that degree, it could be suggested that insurance is criminogenic.

Common sense suggests that, apart from major losses, and particularly in the domestic field, the type of property commonly stolen by burglars will often be replaced relatively quickly irrespective of insurance. After all, which household wants to be without its television or video recorder and which business can afford to be without its computer? While there are indications (Anderson et al., 1995a) that the same perpetrators may be responsible for the bulk of repeated offenses against a victim, we do not know the extant to which the same burglar returns because he expects that similar property will be available again or because he expects another easy entry — although Polvi et al. (1990) have suggested the former. On this evidence we cannot, without specific research, conclude that insurance is criminogenic in this way.

Until recently, there has been little evidence on the question of whether the high levels of repeat victimization are caused by the same burglar returning. Although Maguire (1982), in his interviews with burglars, did not ask the specific question, very little evidence of burglars' returning emerged from what they did tell him. Chenery et al.'s (1994) analysis of British Crime Survey data suggested that the majority of repeat offenses of the same kind are similar in method and circumstances and are presumed by the victims to be the work of the same person. Recent offender surveys (Winkel, 1991; Gill and Matthews, 1993) suggested that criminals do commit repeat offenses against the same targets. Steve Everson (personal communication) found that 80% of repetitions, where there are clearances of at least two of the crimes, feature the same offender — in gross terms, 80% of repeat burglaries are estimated to be the work of the same burglar. What we do not know is why the burglar returns and to what degree this is linked to insurance or the expectation that stolen property will have been replaced through the medium of insurance. Farrell et al. (1995) argued that repetitions involve less effort, lower risk and equivalent reward when compared to a first victimization. They speculated that the reasons a burglar will return include:

(1) knowledge of entry and exit points;

(2) knowledge of the layout of the property;

(3) a possibility that the last entry point will still be insecure;

(4) market for goods seen during the first burglary may have been established; and

(5) it may be expected that goods will have been replaced (possibly by means of insurance).

However, perhaps further research could tell us whether repeats are indeed the result of the same burglar returning and, if so, what his or her motives are.

At a practical level, one U.K. police force has issued a leaflet to businesses on computer crime, containing the explicit advice that, following a burglary, the packing materials from the replacement computer should not be left on view with the rest of the garbage (where the original burglar can easily spot it and decide to pay a return visit) but should be properly disposed of. Given that this is a cost-free crime prevention measure, why are insurers not providing such advice as a service to their policyholders following a burglary? With further research, we could probably be more prescriptive, and helpful, with such advice.

Are Policyholders Less Careful?

If policyholders are less careful of their possessions when they know they are insured, then this will presumably lead to more crime (on the not-unreasonable assumption that taking at least a modicum of care will reduce some of the risk of loss through crime). It is unlikely that there is only a certain amount of crime to go around and, therefore, that more care on the part of one individual will inevitably displace crime to a less-careful one. It is far more likely that there is some opportunism in crime (see, for example, Bennett and Wright, 1984). For example, the fact that a camera left unattended on a beach is likely to disappear probably has no influence on the amount of crime that would have been committed in the vicinity if it had not presented itself as both a temptation and an opportunity.

This question has engaged the attention of insurance writers for many years. Most insurers are convinced that their policyholders relax their standards of care when they have the comfort of knowing that they are insured. However, evidence supporting this assertion is difficult to find. For example, the fact that many claims are submitted for careless losses under the baggage sections of travel insurance policies could be evidence for lack of care, insurance fraud (Alport, 1988), or merely that policyholders are always this careless of their property whether or not they are insured.

In many instances there will be little incentive for insured persons to relax their standard of care. Often, the loss will cost the policyholder much more than the amount of the insurance payment, even if the policy pays in full in accordance with its terms. For example, if a business has a computer stolen, it might have insurance cover for replacement of the hardware. It is far less likely to carry insurance covering the cost of replacing the data or the disruption to the business caused until the replacement is functioning properly. Although insurance against such risks is available, only those businesses with extensive data processing facilities tend to buy it. Most businessmen know that a crime or other loss to the business will involve often-significant uninsured losses so the incentive to try to prevent loss will be substantially unimpaired.

Insurers have a whole raft of measures available to combat what they term "lack of self interest" (Litton, 1990:100-102). The more successful they are in combating this tendency, the less valid will be the argument that insurance is criminogenic because it reduces the incentive to take care. To the extent that policyholders appreciate that insurance will not always recompense them for all the consequences of a loss, the force of the argument is further diminished.

HOW DO INSURERS MOTIVATE CLIENTS TO TAKE PREVENTIVE ACTION?

Perhaps the most significant impact that insurers have on crime, and the one of most interest to criminologists, is by their deliberate attempts to influence crime. They do this partly by general persuasion (through such activities as contributing to crime prevention campaigns or distributing crime prevention leaflets) but, more particularly, by attempting to motivate their policyholders themselves to take measures — often as specified by the insurer — to reduce the risk of their suffering a loss from crime. Insurers motivate their policyholders toward action in various ways, some of which are discussed below.

The Conditional Granting of Insurance

The insurance cover is subject to specific requirements designed to ensure that the policyholder takes risk-reduction measures. For example, flood insurance on contents may be conditional upon goods in a cellar being stored a specified height off the floor or any intruder alarm must be set when the premises are unoccupied. If the condition is not complied with, either the whole policy is voidable by the insurer or the claim affected by the breach is not met. Some requirements also perform an educational function, such as physical security warranties in which door or window locks must be used when the property is unoccupied or when the household retires for the night. Such steps should be common sense, but, in some cases, only if insurers impose these conditions will policyholders use their common sense!

Disincentives

The imposition of special terms as incentives to improve what the insurer regards as an unsatisfactory feature or to obtain for the insurer a contribution in the event of a claim — either coupled with time limits pending improvement of unsatisfactory features or as semi-permanent features of the cover — include the following:

(1) premium loading — a premium in excess of that justified for a normal risk of the type;

(2) deductible ("excess") — the policyholder is required to bear the first £x of any loss;

(3) franchise — the policyholder bears any loss below a specified figure, above which the insurer bears the entire amount;

(4) coinsurance — the policyholder bears a stipulated percentage of any loss (with or without an upper limit);

(5) reinstatement — the refusal to reinstate a policy sum insured after a loss until preventive measures have been taken;

(6) increased sums insured — an increase in values insured or cover on attractive property can be made conditional upon improved security; and

(7) renewal — renewal of the policy (particularly after a claim) being similarly conditional.

The point about reinstatement may merit further explanation. Under material damage insurance, the sum insured applies to all claims during the insurance year. Following a loss, if the policyholder replaces the property, he or she will be under-insured until the insurer agrees to reinstate the sum insured (for which an additional premium may be charged). Withholding the reinstatement can be a valuable weapon to enable the insurer to make stipulations about improved security (unless the insurer contractually guarantees reinstatement).

Stick and Carrot

Some measures are imposed to encourage the policyholder to take specified action. If he or she complies, there is no penalty but, if the person does not, the specified penalty is applied. For example, an insurer might impose a £100 theft deductible on a motor insurance policy that does not apply if the car is garaged or if an immobilizer is operating at the time of the theft. Similarly, a deductible may apply to theft from the home if there is no sign of forcible entry. Here, the insurer hopes that the penalty will encourage the client to act prudently by securing the property but may not wish to withdraw theft cover completely even where elementary precautions are not taken.

Setting Standards

Insurers will usually require that any stipulated measure be to a specified standard. For example, in the U.K., very few insurers will accept an intruder alarm that has not been installed by a member of the National Security Council for Intruder Alarms. Locks must usually comply with the appropriate British standard. Vehicle security devices — either where they are a requirement or used to qualify for a premium discount — must be "Thatcham approved" (see below).

One suggestion in this general area whose time may now have come involves the vexed question of how to deal with false alarms from intruder alarms. The U.K. police are taking measures to combat the problem, including withdrawal of police response to persistent offenders, but it still remains a problem. Litton suggested that

> [w]ith the co-operation … of the police, insurers could keep records of false alarms and other alarm failures and grade alarm companies accordingly. They should recommend only alarm companies with above-average records and make their data available to their policyholders as justification for their recommendation. Such a move should exert the best of all pressures — commercial pressure — on alarm companies to hasten their research and development programmes to eliminate, or at least reduce, alarm failures as it would be apparent that, for the first alarm company to succeed, the rewards

would be enormous. Such a move would cost insurers very little but could yield potentially large benefits [Litton, 1982:18-19].

In the U.K., the idea still has merit. In some cities in America, however, the police are now insisting that intruder alarm installations must be registered with them. Householders are fined on an increasing scale for each false alarm. The police records will thus not only contain details of false alarms but of the alarm companies whose systems are causing them. If those data were to be published with a rank ordering of alarm companies showing false alarm rates, competitive pressures might start to eliminate the causes of false alarms. It would not matter whether these are design faults or operator errors — most operator error can surely be designed out of alarm systems (as the Highway Loss Data Institute demonstrates so well for automobile safety) given the motivation for the alarm company to undertake the design work. If customers, on the basis of a police (or insurance company) ranking of false alarms, were "voting with their feet" and turning to competitors' systems, would that not provide the necessary incentive? With a reduction in false alarms, intruder alarms could begin to regain their position as a significant instrument for burglary prevention.

Exhortation

The insurer may give advice on various measures that will reduce the risk of loss. For example, they may send leaflets to policyholders encouraging them to lock their doors and windows when they leave the property or to mark their possessions. If followed, these suggestions should reduce the risk of burglary (or help the recovery of property), but no penalty would attach if the policyholder did not follow the advice.

Incentives

Not all motivators are negative ones: premium discounts and financial help can provide incentives. Premium discounts can be granted for the installation of approved security devices (with the insurance often being made conditional upon the devices being used), for membership of Neighborhood Watch, or for any other activity that the insurer considers may reduce risk. Financial contributions towards security improvements are relatively new in the U.K. and currently restricted to a few insurers.

ACTION BY INSURERS

To the extent that insurers are insuring the consequences of (non-policyholder) crime — how, therefore, do they react? They react in the property insurance field as they do in any other class of insurance — by trying to select business that is likely to have the fewest claims or, in relation to their existing insurance business, by trying to persuade their policyholders to prevent or minimize claims. Insurers cannot prevent crime directly; they can only act to prevent crime by persuading their policyholders to take the necessary preventive measures.

Insurers, of course, are keen to prevent burglaries because, by preventing burglaries, they can help to prevent claims. There is an argument (see, for example, Pease, 1979) that suggests that insurers welcome claims because higher losses enable them to charge increased premiums. This is, at best, partly true (Litton, 1982). If there were no losses, then obviously there would be no need for insurance. However, we shall never live in that perfect world so prudent businesses and individuals will always need insurance. Even if losses, and therefore claims, are small, insurers will always be able to charge a minimum (reasonable?) premium for the risk and, at that level of losses, they should be able to make a reasonable profit (even though competition will drive premiums down to a low level). Experience shows that, if losses are high and rising, premiums seldom catch up with claims. This has happened in recent years in the U.K. with employers liability insurance where few, if any, insurers are making a profit and can see no prospect of doing so for years to come. To this degree, insurers lose and clients benefit — however, even this is an untrue statement because neither party benefits if burglaries are taking place because there will always be elements of the loss that cannot be insured and can often be as large, or larger, than the amount of the insurance claim.

Insurers are, therefore, concerned to prevent losses in all fields of insurance and, traditionally, have been prepared to devote resources to doing so. Most insurers talk of doing this "in partnership" with their policyholders, although either the reality, or the perception by policyholders, is different. Particularly in the burglary-prevention field, insurers will send their surveyor to "assist" with helpful suggestions for crime prevention measures. How often, though, does this exercise turn into a list of requirements by the insurers, often with short time scales for implementation and the threat of withdrawal of cover if the policyholder does not comply? The solution to this problem is for insurers to offer, and clients to request, this input before there has been a burglary. Insurers are always more sympathetic at this point and their input can be genuinely constructive.

Even though carried out purely from motives of self-interest, the activities of insurers in encouraging target hardening are to be welcomed. While some crimes may be displaced (Barr and Pease, 1990), others may be prevented — and any general increase in security levels is surely a gain. In the burglary field, insurers (and the police) have always traditionally concentrated on target hardening. Within recent years, other fields have either opened to, or been opened by, them so there are now four main areas in which insurers are trying to take action. These are discussed below.

Target Hardening

Given the reliance of both the police and the insurance industry on target hardening — that is, the insistence, whenever they get the chance, on locks, bolts and bars and, increasingly, intruder alarms — a valid question is whether this approach works. For *overall* levels of burglary, research, the opinions of burglars (e.g., Bennett and Wright, 1984; Maguire, 1982), and *UK Criminal Statistics* all suggest that target hardening does not work. There are so many unprotected or poorly protected premises that any thief who wishes to find an easy "mark" will have no difficulty in doing so (although see Tilley and Webb, 1994, for a report of how household security levels in the U.K. appear to be improving, particularly among the better-off sections of the community).

For *individual* premises, or groups of premises, however, target hardening does work. Burglars themselves and academic research both support this view. For example, Allatt (1984) arranged to upgrade the door and window security of the dwellings on an entire local authority housing estate in the North East of England. Burglaries fell dramatically and there was no apparent displacement to neighboring areas. In Kirkholt, in the North of England, improved security (as one of a raft of measures) reduced burglaries significantly (Forrester et al., 1988). The work reported by Tilley and Webb (1994) also provided persuasive evidence of the efficacy of target hardening. Eleven separate schemes, publicly funded under the Safer Cities Initiative in English towns and cities, were analyzed. All the schemes involved target hardening of one or more selected groups of dwellings: victims; those perceived as vulnerable; crime "hot spots;" or entire areas. In most cases, security upgrading was complemented by one or more additional measures (such as publicity, property marking, victim advice or support, Neighborhood Watch). In the majority of the schemes, domestic burglaries fell — in some cases by a significant percentage.

In the non-domestic field, Tilley (1993) reminded us that studies have found that businesses have a higher rate of victimization than dwellings. For example, in a 12-month period: (1) of 50 businesses in one London Borough, 30% had been victims of burglary or attempted burglary; (2) in the Wirral, Merseyside, rates of victimization of businesses in three streets averaged over 50%; (3) in Birkenhead, Merseyside, of 58 businesses, 67% had been victims of some type of crime, 50% had suffered burglary and 33% theft. Nationally, 24% of both retailers and manufacturers had been burgled while 22% of retailers and 18% of manufacturers had had an attempted burglary (Mirrlees-Black and Ross, 1996a; 1996b). These figures can be compared to national estimates from the 1992 British Crime Survey (BCS) of 5.3% for household burglary (Mayhew et al., 1993). Repeat victimization is similarly a problem.

> In Hartlepool [N.E. England]... of the 250 [business] addresses, 40% are reburgled at least once within 12 months of the first incident. Of those reburgled at least once 48% are reburgled at least twice ... of those reburgled at least twice, 57% are reburgled at least three times." [Tilley, 1993:7]

Under the Safer Cities initiative, Hartlepool and Salford offered subsidized security upgrades. In Hartlepool, in the total of 563 months of trading covered by 25 businesses before the upgrades, there were 46 burglaries. In the 270 months of post-upgrade trading, there were none. The results for Salford are shown in Figure 1: there were 645 offenses against the businesses in the 12 months prior to security upgrading and only 194 in the following year (Tilley, 1993).

Figure 1: Results of the Salford Security Upgrade Scheme

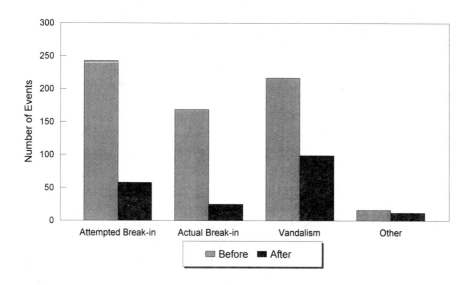

Source: Tilley (1993:16).

Additional evidence that target hardening works is provided by the figures for attempted burglaries. According to police figures, between 1981 and 1987, U.K. burglaries *with* loss rose by around 36%. *Attempted* burglaries rose by between 46% (*Criminal Statistics*) and 78% (BCS). Intuitively, as people will be less inclined to report an attempted, than a completed, burglary to the police than , the BCS figures — which suggest that attempted burglaries have risen at twice the rate of burglaries with loss — appear to be more persuasive than the police figures. Something was operating to prevent entry for those attempted burglaries and, in the absence of other explanations (Litton, 1990), increased crime prevention measures must surely take some of the credit. Similarly, while thefts of motor vehicles have more than doubled in the U.K. since 1981, attempted thefts have increased by between 400% (*Criminal Statistics*) and 600%

(BCS), which may indicate that greater security consciousness (and better vehicle security) is beginning to have an effect.

Given that improving security on individual dwellings does appear to work, there is a question, addressed further below, of how insurers can be guided into recommending target-hardening measures for those properties where they will be most effective. Insurers could only successfully insist that all insured properties be "adequately" protected if this was done as a market agreement between all insurers, as otherwise the "tougher" insurer would lose business to those insurers prepared to take a more lenient view. (There was one successful market agreement in the U.K. in the 1960s not to compete on levels of security for commercial properties — see Litton (1990) for details — but the agreement only subsisted for a short time.) As long as their requirements are not so severe as to drive the business to a competitor, insurers experience few problems in ensuring that their requirements are implemented. Many requirements are imposed (or recommendations agreed to) after a survey and insurers usually demand written confirmation that agreed security improvements have been installed. Insurers would raise difficulties if, at the time of a claim, it was found that the assurances they had been given, and on the basis of which they had granted cover on certain terms, were untrue. In general, therefore, the problem is not that insurers cannot achieve implementation of crime prevention measures, but rather of their knowing with any degree of certainty which measures work, to which properties they should be applied, and when. It is in these areas that criminology has much to offer the insurance industry and, through the industry, the public at large.

It may be that the actions of insurers in actively seeking improved security do not always lead to beneficial results. It is sometimes argued that, because they are commercial organizations, insurers are reluctant to write business in high-risk areas, rendering insurance difficult, if not impossible, to obtain in some inner-city areas. U.K. insurers deny that this happens. Gill and Turbin (1996) undertook research to test this proposition and found little evidence of the refusal of household insurance. What their research did suggest, however, was that the high cost of implementing the minimum security requirements set by insurers was a major disincentive to the purchasing of insurance by some residents. In support of the proposition that good can ensue from cooperation between residents and insurers in tackling crime, they suggested that help with such costs should be made available. Given that a few insurers are beginning to offer financial assistance in the non-domestic field — and at least one insurer offers a modest contribution toward the cost of extra security to new domestic policyholders — is there scope for more active involvement of this nature by insurers?

Property Marking and Property Recording

In the U.K., insurer attention in this area is somewhat patchy. For example, in 1989 Royal Insurance gave £100,000 to police forces to support property-marking campaigns. Other U.K. insurers are encouraging property marking both by publicity literature and, occasionally, by such devices as the free issue of property-marking pens. Little other active support currently seems to be given. Whether property marking is regarded as a deterrent (which it can only be if advertised in such a way that the prospective thief is aware that property is marked) or because it enhances prospects of recovery of property, or both, is unclear — although Laycock's (1992) study supports the deterrence hypothesis. Laycock reported a property-marking project in Wales that achieved a 40% reduction in burglaries. She suggested that at least part of the success of the initiative may have been attributable to the extensive publicity and enthusiastic police involvement, accompanied by extensive local publicity of the project results — a judgment supported by a further reduction in burglary numbers in the second year immediately following publication. Laycock also reported projects in America and Sweden whose results were inconclusive. Whether the type of property marking being promoted by U.K. insurers, typically with no supporting publicity, works is as yet unknown. Intuitively, it can do no harm, but there does appear to be a need for research to demonstrate whether it works. If property marking is an effective means of crime prevention, there would appear to be scope for insurer initiatives, probably at relatively little cost, to encourage it.

Some insurers are encouraging property marking of vehicles and mobile construction equipment, and their components, with coded micro dots. This technology is new in the U.K. so information about its effectiveness is hard to come by.

Some U.K. insurers, particularly those involved in the insurance of high-net-worth individuals, now encourage, by premium discounts, photographic recording of valuables and may provide or subsidize professional surveys or valuations as a permanent record and description of property. Insurers are increasingly issuing security guides that will mention the importance of recording serial numbers of attractive property. Again, there is no relevant research that would tell us whether publicizing the existence of such arrangements would be crime preventive.

Neighborhood Watch

The majority of the large household insurers in the U.K. now give a premium discount for participation in Neighborhood Watch (NW) projects. However, research evidence on their effectiveness, at least in the U.K., is limited (Husain, 1988). One perceived snag with NW projects is that they often appear to cease to function effectively as interest wanes (Husain, 1988). The major U.K. research work is by Bennett (1989:146), who reported on the Metropolitan Police NW initiative launched in 1983, with the depressing conclusion that "the NW programmes had no measured impact on the crime rate in either experimental area." On a more positive note, Tilley and Webb (1994) reported projects where NW, as one of several measures, seemed to have contributed to a reduction in burglary. Bennett and Wright (1984) quoted Titus as reporting that NW schemes in the USA consistently reduced burglary. Cirel et al. (1977) reported on the success of a "block watch" project in Seattle (involving groups of ten to 15 neighbors watching each other's houses and arranging occupancy surrogates) that reduced burglary rates by 50 to 60%. Forrester et al. (1988) also reported considerable success for their "cocoon" Neighborhood Watch (involving, at most, five or six immediate neighbors of a crime victim), albeit, again, as one of a raft of crime prevention measures. There appears to be scope for further research on the effectiveness of NW both when used as a crime prevention tool in its own right and when used with other crime prevention measures.

One insurer, General Accident (GA), has gone further than allowing premium discounts for NW membership. GA has become heavily involved in the NW movement in the U.K. and is a national sponsor of the newly formed National Neighbourhood Watch Association. It is committed to contributing £1,000,000 annually at the local and national level at least until the year 2000. It has developed a household insurance policy available only to NW members through insurance brokers who are appointed by the insurer on an exclusive regional basis to coincide with police areas — an example of how the police are still fundamental in establishing most NW schemes (Husain, 1988). It was hoped that the police would cooperate in making the policy available to members (as a benefit of NW participation) by releasing to the nominated insurance brokers the names and addresses of NW coordinators, but this has only happened in some areas. The broker surveys each dwelling prior to acceptance to assess levels of physical security and make recommendations for improvement. GA contributes toward the cost of security upgrades by premium discounts (from their already discounted NW rates) and a small (£25) cash handout. In its publicity material, GA quotes a reduction in the rate of burglary from one in 12 generally to a rate of one in 78 for those insured on the scheme. Leaving aside the question of whether those who insured on the scheme were typical, Husain (1988) told us that NW schemes are biased towards the middle class who tend not to live in the most burglary-prone areas. The claim is a spectacular one. Is it possible that the effect comes not from participation in a NW scheme, per se, but rather from the security survey (and the subsequent follow-up to ensure that recommended security improvements have been implemented) by the insurance broker required as a prerequisite of participation? Research on this question, using this database, could potentially yield important information on which crime reduction measures work in practice. We should not be deterred from this by the fact that teasing out the relative contributions of the various components (NW membership, an individual survey providing security advice and insurer incentives for security improvements) would probably not be easy.

GA runs an annual series of Crime Check conferences in each region, bringing together NW, police, the business community and insurers with the purpose of encouraging crime awareness. There is typically a session each for business and domestic interests. Insurance is not promoted at the events. It also issues crime prevention material (including videos directed at NW organizers) that make no mention of insurance. Interestingly, GA funds most of its involvement with the scheme not from its advertising budget but from its community projects fund. At least part of the objective must be to sell more, and hopefully more-profitable, insurance, but the objectives go wider than that — as the police cooperation testifies. As a series of crime prevention initiatives, and as an example of the more direct involvement of insurers in this arena for which the present author has long been pleading, the GA scheme is to be heartily welcomed.

Husain (1988) reminded us of another less-tangible effect of NW schemes. The fact that most residents think that NW has a beneficial effect not just on the problem of crime, but also on other related issues, is itself a benefit. To the extent that insurers are encouraging participation in NW schemes, they may be contributing to a reduction in the fear of crime — itself a laudable objective.

Motor Vehicle Security

U.K. motor insurers allocate cars to one of 20 rating groups devised centrally through the ABI and accepted across the insurance industry. Rating groups take account of various factors that contribute to costs of claims including: performance; availability and cost of parts; ease of replacement of parts; and, of particular relevance in the present context, security. Security as a factor was first incorporated in 1991. There is, though, doubt in certain quarters as to whether security factors carry as much weight in the group rating as insurer publicity suggests, principally because insurance payments for personal injury and for vehicle damage considerably outweigh those for theft. Evaluation of the security of new vehicles is carried out according to criteria laid down by the Motor Insurance Repair Research Centre ("Thatcham"), which is funded by the insurance industry. Particular emphasis is placed on "passive" arming of security devices given that research indicates that the public cannot be relied upon to lock their own cars (ABI, 1994).

Many car manufacturers have reacted positively, to the extent that increasing numbers of new models are achieving lower group ratings as a result of the security factor alone. Where, however, the security level is considered inadequate, the group ratings are being increased — again to provide an incentive to manufacturers to do better. Group ratings published since 1994 are accompanied by a special indicator so that manufacturers and, perhaps more importantly, the public are fully aware of the extent to which in-built security has affected the group rating. The rating system is proving to be a powerful spur to vehicle manufacturers to improve the security on their vehicles — which, fortunately, does not bear out Ahlström and Ahlberg's (1994, cited in Niemi, 1995) gloomy suggestion that car manufacturers and insurers have only a limited interest in such improvements since they benefit financially from car thefts. Manufacturers, being keenly interested in the cost of vehicle ownership (including insurance), stand to gain competitive advantages. The public receives benefits in terms of relatively lower premiums and better protected cars. Motor vehicle manufacturers are also reporting an increased awareness of security among car buyers (although we are still a long way from the ready availability of security information on cars that is commonplace in the U.S.A.).

Inadequately protected cars still represent the majority of vehicles on the roads. Thatcham have applied considerable resources to the development of criteria for "after market" devices and publish lists of approved alarms and immobilizers. An increasing number of insurers now offer significant premium discounts as an incentive for policyholders to fit "Thatcham" security to their vehicles. For high-risk vehicles, however, the provision of cover may be conditional upon extra security being fitted. It is this requirement that is credited with the large reduction in the number of thefts of "hot hatches" over the past three years and that has led to their being insurable again. Individual insurers are also linking up with manufacturers and installers to offer discounts from the purchase or installation price. While Thatcham approval operates for the entire insurance industry, individual insurers' reactions to the devices are a matter for them alone so one insurer may offer a discount for a particular device, whereas another may make its fitting a requirement.

Following their recent introduction into the U.K., "Tracker" devices have, from the insurance industry's point of view, been as successful here as in the U.S.A. and other countries. While Thatcham has not yet tested them, many insurers are granting premium discounts for their installation. Again, premium incentives are being used to mold behavior in a desired direction. Some criminologists (R.V. Clarke, personal communication) argue that such devices have not been wholly successful because: (1) they do not prevent thefts by joyriders; (2) while they lead to swifter recovery of a vehicle, they do not prevent its being stolen; and (3) they distort the police response so that they pay more attention to recovering vehicles with these systems than those without. An insurer will always prefer that a vehicle not to be stolen at all and, to this end, will encourage the policyholder to fit adequate mechanical devices to render the vehicle less attractive to thieves. However, once a vehicle is stolen, the insurer will prefer that it is recovered as rapidly as possible either to minimize the opportunity for joyriders to damage it or reduce the time available to professional thieves either to break it up for parts or to deliver it to a waiting purchaser. Tracker devices achieve both of these objectives, which is why they are likely to become increasingly popular with insurers. Insurers (like their clients) will be delighted if the police spend more time recovering "their" stolen vehicles and will be indifferent to any distortion of police response — unless, of course, this should directly impinge on them by delaying a response to another insured crime. It is extremely unlikely that such a relationship would ever be demonstrated. This reaction is no different from insurers' reactions to other measures that can benefit them even though they might have negative effects on society. Thus, for example, as already argued, insurers are indifferent to the displacement effects of their crime prevention activities. Displacement will usually be either to uninsured properties or to properties insured by their competitors.

Most motor insurers have now incorporated into their policies theft deductibles (which sometimes become inoperative if specified security precautions are taken — such as if the car is garaged at the time of a theft) as an incentive to their policyholders to take security precautions. Similar approaches are being taken by household insurers with respect to theft cover; and the insurance market is now beginning to turn its attention by similar means to the theft problem for goods vehicles and motor cycles.

After years of bemoaning increasing levels of car crime but doing little, other than increasing premiums in response, U.K. insurers have, over the last five years, awakened to the fact that, by the provision of incentives and disincentives, they can change the behavior of vehicle manufacturers and the vehicle-buying public so that more emphasis is placed on vehicle security. Because of the number of older cars still on the roads, it will be some time yet before the results of these initiatives are seen, but, by flexing their muscles in this manner, insurers must surely be on the way to changing crime patterns in this field.

U.S. insurers, however, are considerably in advance of these U.K. initiatives. The National Highway Traffic Safety Administration produces an index of each vehicle model stolen each year although the index is restricted to new models. The Insurance Institute for Highway Safety, supported by U.S. automobile insurers, publishes detailed safety information on vehicles. It, in turn, funds the Highway Loss Data Institute, which publishes comprehensive statistics and reports on injury, collision and theft losses for most models of vehicle from data supplied by automobile insurers. The Institute carries considerable influence with vehicle manufacturers and has had notable success in achieving modifications both to unsafe vehicles and to those that present an above-average theft risk. Vehicle manufacturers are, understandably, reluctant to see their models score badly in the regularly published reports.

The Australian insurance organization, NRMA, similarly publishes an annual report on car theft in Eastern Australia. By contrast, similar initiatives in the U.K. are in their infancy. The Home Office has published one car-loss index (Houghton, 1992) and is considering a more comprehensive follow-up. The Association of British Insurers is thought to be adopting a cautious approach to any support for such a project. If true, this is to be regretted. It is apparent that the production of the Home Office index entailed a considerable amount of work in obtaining, translating and consolidating data. The American efforts in this field suggest that insurance data can be more informative at less cost. The only other U.K. work in a related field is the "motor casualty report" published by the Department of Transport.

In contrast with what is being achieved in other countries, notably America, U.K. initiatives can only be described as timid and limited. It is possible that better cooperation between the insurance industry and government would hasten crime prevention efforts in this field. Similarly, the potential for the use of pooled insurance statistics as a crime prevention tool has been more than adequately demonstrated by the U.S. insurance industry. Annually produced league tables of high quality and in accessible form have to be a better spur to crime prevention than that which is available in the U.K..

We still, though, lack research on the deterrent effect of vehicle security devices for the various types of car thieves. Obvious security is more likely to deter the casual thief than the professional who is stealing to order. What types of security measures (such as a central register of Vehicle Identification Numbers (VINs), the mandatory marking of the VIN so that it is visible from outside the vehicle, security etching and trackers) will deter the professional thief? Criminological research could surely help to throw light on this type of question. With such guidance, insurers would be better placed to direct their incentives.

Many vehicle thefts are carried out so that criminals can use the documentation of vehicles "written-off" by insurers to disguise the identity of stolen cars that are then sold to unsuspecting purchasers. For many years, U.K. insurers have voluntarily reported write-offs to the central licensing authorities so that, if a suspect vehicle is re-licensed (and, therefore, ostensibly back on the road), the police can check its authenticity. However, with over 400,000 write-offs per year, the police are unable to carry out such checks effectively given that many vehicles are re-licensed legitimately after repair. In an effort to combat the problem more effectively, insurers now, by agreement with the police and licensing authorities, notify only the higher-value write-offs that are more attractive to "ringers" (see note 1). The vehicle registration documents for the vehicle are returned to the licensing authority for destruction and those vehicles destined for scrap or breaking for spares are identified as such so that the vehicle record is effectively "frozen" to prevent the issue of duplicate licensing documents and their subsequent misuse. A certification scheme to ensure that seriously damaged vehicles are crushed is also planned by the ABI. After years of paying lip-service to the problem of "ringing," are U.K. insurers at last beginning to use their power to help worthwhile action to be taken? Again, though, are U.K. insurers adopting the right measures? What does deter professional car thieves? Would international comparisons be informative? There must be considerable scope for criminological work in this area.

WHERE DO INSURERS GO NOW?

Given that insurers have traditionally concentrated on target hardening and that, realistically, this will probably form the focus of the majority of their crime prevention efforts for the immediate future, and given that insurers cannot insist that all their policyholders' premises be protected to what is perceived to be a good standard, how can insurers identify those premises that are most at risk to help them target their crime prevention efforts? How can the police target their resources? How can the concerned property owner decide on the cost-effectiveness of security measures? Obviously, insurers' own statistics can help and U.K. insurers are already using postal codes to stipulate those premises meriting protection, although this action is often only triggered when the value at risk (the "sum insured," to insurers) reaches a certain figure.

Environmental Risk Index

Are there any other ways in which vulnerable premises can be identified? In the domestic burglary field, the work of Winchester and Jackson (1982) suggests that there are. Their study deserves to be much better known for its practical implications. They surveyed, in the South of England, around 400 burgled dwellings and 400 dwellings that had not been burgled and looked for features that distinguished between them. Their Environmental Risk Index contained 14 surveillability and access features that they found discriminated burgled from non-burgled dwellings (see Table 3).

Table 3: Variables Used to Construct the Environmental Risk Index

1. Situation - located in the country
2. Isolated
3. In a location with few (less than 5) other houses in sight
4. Road type: major town road or village lane
5. Set at a distance from the road in which the house stands
6. Located on the nearest major road
7. Housing plot not adjacent to gardens of other houses
8. Housing plot adjacent to private open space
9. Access at both sides of the house from front to back on the plot
10 Not overlooked at the front by other houses
11. Not overlooked on either side by other houses
12. Majority of sides of house not visible from public areas
13. Set at a distance from the nearest house
14. Road frontage obscured from roadside view

Source: Winchester and Jackson (1982:39)

Winchester and Jackson found that the greater the number of factors possessed by a dwelling, the higher was its chance of having been burgled.

Dwellings with a score of zero on the Index had a one in 1,800 chance of being burgled. Dwellings with nine or more features had, on average, a one in 13 chance of being burgled. Gillian Litton (1992) undertook a small, but successful, replication of this study in the North of England. The two sets of results are detailed in Table 4. Litton also found that dwellings with low scores on the index were at low risk whereas dwellings with high scores were at high risk.

Table 4: Estimated Annual Risk Rates by Environmental Risk of Site

	Index Score	Winchester & Jackson Risk Rates (Kent)	Litton Risk Rates (Harrogate)
High environmental	13	1 in 5	
risk dwellings	12	1 in 12	No samples
	11	1 in 10	
	10	1 in 29	
	9	1 in 11	
	8	1 in 20	1 in 7
	7	1 in 43	
	6	1 in 43	
	5	1 in 92	
	4	1 in 95	1 in 19
	3	1 in 113	
	2	1 in 218	
Low environmental	1	1 in 233	1 in 89
risk dwellings	0	1 in 1,845	
Overall		1 in 99	1 in 23

Source: Winchester & Jackson (1982:39) and Litton (1992:64)

In their interviews with burglary victims, Anderson et al. (1995a) noted how many of the victims' dwellings displayed Index features (such as a secluded rear or side path). Maguire (1982) commented how the views of burglars he interviewed explicitly supported Winchester and Jackson's (1982) findings, particularly on the importance of surveillability and occupancy. Bennett and Wright's (1984) interviews with convicted burglars also revealed that closeness of neighbors, cover and rear access were important situational cues in offender decision making.

We may potentially have a tool that works. Could these be the sorts of factors that insurers could identify and use when they are influencing their policyholders to take crime prevention measures? Even comparing the North of England with the South, some of the individual factors in the index were found to be less relevant and some to be far more important than others. Individual factors may be less important than the fact that identifying factors can be predictive of premises at risk from burglary. This research was conducted on dwellings. There would seem to be an urgent need for similar research in the commercial and industrial field. This might be more difficult because dwellings are far more homogeneous than are commercial premises, but that difficulty should not prevent efforts to refine a tool that would help us in predicting risks of burglary.

Even with the limited material so far at hand, insurers should be acquainting their staff and their policyholders with these findings. The incentive for insurers is that, if they can identify the high-risk premises, they can target their crime prevention activities and possibly avoid some burglary claims.

As will be apparent, the present author adopts a different viewpoint from that adopted by Maguire (1982) who argued, on the basis of Winchester and Jackson's findings and his own interviews with burglars, that levels of security are virtually irrelevant in deterring burglars. The evidence so far reviewed suggests that this is too pessimistic a viewpoint.

Repeat Victimization

Perhaps the most exciting concept that criminological research is making available is, as yet, unknown to insurers. The phenomenon of repeat victimization, whereby only a small proportion of the population and of victims suffer a large proportion of all criminal victimizations, has been recognized in the criminological literature for over two decades. Only comparatively recently, however, have the policy implications of the concept begun to be recognized (Farrell, 1995), particularly following the seminal practical work undertaken by Pease and his co-workers (for example, Forrester et al., 1988; Forrester et al., 1990; Farrell and Pease, 1993;

Lloyd et al., 1994; Anderson et al., 1995a; 1995b). Data from the 1992 British Crime Survey demonstrated that around 60% of the population were *not* victimized during the survey period of just over a year (Farrell and Pease, 1993). Those people victimized on two or more occasions (20% of the surveyed population) reported 80% of all incidents. Pease and Laycock's (in press) analysis of BCS data suggested that some 4% of people suffered about 44% of the offenses and reported an unpublished Stockholm victimization survey that yields almost identical findings.

Concentration on non-victims misses an opportunity. If past victimization is indeed an excellent predictor of rapid future victimization, then insurers can obtain the best return from crime prevention activities by concentrating on those who have already been victims rather than trying to target, inadequately, all of their policyholders in an unfocused way.

The insurance industry (certainly in the U.K. and probably elsewhere) has been dealing with the effects of repeat victimization for many years but appears not to have recognized it as such — although the author's recent attempts (for example, Litton, 1996) to publicize the results of research are beginning to awaken (self-)interest among U.K. insurers. Criminologists are increasingly promoting the message that a concentration on repeat victimization can be a powerful weapon in our crime prevention armory. There is a massive information exercise to be undertaken to inform the insurance industry of the huge potential of the concept for its own crime prevention efforts.

While it does not yet recognize repeat victimization, the U.K. insurance industry has evolved its own particular strategies and even a conceptual framework that it terms accident-proneness. It is a widely held U.K. insurance view that a trait of accident-proneness exists and many underwriting measures are predicated on this belief. All insurance proposal forms ask for details of previous claims and many require details of previous incidents of the type to be covered by the proposed insurance, whether or not an insurance claim was made. Even one previous claim will be noted by the underwriter and, if it is a large claim, some underwriting action may be taken. A series of trivial incidents will usually lead to the presumption that the proposer is accident-prone and to appropriate underwriting action (such as a deductible, a premium loading, the exclusion of certain risks or perils, or even the declinature of the insurance). The underwriter will often assume, first, that the series of incidents is predictive of the likelihood of future incidents and, second, that the revealed accident-proneness is likely to result, in the future, in at least one large claim.

If the evidence about repeat victimization is valid, then perhaps insurers should think again about their underwriting approach. It is at least possible that the risk inheres in the insured property rather than (solely) in the insured person. It appears that insurers are correct in assuming that past events can predict the future but possibly should reorient their thinking so that they become agencies in enabling the avoidance of that particular future.

Research has identified a remarkable prevalence of repeat victimization across the whole spectrum of criminal activity (Bridgeman and Sampson, 1994), of which the following are relevant to the present topic:

(1) motor vehicle theft — a quarter of respondents experienced more than one incident, with 8% of the victims accounting for 22% of the incidents measured in three surveys (Mayhew et al., 1993);

(2) crime against small business — 39% of businesses were found to have been burgled again at least once in a year (Tilley, 1993);

(3) retail burglary — 2% of retailers surveyed sustained 25% of the burglaries (Mirrlees-Black and Ross, 1995b);

(4) manufacturers — 2% of manufacturers surveyed sustained 26% of the burglaries (Mirrlees-Black and Ross, 1995a); and

(5) crime on industrial estates — on the worst estates, businesses could expect to be victimized five times per year (Johnson et al., 1991).

Domestic burglaries on a local authority housing estate in the North West of England in 1985 were equivalent to an annual rate of 24.6% — that is, a risk of burglary of one in four (Forrester et al., 1988). The researchers found a substantial problem of repeat victimizations: the chance of a second or subsequent burglary was over four times the chance of sustaining a first burglary. A raft of measures, targeted on people who had already been burgled, was implemented. These included: (1) up-rating of household security; (2) property postal-code marking; (3) Neighborhood Watch; and (4) Homewatch by the police. Table 5 shows the dramatic 75% fall in the number of residential burglaries over the three years of the project; however, the degree to which these figures were inflated by the effects of another of the project initiatives — the replacement of gas and electric *cash* pre-payment meters — is unknown. The reduction applied to the whole estate and not just to the protected houses. There, therefore, appear to be beneficial diffusion effects.

Table 5: Kirkholt: Domestic Burglary — Pre- and Post-Initiative

	PERIOD			
	1986/87 (PRE)	1987/88 (POST 1)	1988/89 (POST 2)	1989/90 (POST 3)
TOTAL FOR PERIOD	526	223	167	132
Average per month	44	19	14	11
% fall on previous year		58%	25%	21%
% fall on two years previous		68%	68%	41%
% fall on three years previous				75%

Source: Forrester et al. (1990:20)

Given that businesses can suffer even higher rates of repeat victimization than residences (Johnston et al., 1994; Mirrlees-Black and Ross, 1995a; 1995b; Tilley, 1993), could a similar targeting of resources on those who have recently been victimized be equally successful against business crime? Insurers, at least in the U.K., devote far more resources to encouraging their business policyholders to prevent burglary than they do to their domestic policyholders. In the light of insurers' almost total lack of knowledge of the research on repeat victimization, much of their effort may be inappropriately directed.

Polvi et al.'s (1990) analysis of repeat burglaries in Saskatoon, Canada, provides a valuable insight into when repeat burglaries occur. The risk of being burgled a second time was highest within one month of the first burglary. Specifically, a dwelling was 12.42 times more likely to be burgled a second time within a one-month period (see Figure 2).

Figure 2: Cumulative Frequency, Repeat Domestic Burglaries, Saskatoon 1987 (by Days Between Crimes)

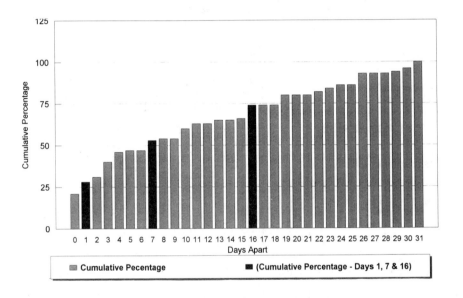

As Figure 2 shows, there were 42 double burglaries within this 30-day period (shown here as the cumulative proportion of the 42 events by days between crimes) of which:

(1) at day one, 28% of repeat burglaries occurred in the same or adjacent day;

(2) 50% have occurred by day 7; and

(3) 74% have occurred by day 16.

The researchers suggested that these figures justify extraordinary measures being taken to protect the dwelling for one or, at most, two days. Our problem is — how do we disseminate this information to those who can act upon it? The information is unlikely to be of interest to individual businesses prior to their being burgled — since burglary is something that only happens to other people! — but it should be of enormous interest to insurers and the police. Knowledge of this research might enable insurers to direct their crime prevention advice in a better fashion.

It is obviously impracticable for insurers to initiate a response within the first day or two — it will usually be longer than that before they even learn of a burglary, much less respond to it. However, given the will, there is no reason why insurers should not gear themselves up to be able to respond within seven days — which could target a substantial proportion of repeats. The benefit to insurers (and, therefore, to their clients) is obvious — even if they will not succeed on every occasion in influencing prompt remedial measures on the part of their policyholders. It is apparent that previous attitudes to repeat victimization, exemplified by Maguire's (1982:169) comment that "the police can do a great deal for the welfare of victims ... reassure them that ... the chances of a burglar returning are small," are now outdated and perhaps the best service we can render to victims is to tell them that a swift repeat is likely and recommend rapid security improvements.

Insurers are not the only agency in a position to influence remedial measures. The insurance broker is uniquely positioned to give prompt advice at a time when clients are likely to be at their most receptive — at the time of notifying the loss. Leaving aside the delays caused by holidays and weekends, this will typically be on the day of, or the day following, the burglary. However, the client's first call is likely to be to the police who should be able to give advice even closer in time to the first incident. Is there any reason why all three parties — insurer, insurance broker and police — should not have in place guidelines for giving immediate practical advice to the victim? Let us also not forget the loss adjuster who, for larger losses, might be on the scene relatively quickly. Four potential sources of advice on the need to take remedial measures, the necessity of taking them rapidly and on the measures to take might succeed in driving home the message that a repeat burglary is likely and that, if it happens, it will probably happen very quickly.

Given the self-interest which the insurance industry has in preventing burglaries, would it be worth their while investing resources in helping their policyholders to prevent burglaries — by targeting repeat burglaries?

It has long been an article of faith in British insurance circles that policyholders should be encouraged to improve their physical protections in the hope that burglary will be prevented. This natural inclination among insurers has to be tempered somewhat because, for smaller and less hazardous risks, competition will stop an insurer from being too severe in his requirements. For larger and more hazardous risks — and the suffering of a burglary dramatically increases the perceived hazard — insurers actively promote target hardening either by leaflets, letters, or surveys.

A burglary will often provide the opportunity (excuse) for the insurer to conduct a security survey. The trouble with insurers, though, is that they are far too slow. By the time their bureaucracy has ground into action, weeks, or even months, have gone by. The research evidence for the predictive power of repeat victimization is persuasive and demonstrates that action should be taken quickly. Insurers, their policyholders and the police should take these lessons on board. They should target their crime prevention efforts on those who have already been victimized and should do so promptly. Where we are concerned with scarce resources — and police crime prevention surveys or insurer security surveys are scarce resources — it behooves us to allocate them in the most effective way. If the above research shows one thing, it is that action must be taken quickly. Perhaps insurers — out of self-interest — can be persuaded to move more quickly. Maguire's (1982) research demonstrates that prompt upgrading of security can reassure and comfort worried victims so prompt action by insurers might have more than one beneficial effect.

CONCLUSION

Crime and insurance interact. Not only can crime affect insurers, insurers can affect crime. The influence of an insurer is potentially critical as insurers are probably the only agencies in a position to offer a property owner financial incentives for taking crime prevention measures. There is substantial evidence that, when they do choose to act, insurers can function to help prevent crime or to change the type of crime that occurs (Litton, 1982).

Insurers have the power to motivate their policyholders to take crime prevention measures by the best of motivators — financial incentives or disincentives. Initiatives, such as those described in this paper, surely give insurers the opportunity to use their power in a focused way. Insurers are interested in anything that will help them pay out less in claims, give them an edge over the competition, or help them identify a niche market with an improved probability of profit. Criminologists can help them in these goals by identifying those crime prevention techniques that will lead to fewer, or less expensive, burglaries. The motivation for the insurance industry is enhanced profits, but the beauty of such an approach is that everyone — except, that is, the criminal — will benefit. The problem appears to be that much of insurers' efforts are intuitive rather than founded upon research findings. This is not to suggest that insurers are ineffective in what they do in this field, only that, with good research (or better knowledge of existing research), they could achieve better results. Much criminological research, valid though it is, often does not seem to lead to action (for example, the Environmental Risk Index (Winchester and Jackson, 1982), which appears to provide pointers for practical action, has been largely ignored). Criminologists generally appear to have neglected the insurance industry as a major source of motivation for the taking of crime prevention measures.

Most businesses carry crime insurance (and the exceptions are usually the larger companies who self-insure such risks but who will tend to be more receptive to crime prevention measures and will frequently have their own risk-management resource). In the U.K., the number of households carrying insurance is increasing. The potential crime-preventive influence of insurers is large and increasing. What would, perhaps, be helpful for crime prevention generally is greater cooperation and communication between insurers and researchers. If crime prevention research were relevant to the activities of insurers, and were presented in a form, and a forum, that was accessible to them (few insurance people read academic writings), the insurance industry might prove to be the mechanism by which behavior of the insuring public might be changed. Insurers, though, will not take the initiative in this exchange — most insurance people do not even know that criminological research is being conducted so will be unaware that it can be of relevance to them. Criminologists have a product that is potentially of use to the insurance industry, but the onus is on them to promulgate it. As well as the usual academic journals, criminologists might find that useful results could follow from finding out what publications insurers read and publishing there as well. Similarly, criminological findings could be presented at gatherings of the local insurance institute or at insurance conferences. Insurers are probably uniquely positioned to intervene effectively to influence crime prevention — given that the ability can be recognized, appreciated and mobilized, and that their efforts can be correctly directed in ways that are likely to be effective. The insurance industry could act as a conduit whereby the results of criminological research become translated into crime prevention action. What is currently lacking is input from criminologists to enable insurers to direct their potential for motivation to help prevent crime.

***

NOTES

1. "Ringing" of motor vehicles is the procedure of giving to a stolen vehicle the identity of another vehicle — often one that has been the subject of an insurance write-off.

REFERENCES

ABI (1994). *Motor Insurance Anti-Fraud and Theft Register*. London, UK: Association of British Insurers.

—— (1996). *Newsletter, January, 5; March, 7*. Crime and Fraud Prevention Bureau. London, UK: Association of British Insurers.

Allatt, P. (1984). "Residential Security: Containment and Displacement of Burglary." *The Howard Journal of Criminal Justice* 23(2):99-116.

Anderson, D., S. Chenery and K. Pease (1995a). *Biting Back: Tackling Repeat Burglary and Car Crime*. Police Research Group. Crime Detection and Prevention Series, Paper No. 58. London, UK: Home Office.

—— S. Chenery and K. Pease (1995b). *Preventing Repeat Victimisation: A Report on Progress in Huddersfield*. London, UK: Home Office Police Research Group.

Barr, R. and K. Pease (1990). "Crime Placement, Displacement and Deflection." In: M. Tonry and N. Morris (eds.), *Crime and Justice: A Review of the Research*, vol. 12. Chicago, IL: University of Chicago Press.

Bennett, T. (1989). "The Neighbourhood Watch Experiment." In: R. Morgan and D.J. Smith (eds.), *Coming To Terms With Policing*. London, UK: Routledge.

—— and R. Wright (1984). *Burglars on Burglary: Prevention and the Offender*. Aldershot, UK: Gower.

Blunt, H.P. (1907). The Moral Hazard in Fire Insurance. *Journal of the Insurance Institute of Great Britain and Ireland* 10:97-126.

Bridgeman, C. and A. Sampson (1994). *Wise After the Event: Tackling Repeat Victimisation*. A report by the National Board for Crime Prevention. London, UK: Home Office Police Research Group.

Chenery, S., A. Tseloni and K. Pease (1994). *Series Events in the 1992 British Crime Survey*. Paper presented at the annual meeting of the American Society of Criminology, Miami, November.

Clarke, M.J. (1989). Insurance Fraud. *British Journal of Criminology* 29:1-20.

—— (1990). The Control of Insurance Fraud: A Comparative View. *British Journal of Criminology* 30:1-23.

Cirel, P., P. Evans, D. McGillis and D. Whitcomb (1977). *Community Crime Prevention, Seattle, Washington: An Exemplary Project*. Law Enforcement Assistance Administration, U.S. Department of Justice. Washington, DC: U.S. Government Printing Office.

Criminal Statistics. Annually. London, UK: Home Office.

Davidson, N. (1984). "Burglary in the Community: Patterns of Localisation in Offender-Victim Relations." In: R. Clarke and T. Hope (eds.), *Coping with Burglary*. Boston, MA: Kluwer-Nijhoff.

Duncan, J. (1982). "How Do You Spot a Leopard?" *Policy Holder Insurance News* January 15: 27-29.

Farrell, G. (1995). Preventing Repeat Victimization. In: M. Tonry and D.P. Farrington (eds.), *Building a Safer Society: Strategic Approaches to Crime Prevention. Crime and Justice: A Review of Research*, vol. 19. Chicago, IL: University of Chicago Press.

—— and K. Pease (1993). *Once Bitten. Twice Bitten: Repeat Victimisation and its Implications for Crime Prevention*. Crime Prevention Unit, Paper No. 46. London, UK: U.K. Home Office.

—— C. Phillips and K. Pease (1995). "Like Taking Candy: Why Does Repeat Victimization Occur?" *British Journal of Criminology* 35(3):384-399.

Forrester, D., M. Chatterton and K. Pease (1988). *The Kirkholt Burglary Prevention Project, Rochdale*. Crime Prevention Unit, Paper No. 13. London, UK: Home Office.

—— S. Frenz, M. O'Connell and K. Pease (1990). *The Kirkholt Burglary Prevention Project: Phase II*. Crime Prevention Unit Paper 23. London: Home Office.

Gill, M. and R. Matthews (1993). *Raids On Banks*. Leicester, UK: Centre for the Study of Public Order, University of Leicester.

—— and V. Turbin (1996). "Insurance and Security in the Inner-City: A Report to Birmingham City Challenge Group." Leicester, UK: Centre for the Study of Public Order, University of Leicester.

Houghton, G. (1992). *Car Theft in England and Wales: The Home Office Car Theft Index*. Crime Prevention Unit, Paper No. 33. London, UK: Home Office.

Hughes, T. (1995). "Claims: Fact or Fiction." *The BROKER* April.

Husain, S. (1988). *Neighbourhood Watch in England and Wales.* Crime Prevention Unit, Paper No. 12. London, UK: Home Office.

Johnston, V., M. Leek, J. Shapland and P. Wiles (1991). *Crimes and Other Problems on Industrial Estates.* Sheffield, UK: University of Sheffield, Faculty of Law.

—— M. Leitner, J. Shapland and P. Wiles (1994*). Crime on Industrial Estates.* Police Research Group. Crime Prevention Unit, Series Paper No. 54. London, UK: Home Office.

Kelly, N. (1993). "Damping the Flames of Fraudulent Claims." *Corporate Cover* May, 23-24.

Laycock, G. (1992). "Operation Identification, Or the Power of Publicity?" In: R.V. Clarke (ed.), *Situational Crime Prevention: Successful Case Studies.* Albany, NY: Harrow and Heston.

Litton, G.S. (1992). "Insurers and Domestic Burglary: The Environmental Risk Index Revisited." In: *Journal of the Society of Fellows.* London, UK: The Chartered Insurance Institute.

Litton, R.A. (1982). "Crime Prevention and Insurance." *The Howard Journal of Penology and Crime Prevention* 21:6-22.

—— (1985). *Crime, Crime Prevention and Insurance.* Unpublished Ph.D. Thesis. Milton Keynes, UK: The Open University.

—— (1990). *Crime and Crime Prevention for Insurance Practice.* Aldershot, UK: Gower.

—— (1995). "Moral Hazard and Insurance Fraud." *European Journal on Criminal Policy and Research* 3(1):30-47.

—— (1996). "Burglary Insurance Fraud." *Journal of the Society of Fellows.* London: The Chartered Insurance Institute.

—— (1996). "Repeat Victimisation: Its Implications and Opportunities for the Insurance Industry." In: *Journal of the Society of Fellows.* London: The Chartered Insurance Institute.

Lloyd, S., G. Farrell and K. Pease (1994). *Preventing Repeated Domestic Violence: A Demonstration Project on Merseyside.* Crime Prevention Unit, Paper No. 49. London: U.K. Home Office.

Maguire, M. in collaboration with T. Bennett (1982). *Burglary in a Dwelling: The Offence, The Offender and The Victim.* London, UK: Heinemann.

Mayhew, P., N. Aye Maung and C. Mirrlees-Black (1993*). The 1992 British Crime Survey.* London, UK: Her Majesty's Stationery Office.

Mirrlees-Black, C. and A. Ross (1995a). *Crime Against Manufacturing Premises in 1993.* Research Findings No. 27. London, UK: Home Office Research and Statistics Department.

—— and A. Ross (1995b). *Crime Against Retail Premises in 1993.* Research Findings No. 26. London, UK: Home Office Research and Statistics Department.

Niemi, H. (1995). "Insurance Fraud." *European Journal on Criminal Policy and Research* 3(1):48-71.

Pease, K. (1979). *Reflections on the Development of Crime Prevention Strategies and Techniques In Western Europe, Excluding Roman Law Countries.* Report to the

United Nations Centre for Social Development and Humanitarian Affairs, 31 October. Manchester, UK: Department of Social Administration, University of Manchester.

—— and G. Laycock (in press). "Reducing the Heat on Hot Victims."

Polvi, N., T. Looman, C. Humphries and K. Pease (1990). Repeat Break-and-Enter Victimisation: Time Course and Crime Prevention Opportunity. *Journal of Police Science* 17:8-11.

Reppetto, T.A. (1974). *Residential Crime*. Cambridge, MA: Ballinger.

Scarr, H.A. (1973). *Patterns of Burglary*. National Institute of Law Enforcement and Criminal Justice. Washington, DC: Government Printing Office.

Stockdale, J.E. and P.J. Gresham (1995). *Combating Burglary: An Evaluation Of Three Strategies*. Police Research Group. Crime Detection and Prevention Series: Paper No 59. London, UK: Home Office.

Tilley, N. (1993). *The Prevention of Crime Against Small Businesses: The Safer Cities Experience*. Crime Prevention Unit, Paper No. 45. London, UK: Home Office.

—— and J. Webb (1994). *Burglary Reduction: Findings from Safer Cities Schemes*. Police Research Group. Crime Prevention Unit, Series Paper 51. London, UK: Home Office.

Waller, I. and N. Okihiro (1978). *Burglary: The Victim and the Public*. Toronto, Canada: University of Toronto Press.

Winchester, S. and H. Jackson (1982). *Residential Burglary: The Limits of Prevention*. Home Office Research Study No. 74. London, UK: Her Majesty's Stationery Office.

Winkel, F.W. (1991). "Police, Victims and Crime Prevention: Some Research-based Recommendations on Victim-Orientated Interventions." *British Journal of Criminology* 31:250-265.

A BRIEF HISTORY OF THE SECURITY INDUSTRY IN THE UNITED STATES

by Robert D. McCrie

John Jay College of Criminal Justice,
The City University of New York

Abstract: *The modern security services industry — guarding, investigations, alarm monitoring and armored courier — evolved in the United States during the second half of the nineteenth century. By the mid-1990s the industry represents almost three times the number of personnel employed as those in local, state and federal law enforcement combined. The efforts to create uniform standards in the industry have been uneven. Historical antecedents for major industrial components are discussed. Problems and opportunities are identified.*

Private security, defined as the non-governmental protection of assets from loss, antedates public measures taken to safeguard people and property. For most of recorded history, people depended largely on themselves and their associations to keep the peace and protect lives from danger and capital assets from depreciation. Public intervention in such matters arrived in modern times (South, 1988).

Assets came to be concentrated within cities and were protected with the walls, animals, locks, sentries and elaborate protocols required to organize life within confined areas. Protecting assets in the workplace depended on physical security measures supported by alert workers who would discourage crime and would mete summary judgment to those caught stealing or cheating their masters or employers.

All of this was to change, however, with the industrial revolution, beginning in England about 1750. Cities grew larger because the city walls became redundant and physical growth could explode beyond historic confines. A night watch had protected the community after sundown and a constable with deputies, or their equivalents, served the rudimentary needs of populated areas from the pre-Norman Conquest through the early nineteenth century. Organized commerce, however, provided its own protective measures to safeguard assets, using manpower, loss reduction strategies, and physical means to protect assets. If something was stolen, often the victim would not turn to the fragmented constabulary system, but rather to entrepreneurs who would seek to retrieve "stolen" items for a reward (Johnson and Wolfe, 1996).

In such a burgeoning environment, the ascendant city required innovation to support order and justice within the community. That innovation was the modern policing and criminal justice system that subsumed many of the task of private protection. An urban scholar (Monkkonen, 1996:201) has written: "Historians working in the field of American crime and justice have produced a massive body of scholarship; a recent, selected collection of articles alone consumed over 7,000 pages in sixteen bound volumes." However, no such largesse of literature exists for the security services industry which grew as a modern business not in the industrial cities of Britain or the Continent but in urban centers of the eastern United States. By the mid-1990s the sentries of American corporatism had outnumbered their public-sector counterparts by about three-to-one with more growth expected, as has been posited by Cunningham et al. (1990) in *The Hallcrest Report II.*

The security industry merits interest from historians, criminologists, and scholars from other fields, not only because of its size relative to contemporary policing, but also because political debate about privatizing criminal justice services raises many fundamental issues about society. The growth of privatization serves further to enhance expansion of the security-services industry in the United States, according to Bowman and colleagues (1992; 1993). Security, as an industry in the United States, grew in response to private-sector needs in the second half of the nineteenth century. Separate categories of business emerged to control different types of industrial problems. For that reason, distinct components of the industry will be reviewed individually.

GUARDING, INVESTIGATIONS AND PERSONAL PROTECTION

During the mid-nineteenth century in the United States, counterfeiting was a commercial problem of vexatious frequency and measurable cost to industry and commerce. The federal government did not yet produce its own banknotes but allowed individual banks to do so, providing that the notes issued were backed by adequate hard reserves. This situation permitted counterfeiters in one area to produce notes that could be successfully passed elsewhere, if not locally, because the public would be unfamiliar with various features of different banknotes. Investigation and arrest of counterfeiters was a duty of county sheriffs and local police as well as United States marshals, though the extent of the problem far exceeded the marshals' ability to control such losses (Scott, 1957). While other problems of lawlessness infected the growing nation, counterfeiting threatened the confidence and stability of daily commerce throughout the nation from large cities to small communities like Dundee, Illinois.

In 1843, Allan Pinkerton and his wife, emigrants from Glasgow, settled in this small community, 50 miles from Chicago, where he founded a cooperage. The business grew. In 1847, Pinkerton was on an island in the Fox River near Dundee searching for trees that would make good barrel staves. According to Horan (1967), the cooper spotted a cooking fire indicating that someone else had been using the island. Pinkerton was curious about the campers and returned several times until one night he discovered a band of counterfeiters who had selected the presumably private locale as their base of operations. Informing the sheriff of Kane County of the discovery, Pinkerton and the sheriff, by one account, headed a posse that arrested the band with "a bag of bogus dimes and the tools used in their manufacture" (Horan, 1967:16).

A few months later Pinkerton was asked if he would undertake "a little job in the detective line." The only scrip (banknotes) the settlements in the area trusted was issued by the Wisconsin Marine and Fire Insurance Company, owned by frontier banker George Smith. But two counterfeit ten-dollar bills from Smith's bank had passed successfully in Dundee. The operator of the general store suspected a villager as the false note passer, but no evidence of the equipment needed to make the notes could be found, despite fruitless searches of the suspect's farmhouse. Suspicions of the source of these counterfeits turned to a well-dressed stranger still in the region. Pinkerton eventually located the man and engaged him in a conversation in which he portrayed himself as being a hard working man yet willing to make some extra cash with "a good scheme." The initially reluctant stranger eventually offered to sell Pinkerton 50 ten-dollar bills for 25% cash of their face value. A sale was agreed to and the bills were left nearby for Pinkerton under a rock. But to effect a successful arrest and conviction, the suspect had to be seized with the counterfeits in his possession; therefore, after consulting with lawmen, Pinkerton arranged to make a bigger purchase in Chicago. This time the counterfeiter was arrested and jailed, and Pinkerton was compensated for his expenses by the victimized banker. Soon tired of the fractional nature of small town life he encountered in Dundee, Pinkerton sold his cooperage and accepted a deputyship from the sheriff of Cook County, moving to Chicago.

Pinkerton served as Chicago's sole detective for a year, resigned, and became an agent of the United States Post Office with a mandate to solve a series of postal thefts and robberies in the area. He arranged to be hired as a postal clerk where he toiled for several weeks. Eventually, Pinkerton identified a mail clerk who surreptitiously manipulated envelopes to see if they contained money. If they did, he deftly removed it and slipped the cash into his pocket. The clerk was arrested and a search of his room revealed almost $4,000. This arrest and its subsequent publicity made young Pinkerton a hero. He decided to form a business, the North-Western Police Agency, taking a Chicago attorney briefly as a partner (Morn, 1982). The business flourished and Pinkerton's fame increased with it. The firm began providing services to the Illinois Central Railroad. In 1854, Pinkerton received a contract guaranteeing his firm a yearly retainer of $10,000, a large sum at the time. The next year he signed a further contract to provide protection to a group of other railroads, permitting expansion of the business. Meanwhile, Pinkerton continued as a "mail agent" for the post office.

During the Civil War, Pinkerton organized a counter-surveillance network behind Confederate battle lines and briefly provided personal security services to Abraham Lincoln. With the ending of the Civil War, industrial growth in the north surged and with it grew the fortunes and prominence of the Pinkerton agency. Relying on its reputation as a creative and tireless investigative group — the "eye" that never sleeps — Pinkerton's term "private eye" came into popular use. But the agency's services included industrial guarding and protecting property during strikes in addition to investigations of losses. A turning point was 1892 when the agency was inveighed into breaking a strike of the Carnegie, Phipps Steel Company at Homestead, near Pittsburgh. A gun battle ensued between "the Pinkertons" and strikers who seized the plant and were supposed to be removed by the security forces who expected to surprise the strikers by arrival on barges. Before order was restored following a 12-hour siege, three guards and ten workers were dead (McCrie, 1988).

Homestead was not a holocaust, but neither was it the first time that knights of labor had shot strikers dead. In the aftermath to the deadly labor-capital conflict, Congress passed an "Anti-Pinkerton Act" (1893) prohibiting the federal government from employing the services of a private investigative firm. This measure would have had no effect per se in preventing the Homestead carnage but may be seen as a law to express revulsion against a private services provider that used deadly force in the interest of private enterprise. The Pinkerton agency subsequently vowed never again to accept strike-related assignments.

By the early twentieth century, Pinkerton was the nation's leading investigative and security agency but was only one among many. Scores of detectives sought business in the growing cities, attracted to the glamorous and often profitable vocation of detective or private investigator. Moses King's *Handbook of New York City* for 1892 stated "private detective agencies are numerous," and cited Pinkerton's among the "leading agencies" (King, 1892:488). But few of them were organized into multi-office commercial ventures as "the Pinkertons" were.

Another investigative firm that grew to national, sustained prominence was founded by a resourceful treasury department investigator, William J. Burns. Like Allan Pinkerton a half century earlier, Burns's earliest experiences in law enforcement related to investigations of counterfeiting, noted biographer Gene Caesar (1968). The sleuth's successful career in arresting notorious criminals, following painstaking fact-finding, earned Burns a reputation of reliability, persistence and eventual success in pursuing cases that were becoming more complex in the early twentieth century. When Burns opened a private office for "detective services," he was by no means pioneering a field. But Burns produced a rigor and organization to the investigative-services business and quickly agreed to provide protective services for the American Bankers Association, winning the contract from the Pinkerton firm (Caesar, 1968).

By the end of World War II, American commerce and industry were served by scores of well-established investigative agencies and by hundreds of companies that provided watch, guard and patrol services. For industrial clients, detectives primarily undertook specific-loss investigations. When solved, the client could pursue criminal charges, institute a civil suit for recovery of losses, or both. Generally, the larger and better established investigative firms eschewed matrimonial assignments and refused to conduct industrial spying for a client against competitors. However, freelance detectives operated without such a code, sometimes providing services of dubious legality. In addition to assignments on business and matrimonial cases, some "dicks" provided bounty hunting, assisted lawyers in preparing cases for trials, collected debts, acted as bodyguards and conducted undercover operations.

By the 1950s, large-scale personnel protection had become the main revenue source for many traditionally investigative-oriented services. While most manufacturing corporations maintained their own security departments, increasingly these services were contracting out this function to existing security guard and patrol companies. Never as profitable as investigations on an hourly basis, guard and patrol services nevertheless provided larger gross revenues. These could create substantial businesses; and they did. By the end of the 1960s, the government-financed Rand Report written by James S. Kakalik and Sorrel Wildhorn (1972) made it clear that the industry was growing rapidly without there being any understanding about how its practices might impinge upon public concerns.

The funding of the U.S. Law Enforcement Assistance Administration (LEAA) in 1968 was meant to respond to a daunting increase in major violent and property crime during the decade. Most LEAA money was channeled to a wide variety of police-oriented studies and programs; however, LEAA also allocated funds to study "private police" in the United States for the first time. The Rand Corporation, in Santa Monica, California, received a grant from LEAA — which was within the National Institute of Law Enforcement and Criminal Justice, itself a part of the Department of Justice — to conduct "a broad study of private police in the United States" that would be "both descriptive and policy-relevant" (Kakalik and Wildhorn, 1972:v). Five thin volumes by the researchers composed the Rand Report. Concerning the burgeoning security-guard industry, the first volume of the Report issued a damning and widely quoted observation:

> The typical private guard is an aging white male, poorly educated, usually untrained and very poorly paid. Depending on where in the country he works, what type of employer he works for (contract guard agency, in-house firm, or government), and similar factor, he averages between 40 and 55 years of age, has had little education beyond the ninth grade, and has had a few years of experience in private security. Contract guards earn a marginal wage—between $1.60 and $2.25 per hour, with premium-quality contract guards earning $2.75 per hour—

and often work a 48-hour or 56-hour week to make ends meet [Kakalik and Wildhorn, 1972:30].

The report documented a chasm between private security and public law enforcement. The two sectors cooperated only when they had to and were conceptually and administratively quite different, drawing from separate labor pools and following substantially different vetting (pre-employment screening) and training practices. While security directors often had law enforcement experience, still there seemed to be no constructive basis of interaction with public law enforcement. During the period between 1960 and 1969, as the population rose only 12%, public law enforcement grew 42%; meanwhile, privately employed guards and watchmen rose only 7%. Yet the contract segment almost doubled during these same years. Kakalik and Wildhorn saw that in the future a wide variety of issues involving the security industry and the public would emerge as broad public matters.

By the mid-1970s the range of matters identified in the Rand Report produced no substantial changes in federal, state, or local policies relating to guards, watchmen and private investigators; however, it was not forgotten. Another LEAA-sponsored initiative sought to put some of the concerns identified in the Rand Report into more concrete action: the National Advisory Committee on Criminal Justice Standards and Goals convened a Task Force on Private Security (1976) to study the industry and to offer public and private sector guidance and report their findings to the public.

About 80 specific standards and goals were identified in such categories as state licensing, other types of regulations, nature of services, selection and training of personnel, crime prevention methods, industry conduct and ethics. An additional objective of the Task Force was to encourage greater cooperation between public law enforcement and the private security industry. Members from private security, public law enforcement and others serving on the panel agreed that this was desirable.

An indication of how the security industry changed since then is reflected in the evolution of the American Society for Industrial Security (ASIS). This professional group was founded in 1955 when the chill of the Cold War brought together industrial security practitioners who largely were charged to manage government-mandated protective measures for federally financed research and development, military and technical armaments and materials providers. Soon, membership broadened to include security directors in non-military-oriented industrial categories and eventually protection managers from other manufacturing, service businesses and institutions dominated local chapter meetings. ASIS became a meeting place where the tensions and mistrusts among local police, federal security authorities and local private protection executives came to be discussed and minimized. Representatives of the security industry itself, including guard company and alarm business operators and sales personnel, were accepted as associate members but were not permitted to hold national offices in the Society. However, by the mid-1990s, many ASIS chapters were chaired by security-industry members. Following a decline in security director ASIS members due to corporate downsizing from the later 1980s through the mid-1990s, the Society sought aggressively to expand membership to new managers whose corporate duties might include security oversight, among other responsibilities.

By the mid-1990s, much of the direction provided by Rand Report and the Task Force on Private Security resulted in measurable changes within the industry. While the improvement in relations between police officials and private security practitioners was apparent everywhere, other substantive changes also occurred:

(1) the model code for guard regulation proposed in the Task Force report has served as a guide to state legislatures to rationalize the public management of private security guard and investigative companies;

(2) the legal burden of effective security service has been underscored by extensive plaintiff's litigation emphasizing that a property owner or facility operator has a reasonable "duty to protect" invitees, employees, and others while they are on the premises; and

(3) making the public feel safe has become a function of private security forces during a time when the public feels threatened by the potential of random crime and disorder.

By 1996, two companies had achieved annual revenues of over $1 billion dollars from security guard, patrol and investigative services alone

— a growth achieved internally and through external acquisitions. The dour picture of the "aging while male...poorly educated and poorly paid" painted by the Rand Report no longer was wholly accurate. And one national security-services business emphasized that "over half" of its personnel had "some college." But the ease of entry to the security guard and investigative industry remains low. Hence, perhaps 10,000 operating private security guard and patrol companies exist and about 67,000 private investigators registered with state regulators in 37 states seek business. Total industry revenues for guard services were estimated at $9.8 billion in 1990 and projected to grow to $21 billion by the year 2000, at an annual growth rate of 8%. Additionally, revenues for private investigations were estimated to be $2.4 billion in 1990, growing to about $4.6 billion by the year 2000 (Cunningham et al., 1990).

ALARMING A NEW NATION

The protection of assets from loss — that is, security — generally is achieved with adequate physical protection supplemented by human presence as a deterrent. However, even with the modest wages paid most guards and watchmen over the years, alarms have been a means to decrease dependence on hourly employees who are, nonetheless, a substantial aggregate cost over time and sometimes are less reliable than a systems approach to security. Alarms also serve the purposes of alerting guards, property owners, or the public at large to investigate and respond to the signal. They also deter burglars from attacking premises fitted with alarms.

Animals provided the earliest alarms. The Roman historian Livy described how in 386 B.C. many Romans had taken refuge atop the Palatine Hill while the city was under siege from the Gauls. One starlit night, the Gauls sought to surprise the natives by climbing a steep slope of the hill that was poorly protected by sleeping sentries and dogs. The Gauls were on the verge of succeeding when they encountered a flock of Juno's sacred geese that, despite the hunger of those besieged, had been spared. As the invaders climbed to the summit, however, the geese began to cackle and clap their wings, awakening Marcus Manilius and others with him who rushed for a timely counteroffensive.

Over the centuries offensive and defensive armies used animals, runners, smoke, noise, mirrored surfaces and other means to warn against invaders. The private sector relied mostly on animals and watchmen. By the time of the industrial revolution, mechanical alarms became available. An English inventor, Tildesley, described a set of chimes mechanically linked to a door lock. The inventor's promotional literature proclaimed:

> The bells associated with it are constructed in such a manner that no sooner is the skeleton key of an intruder applied to the lock than the [bells] begin to chime a plaintive air that inspires such a sentiment in the mind of the housebreaker that will doubtlessly prompt him to take precipitative flight [Greer, 1991:7].

The first known application of a mechanical chimes alarm in the United States was installed during the eighteenth century in a bank in Plymouth, Massachusetts. The unauthorized opening of the vault door tripped a lever that jerked a wire running underground to the cashier's home next door where it pulled on bells. The nineteenth century produced an array of dubious mechanical devices that would signal chimes, trap the unsuspected, or automatically fire a shot at the unsuspecting burglar. Electricity would improve reliability substantially.

By the early part of the nineteenth century, the Italian physicist Alessandro Volta developed a prototypical battery. This "pile" of copper, moist pasteboard and zinc layers provided a constant current offering inventors a steady source of electricity to power devices. The Englishman Michael Faraday discovered that electric currents could be altered by magnets through which two persons could exchange messages with each other. The telegraph was made possible as a result. English physicist Charles Wheatstone and a decommissioned army officer, William P. Cooke, applied for the first patent for a telegraphic signal in June 1837. The same year Samuel F.B. Morse, working with Alfred Lewis Vail, developed a working model of a telegraph and created a code through the rhythmic interruption of electrical current for longer or shorter intervals that corresponded to letters of the alphabet. Morse and his associates required financing to build a prototypical telegraphic line between Baltimore and Washington. Congress narrowly approved the request for $30,000 in February 1842, and a working line between the two cities was inaugurated in January 1845. These developments made possible modern burglar and fire alarm transmissions.

The intellectual climate of Boston at the time provided the ferment for studying electricity and telegraphy and putting these discoveries to commercial use (Bruce, 1987). A student at Harvard University, William F. Channing, suggested the telegraph to signal occurrence of the greatest scourge of nineteenth century urban centers: fire. Still, New York City became the first urban locale to install a fire alarm telegraphy system. It was not only faster than the status quo, but also it was more reliable and democratic. In addition to frequent conflagrations, "mischievous rogues" and youths rang fire bells as pranks, and the system depended upon the church sextons, who were supposed to ring fire bells, which disturbed the ideology of church-state separation. Alarm towers became linked by a single telegraph circuit with an ordinance in 1847. The system was awkward, requiring someone with knowledge of the Morse code to tap precise information about the alarm into the system, but the scheme provided a definite improvement over the manual ringing of bells.

Bostonian Edwin Holmes was a retailer of notions. The financial panic of 1857 convinced him to find a more recession-resilient business in which to invest. In nearby Somerville, Augustus R. Pope had filed for a patent in October 1852, for an "Improvement in Electromagnetic Alarms" (Holmes, 1990). Pope's simple magnetic contacts were wired in an open circuit so that the opening of any door or window that was supposed to be closed would make a contact and trigger the bell. A battery provided the power. But Pope's marketing of the device appears to have been unsuccessful and Holmes bought the patent in 1857 as an investment. Within a few years, Holmes concentrated on the alarm business, making incremental improvements in transmission reliability and moving the headquarters to New York City.

The development of an obscure patent into a functioning central alarm station business was arduous but eventually was realized. By the twentieth century a "Holmes" was synonymous with an alarm installed and centrally monitored by the Holmes Burglar Alarm Company. While the initial application of telegraphy was for fire protection, defense against burglary soon became an important reason for installing alarm systems. Part of the success of the Holmes organization was an early personal association established in Boston between Holmes and telephone inventor Alexander Graham Bell who met when both patronized the services of a master electrician, Thomas A. Watson, whose services they required. With the growth of both businesses — burglary alarms and telephones, which needed the costly laying of wire, Bell's company agreed to lay subvoice-grade lines at the same time they laid voice grade wires for their own growing service requirements. Holmes held an equity position in the telephone business for years, but eventually divested it to concentrate capital on his own business. Nonetheless, the two businesses continued to cooperate.

The early twentieth century was a time of both rapid growth of telegraphic-based burglary alarm services among businesses and of the consolidation of many such operations into a single holding company. In 1901, the president of Western Union, Colonel R.C. Clowry, began acquiring independent alarm companies. He quickly purchased 80 independent firms that were incorporated in New Jersey as the American District Telegraph Company, later known as ADT. Clowry also sought to purchase the Holmes firm, but the founder's son demurred. In 1905, an agent of American Telephone and Telegraph (AT&T), Charles F. Cutler, who headed the New York Telephone Company, succeeded in purchasing the Holmes entity. Then just four years later, AT&T bought a controlling interest in Western Union: thus, the leading alarm businesses were owned by the same consolidating company or trust. The monopolization of the communications industry resulted in a Justice Department investigation, and in 1914, a federal court ordered AT&T to divest itself of Western Union.

By the mid-twentieth century, the alarm business had continued to expand, but another monopolistic pattern emerged. James Douglas Fleming, president of the Grinnell Company, a leading fire-suppression products supplier, over a four-year period beginning in 1949, purchased the assets of Holmes, ADT, and AFA (Automatic Fire Alarm of New York). Many hundreds of alarm companies also competed in the marketplace. But Fleming's assemblage dominated the most profitable, regulated service response category of alarm businesses: those which provided certificated services listed by the standards group, Underwriters Laboratories (UL). Federal Judge J. Wyzanski invoked the Sherman Antitrust Act in his 1964 opinion ordering the break up of this alarm businesses (Greer, 1991).

By the mid-1990s, the burglar alarm industry remains a dynamic industrial component of the security industry. For most of the century, reliable alarm systems necessitated a costly installation of sensors for the perimeter (doors and windows) and the space inside (volumetric detectors), often requiring the supervision of a licensed electrician. These requirements limited alarm services to industrial and large commercial and retail applications and excluded most residential installations. However, since the advent of radio frequency-communicating sensors, cheaper telephonic communications and modular central monitoring stations, residential and smaller commercial and retail alarm installations have proliferated. In 1990, the industry generated about $4.5 billion in revenues and is predicted to grow at a 12% compound rate to $14 billion by 2000. About 100 alarm companies provide UL-certificated services, while an additional 12,600 companies in 1990 provided uncertificated and less costly alarm services (Cunningham et al., 1990).

ARMORED CARRIERS

In May 1859, Washington Perry Brink bought a horse and light wagon to collect and deliver parcels, baggage and merchandise in Chicago. The 26-year-old transplanted Vermonter was not the only person with the idea of delivering packages. Brink had to find ways to make his business distinctive for it to succeed in the crowded package-delivery marketplace. Previously, pioneer expressmen Henry Wells and Alvin Adams, fellow Vermonters, had founded the American Express Company in 1850. Adams and others began The Adams Express Company in 1854. And Wells with William G. Fargo organized Wells Fargo and Company in 1852 "to move packages, money, and valuables" (Seng and Gilmour, 1959:17).

As his business grew, Brink hired only single men of presumed honesty who would agree to board within the Brink household. This assured that the horses were properly stabled at night and that the last run had been completed by the deliverymen who could be questioned as they gathered around the boardinghouse dining table. Thus, the chancy delivery of packages entrusted to competitors' hands could be avoided if Brink's men received them. With the death of the founder, his son, Arthur Perry Brink, assumed control of the business and incorporated it in February 1879. Two of Brink's directors had connections with large express companies operating over thousands of miles and in numerous cities. Brink City Express was able to complement these businesses by handling downtown Chicago deliveries that the larger express companies, represented by the Brink's board members, could not serve themselves. The urban-centered business grew steadily from this board-nurtured patronage.

In 1891, the directors moved to have the company bond its own men exclusive of hostlers (grooms). This permitted the company to handle custom-house goods. The same decade the firm appointed a manager and superintendent to arrange for the conveyance of payrolls. The firm's first recorded payroll delivery, made possible by the previous decision to bond employees, was for a Western Electric plant in 1891. Security was not a major issue during the first years of operations. Brink's guards picking up money would wrap it loosely in a pair of overalls or in a newspaper and place it under the seat of the wagon. If a large sum of money were to be carried, a shotgun would also make the trip, tucked under the seat.

In 1900, the company recorded its first delivery of bank funds: six bags of silver dollars, each weighing 60 pounds, moved from the Home National Bank to the Federal Building. No effort at concealing the money was made. Four years later the company moved into the automotive age with its first vehicular purchase.

The initial instance of a criminal attack on Brink's deliverers occurred on August 28, 1917, when four bandits surprised them. Three of the bandits were quickly arrested and most of the money was recovered; however, it was clear after 26 years of operating without an external criminal incident that times had changed. A strategy for better protecting the delivery vehicles was needed and training deliverers to be more cautious was apparent.

Over the next several decades the Brink's firm continued to expand steadily, entering new markets one at a time. The company offered to move money for banks and other businesses at rates that were less than the cost of operating their own vehicles or less than what local deliverers would charge for the same service. Moving steadily to consolidate its growth, Brink's received its first regular contract from a Federal Reserve Bank in Cleveland in 1949. Because of its insurance strength, operational efficiencies, and extensive transport networks, Brink's increasingly became a supplier of choice to the banking, commercial and industrial markets for the movement of money. By the early 1960s, Brink's controlled over half of the entire armored-car services market in the United States. The next two largest firms, Wells Fargo Armored and Purolator Armored, together totaled an additional 16% or so of the market.

As a result of the business concentration primarily represented by Brink's and Wells Fargo, the Antitrust Division of the Justice Department began a protracted investigation of monopolistic practices in the armored-carrier business. The companies were forced to divest some accounts, and competitors and customers instituted civil actions for damages. The last class action and antitrust suit was settled by Brink's in 1978. Trucking deregulation in 1980 and changes in procedures of the Federal Reserve Board, permitting newer and smaller armored car companies to use its facilities, enlarged the competitive market for this segment of the security industry. Revenues in 1990 were about $1.25 billion derived from perhaps 70 armored car companies with flat growth anticipated through 2000 (Cunningham et al., 1990).

PRODUCTS, SYSTEMS AND SERVICES

The security industry also includes separate categories of companies that design, manufacture, distribute and sell a wide variety of products, components and systems. In some of these categories, security is one market segment among many, particularly in newer technological industries. As with other industrial divisions discussed here, all have earlier historical antecedents.

Locks

The oldest locks appeared in ancient Egypt. These were made of hard wood and worked with combinations of cylindrical pins having unequal lengths. They have marked similarities with modern cylinder locks. Safety locks invented in the eighteenth century were enhanced through the nineteenth century in Europe.

But the American lock industry, centered initially in Connecticut, made numerous advances in mechanical locking. While Linus Yale, Sr., received several patents including, one on a pin-tumbler padlock in 1857, his son Linus, Jr., received a patent in 1865 that, according to lock-museum curator Thomas F. Hennessey (1976), was one of the most important developments in locks ever made. This was a mortise lock in which the pin tumbler cylinder was screwed into the side of the lock according to the depth of the door. The plug had a cam to operate the dead bolt and became widely used in the United States and elsewhere.

Electronic locks have been integrated into access-control systems in recent decades.

The locking industry and locksmiths are often classified in the hardware industry; however, they may also be considered part of the security industry. In 1990, *The Hallcrest Report II* determined that almost 70,000 persons were employed as locksmiths with revenues of about $2.9 billion. The industry sector is expected to grow at a 7% compound rate to the year 2000 (Cunningham et al., 1990).

Safes and Vaults

The creation of locked chests, safes (four-sided secured containers) and vaults (secured chambers capable of being walked into) is centuries old. In the United States, the industry traces its origins to enduring businesses like Diebold (founded in 1858), the Mosler Company (begun in 1867) and Lefebure (started in 1892). In 1995, 23 companies based in the United States possessed Underwriters Laboratories' (UL) certification for burglary-resistive safes and another 12 based abroad sought UL certification and marketing opportunity in the United States (Underwriters Laboratories, 1995).

Access Control, Communications and Identification

The security industry in the United States has been energized by rapid increases in a wide variety of electronic products and systems, aided by the advent of the personal computer, innovative software, semi-conductor technology and advances in radio frequency and microwave communication. In some cases (such as access control and identification products and systems), the businesses are primarily oriented to security. In others (such as cameras, closed-circuit television, communications and lighting), security is only one of several markets in these rapidly growing components of the industry.

Among the industrial categories discussed in this chapter, the newest — access control with its ramifications — is the one that is reshaping the security industry in the United States most resolutely. For 1990, *The Hallcrest Report II* identified annual revenues among equipment sales providers of $11.7 billion with an average growth rate for the decade 1980 to 1990 of 15%.

Services

A broad variety of specialist security consulting services have evolved over the years. *The Hallcrest Report II* estimate that 800 security consultants and engineers were active in 1990, operating in a myriad of specialties. The consultants are available for private, public and institutional clientele to help resolve a wide variety of problems.

ASSESSMENT OF AN INDUSTRY

How may this industry — or more accurately a group of related industries — be assessed at this time? The guarding and investigations businesses remain the largest, as measured by revenues, and the most visible. Companies in this sector are characterized generally as having ease-of-entry to the marketplace; thus, they tend to be highly competitive, low profit and flexible at meeting changing market needs. An example of this is the expansion of privatization of government services, such as prisons for profit, that have benefited this sector. The clients of most guarding companies claim they cannot afford the level of training and supervision that legislative proposals threaten to impose and, thus, the "professionalism" of the industry has been impeded. Vetting of guards and investigators has improved in some states, though federal standards have, at this writing, insufficient Congressional support to change standards nationally.

The alarm industry has expanded robustly for two decades, driven by technologically based efficiencies and the expansion of the residential security market. The future and certain entry to the market of at least some Regional Bell Operating Companies (RBOCs) as security-alarm services providers will assure, in the meantime, the continued shuffling of alarm accounts among consolidating service operators.

The armored-carrier and security-hardware businesses have been marked by steady and modest growth in recent decades. Both require access to capital to finance their activities (purchasing and maintaining trucks and manufacturing and distributing products) and have experienced variable profitability. The electronic access-control industry is highly dynamic and can affect substantially other segments of the industry in a period of growth, innovation and consolidation.

A question may be raised: Why did major parts of the security industry originate in the United States instead of Europe where the Industrial Revolution had a head start? Two factors may be cited. First, as observed by Steven Spitzer and Andrew T. Scull (1977), the development of the American capitalist economic system in the nineteenth century occurred while public controls against private losses were weak relative to England and the Continent. American industry had to invent its own counter-measures to survive. Second, the dynamic flourishing of American corporatism and individual technical ingenuity found means to provide solutions to urgent market requirements that saved money operationally for security-business customers. For the future, such factors as the growth of privatization, corporate downsizing that benefits the private security industry and a legally supported "duty to protect" litigious environment augurs for continued growth in the years ahead.

With assurances of likely continued energetic growth of the private security business in the years ahead, fundamental questions may be raised about the industry with its relationships to and responsibilities for a larger society. Among the issues are: (1) is the security industry beneficial for public law enforcement while it serves private industry? (2) does the industry work against public interests as it pursues or abets a profit-driven strategy of the client? and (3) how might academic security ameliorate not only the tasks of industry but also the concerns of society as a whole? These issues, selected among many, will be examined succinctly.

The problem about the utility of private security to public policing begins with the assumption that the security business successfully serves, generally, requirements of its clientele. That assumption is regarded as a settled matter since a client would not pay consistently for security services and products — which this chapter demonstrates is the historical reality and pattern — if it were not in the client's self-interest to do so. The reasons why the private sector requires security services are complex: vulnerability to criminal deprivation is only one of the considerations, though a significant one. But it is in the analysis of crime causation that a nexus exists between the public and private police interests.

It is self-evident that law enforcement serves the public by maintaining order and through such actions as, say, arresting a thief; but it is equally true that viable security programs also aid public police efforts. These benefits are mainly created by mitigating the attractiveness of crime through opportunity-reducing measures that "harden the target" for losses to occur. This, in turn, permits a diminution of police resources required to respond to criminal incidents that might be expected to have occurred but did not due to the crime-reduction actions imposed.

An example of this benefit is illustrated from research conducted by William F. Walsh and Edwin J. Donovan of Pennsylvania State University and James F. McNicholas of Starrett Realty Corporation (1992). Starrett City was developed and is operated by a commercial property development and management business listed on a national stock exchange. The apartment complex opened for occupancy in 1974, and by a dozen years later contained 46 residential building, nine parking lots, two public schools, two nursery schools, a power plant and a recreation center. When research began in 1984, the community housed approximately 20,000 residents with a mean income of $24,000. The majority of residents were office or blue collar workers, or city employees. The racial distribution of the precinct including Starrett City in 1984 was: 42% black; 32% Hispanic; 22% white, and 4% other.

Starrett City was constructed within one of the highest crime areas of Brooklyn, the 75th precinct. On a population-adjusted basis for 1985, the precinct exceeded the United States as a whole in six or seven major incidents as reported to the Federal Bureau of Investigation's Uniform Crime Reports (UCR). In some cases the differences were substantial: for example, the precinct had a murder rate of 0.22 per 1,000 population compared with 0.08 for the United States as a whole; robberies were 15.51 compared with 2.14 (again, for the U.S. as a whole). Apparently, this was not a promising area for a major corporation to risk capital in developing a sprawling community, but it did.

The difference was that Starrett City created an effective security patrol service that engendered a crime rate considerably lower than what existed immediately outside the development. In all seven UCR incidents studied by the researchers, Starrett City was significantly lower than the precinct as a whole: more remarkable was the fact that Starrett City was lower on all seven types of serious crime than the national averages. Further, the buildings were graffiti free; trees and shrubs were healthy and undisturbed; litter did not clog the streets. Questionnaires established that residents and retail business operators felt safe there. The authors concluded Starrett City would not exist as a secure residential community without its private policing service. Because of the reduced need for police presence in the community, the authors estimated that Starrett City saved the City of New York at least $750,000 per year in policing costs than would otherwise be expected. The New York City Police Department presented the private force with an award in recognition of its service to the City. Beginning as a departmental unit within the corporation, Starrett Protective Services (now Security Plus Services) has since been created as a profit center whose services are contracted to other corporations.

Nonetheless, does the security industry inherently work against public interests in some ways? The answer may depend upon which public interests are considered. As demonstrated above, effective private security services decrease costs to the public by lowering need for policing due to effective crime mitigation and order maintenance. This, in turn, creates additional savings that are real, but difficult to accurately estimate (for example, diminished criminal justice system costs). In other regards, however, effective private security could have some deleterious social effects.

One possibility is the displacement of crime from an area with good security (the "haves") into one where little or no security exists (the "have nots"), causing social distress to these areas underserved by public police or private control measures. This displacement theory must be regarded as a reasonable speculation, but one that has not been demonstrated through vetted studies. Crime that might have occurred in an area but does not, due to a crime-reduction program, is not necessarily displaced onto nearby areas. For example, when Starrett City was constructed in the early 1970s, the 75th precinct was then above average in the occurrence of major violent and property crimes. The presence of the development did not effect crime patterns subsequently through displacement in any measurable fashion.

Another concern might be that security threatens individual rights. Guards and investigators may detain individuals, search them and invade their privacy. But when an individual is incorrectly affected by such behavior, such as when an apprehended suspect is actually innocent, he or she can bring a civil action against the offending security officers, their employers and the organization, if any, for whom the security business is performing work. If pursued successfully at court, the plaintiff could receive substantial monetary damages.

Finally, the issue of how academic security programs may serve the needs of the protection industry and the community at large deserves a discursive review elsewhere. What may be stated is that, for the present, academic security is fragile. Bereft of guiding ideology, hampered by a meager though steadily growing research base, ignored by graduate schools of business administration and misunderstood by many conventional criminal justice program administrators, security management, nonetheless, seems to be managing the transition from being a vocational subject area to an accepted academic discipline. A directory of academic security offerings listed in the *Security Letter Source Book* (1993) identified 148 programs, most of which offered only a few courses. However, 26 institutions offered bachelors degrees in security and an additional 13 offered masters degrees. The number is likely to have increased since then. With the growth of academic interest, support for research, analysis and applied learning for improved security understanding and practices should ensue. In the end, programs are driven by student desire and market need: the jobs are there; the programs will grow; the students will come.

*** *

REFERENCES

"Anti-Pinkerton Act" (5 U.S.C. 3108, then 5 U.S.C. 53 of 1893).

Bowman, G.W. S. Hakim and P. Seidenstat (eds.)(1992). *Privatizing the United States Justice System: Police, Adjudication, and Corrections Services from the Private Sector.* Jefferson, NC: McFarland & Co.

—— S. Hakim and P. Seidenstat (1993). *Privatizing Correctional Institutions.* New Brunswick, NJ and London, UK: Transaction Publishers.

Bruce, R.V. (1987). *Launching of Modern American Science: 1846-1876.* Ithaca, NY: Cornell University Press.

Caesar, G. (1968). *Incredible Detective: The Biography of William J. Burns.* Englewood Cliffs, NJ: Prentice-Hall.

Cunningham, W.C., J.J. Strauchs and C.W. Van Meter (1990). *Private Security Trends: 1970 to 2000. The Hallcrest Report II.* Stoneham, MA: Butterworth-Heinemann.

Greer, W. (1991). *A History of Alarm Security.* (2nd ed.) Bethesda, MD: National Burglar & Fire Alarm Association.

Hennessey, T.F. (1976). *Early Locks and Lockmakers of America.* Des Plaines, IL: Nickerson & Collins.

Holmes, E.T. (1990). *A Wonderful Fifty Years.* New York, NY: Holmes Protection. [Originally published in 1917.]

Horan, J.D. (1967). *The Pinkertons: The Dynasty that Made History.* New York, NY: Bonanza Books.

Johnson, H.A. and N.T. Wolfe (1996). *History of Criminal Justice.* (2nd ed.) Cincinnati, OH: Anderson Publishing.

Kakalik, J.S. and S. Wildhorn (1972). *Private Police in the United States: Findings and Recommendations.* Washington, DC: U.S. Government Printing Office.

King, M. (1892). *King's Handbook of New York City.* Boston, MA: Moses King.

Livy. (1960). *The Early History of Rome.* Baltimore, MD: Penguin Books.

McCrie, R.D. (1988). "The Development of the U.S. Security Industry." *Annals of the American Academy of Political and Social Sciences* 498:28-33.

Monkkonen, E.M. (1996). "The Urban Police in the United States." In: C. Emsley and L.A. Knafla (eds.), *Crime History and the Histories of Crime: Studies in the Historiography of Crime and Criminal Justice in Modern History.* Contributions in Criminology and Penology. Westport, CT: Greenwood Press.

Morn, F. (1982). *"The Eye that Never Sleeps": A History of the Pinkerton National Detective Agency.* Bloomington, IN: Indiana University Press.

National Advisory Committee on Criminal Justice Standards and Goals (1976). *Private Security: Report of the Task Force on Private Security.* Washington, DC: U.S. Government Printing Office.

Scott, K. (1957). *Counterfeiting in Colonial America.* New York, NY: Oxford University Press.

Security Letter Source Book: 1993 (1993). Stoneham, MA: Butterworth Heinemann.

Seng, R.A. and J.V. Gilmour (1959). *Brink's the Money Movers: The Story of a Century of Service.* Chicago, IL: Lakeside Press.

South, N. (1988). *Policing for Profit: The Private Security Sector.* London, UK: Sage Publications.

Spitzer, S. and A.T. Scull (1977). "Privatization and Capitalist Development: The Case of the Private Police." *Social Problems* 25:18-29.

Underwriters Laboratories (1995). *Automotive, Burglary Protection, Mechanical Equipment.* Northbrook, IL: Underwriters Laboratories.

Walsh, W., E.J. Donovan and J.F. McNicholas (1992). "The Starrett Protective Service: Private Policing in an Urban Community." In: G.W. Bowman, S. Hakim, and P. Seidenstat (eds.), *Privatizing the United States Justice System: Police, Adjudication, and Corrections Services from the Private Sector.* Jefferson, NC and London: McFarland & Company.

THE UNRECOGNIZED ORIGINS OF THE NEW POLICING: LINKAGES BETWEEN PRIVATE AND PUBLIC POLICING

by Clifford Shearing

University of Toronto and University of the Western Cape

Abstract: *The paper contrasts two stories about the origins of community policing, one that locates its emergence within the police and the other that locates it within private security. It argues that both stories need to be recognized if community policing is to be understood.*

INTRODUCTION

To say that community policing has emerged as *the* new development in policing is to state the obvious. It is to be found everywhere — in North America, in Central and South America, in Europe and in Africa. At the heart of community policing lies a future-oriented, risk-focused approach to security that seeks to make "problem solving" rather than "bandit catching" the central feature of contemporary policing. The established understanding of this shift is that it arises out of an assessment by the police and the scholars who have worked with them of their role and strategies.

This assessment, it is argued, led to a series of innovative practices in a few police departments in problem-oriented policing. This, in turn, led to the emergence of a new paradigm of policing. This police-centered story of community policing arises out of, and nicely illustrates, what Johnston (1992:184) has recently termed "an obsessive preoccupation with the study of public police personnel" that insists on identifying contemporary policing with "the police."

This story of community policing is being vigorously promoted on a global basis by a host of "police experts" who are painting a police- and state-centered picture of policing reform around the world. If policing is to do what it is supposed to do — that is, provide security — rather than simply respond to insecurity, what is required, so the story goes, is a massive change in the way in which police departments operate. This is as true in Canada as it is in South Africa. In both places, the same story is told and the same prognosis for the reform of policing is offered. What is wrong with this story is not that it does not say much that is true, but rather that, in presenting this truth, it leaves out much. These omissions prove to be very important because they fundamentally skew the whole reform process by insisting that it is the police who are and should be the center of this process. This skewing may be very good for the police, as a profession, and for the state, as an agency of governance. The cost is a more limited view of police reform than is necessary or desirable.

Our perspective on policing, and police reform, is immediately broadened once one recognizes that there is a second story of community policing that can be told. There are many similarities between this story and the one we have just reviewed, but it is not the same story and its implications are not the same. This second story takes the form of a revisionist account that challenges the first story's "obsessive preoccupation" with the state. The critique this story offers is that the first story fails to acknowledge the enormously consequential change in the structure of governance that has resulted from the emergence of strategies for the provision of security outside the state and the police. While this is something that is occasionally recognized in discussion of community policing — for example, Sherman (1995:338) talked about community policing as "police as security guards," it is, by and large, a phenomena that is seldom reflected upon within this context.[1]

The First Story: A Narrative of the Police as Problem Solvers

The first story provides an account of the emergence of a "new police," at the turn of the nineteenth century, in response to the inadequacy of earlier private policing initiatives to cope with the force of industrialization and its control problems (Reiner, 1995). It traces the way in which this new specialized police struggled, over many decades, to become an effective keeper of the peace. In outlining these developments, Sherman (1992) identified the American police scholar Herman Goldstein as the source the consequential move from bandit-catching policing, which characterized the "new police," to problem solving to create a "new policing" through changes in the way in which the police operate. This "new policing"

advocated an abandonment of policing premised on responses to violations in the criminal law and its replacement with a risk-focused approach
that would identify the sources of problems and address them directly. The
watch word was to be prudence, not after-the-fact detection and punishment.

Policing was to identify problems and then take them apart so that their
causes could be identified and solutions found. Within this new strategy,
the police were encouraged to recognize that it is disorder, rather than
crime, that should be their principal concern (Wilson and Kelling, 1982;
1989; Skogan, 1990). Eck and Spelman (1987) made this point, in the course
of a critique of the crime-control mentality that has come to characterize
state policing: most citizen concerns are not directly related to crime.
Rubbish on the streets, noise, abandoned and ill-maintained buildings,
barking dogs and the like, form the bulk of calls for police service. In many
areas residents judge these problems to be more serious than street crime.
But still the police have for decades been oriented to crime control. They
have in Jonathan Simon's (personal communication) words dealt with
disorder by "governing through crime." As Eck and Spelman (1987:34)
argued: "Given the attention police have paid to crime over the years, one
would have expected that they would have learned to control it. In fact
the opposite is true."

A second feature of this new community-based policing was that the
shift from crime to disorder served to deemphasize the importance of
physical force, which becomes less critical as a resource. While bandit
catching, with its focus on detention, might require physical force as its
essential resource, this is not true when disorder is the central concern.
This feature of this new policing paradigm, which the police were ex-
perimenting with and which has now coalesced as community policing,
is illustrated by Eck and Spelman (1987) in an anecdote they tell. It nicely
captures this new style of policing while drawing attention to the ways in
which it differs from the more conventional bandit-catching policing style.

The story is as follows. A person they call Charles Bedford was having
trouble sleeping on Friday and Saturday nights because rowdy teenagers
walking past his house at night were keeping him awake. In response,
Charles called the cops. Normally, such a call would have brought police
to the scene. They would probably have controlled the situation by moving
the kids on and, if they had found evidence of criminal behavior (for
example, vandalism), they would very likely have charged some of the

teenagers. The responding officer in this case, whom Eck and Spelman call Office Summerfield, operated out of a different paradigm or mentality of policing and acted differently. Summerfield, instead of seeking simply to control the problem — a command and control response — began to take the problem apart. His hypothesis, as he began to think about the problem, was that its source was a nearby roller skating rink that had been promoting itself by offering reduced rates. Summerfield drove to the rink at closing time early in the morning and talked to the kids who were leaving. Some kids he discovered were waiting for a bus while others had decided to walk home through Charles' neighborhood. Summerfield expanded his inquiries by talking to the owner of the rink. The owner had sought to assist kids with their transportation and had hired a bus to bring kids to the rink and to take them home, but there were more kids than his bus would hold. After considering this situation, Summerfield spoke to the owner, explained what was happening, and suggested that he provide more transportation so that kids did not need to walk home. The owner agreed and the problem was solved. Summerfield summed it up like this:

> Look, we can have the best of both worlds. People here can get their sleep and the kids can still have fun. But we can't do it by tying up officers and chasing kids every Friday and Saturday night. There has to be a way of getting rid of the problem once and for all [Eck and Spelman, 1987:49].

In this story, the police still "own" policing though they are now more willing to enlist the help of citizens. What has changed is the way they think about their role. They now see policing as colonizing a future rather than as simply repairing a past. Their concern in this anecdote was not with setting right the peace that had been disturbed, but with reducing the probability of peace being disturbed in a similar way in the future. Problem-solving policing rediscovers peacekeeping as the central role of the police and recognizes that this requires other resources than their own. In this account, the police become brokers who network resources to promote their own and the state's objectives.

This story, and its message, dominates contemporary police and scholarly understandings of policing. Indeed, it is so hegemonic that the second story, which I will outline below, about the growth of civil policing is not even acknowledged. For these reformers, the second story simply does not exist. There is only one narrative and it is a police-focused story in which the police and their advisors are presented as the heroes of a reform process initiated by them. For them, it is the police who have discovered risk-based policing.

The policy implications of this story are straightforward. Now that the bankruptcy of bandit-catching policing has been recognized, innovative thinking within the police community has realized a new vision. What is required is: first, to refine this new way of thinking; and second, to spread this conceptual revolution throughout the police community. For any police organization caught in the grip of a bandit-catching mentality, the reform path is straight forward: adopt community policing as a central policing philosophy. What policing needs is a new generation of future-focused police who think about policing differently. Police everywhere should be adopting a problem-solving "community-oriented" policing style. Anyone who knows anything about what has been happening to policing knows that this message has not only been heard but is being acted upon globally.

In summary, the crux of the first narrative, is that it sets up the problem, so that it appears that the only way in which disorder can be adequately addressed is by accepting direct police involvement in people's lives as problem solvers. Promoting problem-solving policing becomes the same thing as promoting the police as all-purpose problem solvers. It is just this collapsing of the police and problem solving that the second story challenges. In doing so, it opens up policy options and opportunities for reform that this first story eludes.

The Story of Private Policing

This brings me to the second narrative, which is about how problem solving has developed as a central feature of policing without an insistence that this requires a continuing, and indeed an increased, reliance on state policing as the central players in the production of security. It will be no surprise to the reader that this is not a "police story." It is a story of how people, organizations and communities, with access to the means required to develop policing outside the conventional state structures, have very effectively — and without fanfare or direct state funding — moved their policing from bandit catching to problem solving in ways that have limited, rather than expanded, state police interventions in their lives. This narrative challenges the first story on four fundamental grounds. It argues that:

(1) policing is not understood as something that the police "own";

(2) the move from bandit catching to problem solving is presented as something that has taken place on a massive scale without requiring a change in the police role;

(3) the impact of this change has, to date, been limited primarily to policing relatively affluent communities; and

(4) perhaps most important, the move to problem-solving policing has not been driven by the vision of "police" reformers but has emerged as a result of global changes that have, and are, providing for the emergence of what Macauley (1986) called "private governments."

What differentiates this narrative is that it is a story about "policing" rather than "police" (Johnston, 1992; Shearing, 1992) in which it is increasingly difficult to establish "where state regulation ends and where non-state regulation begins" (Santos, 1992:132). It is an account of a "quiet revolution" (Stenning and Shearing, 1980), that finds visible expression in a "rebirth of private policing" (Johnston, 1992) and that has enabled policing to become the responsibility of corporate entities and the communities associated with them.

This story recognizes the conceptual changes that have shifted the focus of policing from bandit-catching to problem-solving policing, which the first story identifies. It argues, however, that these changes have taken place within the context of, and because of, structural changes — "a transnationalization of the legal field" (Santos 1992:135) — to do with the expansion of corporate entities and their role as sites of social life. This has resulted in policing becoming increasingly the responsibility of "corporate communities" that often exist within "gated cities." These communities may be stable over space and time, as is the case with many such residential communities. On the other hand, they may be as temporary as the communities created by visitors to recreational sites, such as Disney

World, or they may be "deterritorialized" (Santos, 1992:136) virtual communities based on shared interests or identities.

These changes, this narrative argues, have fundamentally reshaped modern policing from something that is "owned" by one institution, the state police, to something that is located in a whole variety of institutional contexts. Policing has been "pluralized" within a "world system" (Santos, 1992) so that it is now something that is "owned" by, and done by, a variety of entities (Macauley, 1986). Commercial banks, for instance — which may or may not be transnational — have responded to disorder, including the disorder of crime, on behalf of their shareholders, staff and customers in ways that seldom involve the state police. In doing so, they govern a corporate community.

It is here that the origins and development of the shift to risk-focused, prudential policing, that problem solving realizes, are located. It is these structural changes, the story maintains, that have prompted the change in the way policing has come to be viewed. This is so because, from the perspective of corporate communities — be this a bank or a homeless peoples' federation — it is not the criminal law that is the most relevant source of definitions of disorder but rather the values and objectives that define the "community."

In this paper, I want to tell both of these stories and to argue that both need to be recognized if community policing is to live up to its name and develop as a strategy whereby communities will be empowered not only to do policing themselves but to control the way in which their policing is done. In this story, the state police are seen as one player among many in the business of policing — and as the player who is very often the least important. In this context, the first story is identified as a response to changes outside the police through which they are seeking to recapture ground they have lost to corporate policing.

It is the structural change signaled by the emergence of, among other things, "mass private property" (Shearing and Stenning, 1983) that has driven and facilitated a shift in focus from bandit catching to problem solving. This shift has as its basis a focus on disorder as well as the will and capacity to solve problems. These developments pioneered the problem-solving approach to policing that the first story claims as the product of the police and their advisors. This argument is nicely illustrated in a anecdote (circa 1980) that I heard at a meeting of private security persons about the way in which corporate policing was challenging a bandit-catching mentality. This tale concerns a large steel manufacturer based in Canada that was losing power tools, such as drills and saws, to employees. This had resulted in significant loses to the company. In response, the company's directory of security — an ex-policing officer — was asked to come up with a solution to the problem. His response to this "theft" was to adopt the "hunter mentality" that the notion of a "war on crime" captures so well. He decided that he would arrange for undercover agents to gather evidence on who was stealing the tools. He would then arrange for these people to be stopped and searched as they left the plant in a sweep on a particular day.

When he presented this proposal to the company's chief executive officer (CEO), instead of getting the approval he had anticipated, he was chastised for not understanding the values, interests and objectives of his corporate community. The CEO explained to him that the criteria he was using, and that the director of security should have been using, to assess the value of his plan were company profits and staff morale. The solution the security director had proposed, it was pointed out, did not measure up on either count. Its implementation would mean that costly time and energy would have to be spent on bandit catching and as a consequence highly trained people were likely to be lost to the company. New employees would have to be hired to replace those lost and these new employees would be just as likely to take tools home with them in the future. They would have to be trained, morale would be damaged, and so on. In short, far from solving the problem he was asked to address, his actions would contribute to it. The director of security was asked to come up with a problem-solving rather than a problem-exacerbating course of action. His new solution, which saved him his job, was to open a tool library from which tools could be borrowed.

There are many, many such stories that can be told about private security, for example, stories about Disney World as a place in which the problem-solving approach to policing has been fine tuned and in which policing has been made the responsibility of every person — employee and customer alike — who frequents it.

These stories share the first narrative's emphasis on a change from crime-focused to a more prudential, problem-focused policing. However, it conceives of this, not as something that the police should own, but as necessitating a shift in the location of responsibility for security away from the police to sites where problem solving can take place. This story decenters policing by conceiving of the police as part of a network of resources, without the assumption that they should control the work of the networked.

In this context, the "discovery" of problem solving by the state police, is seen, at best, as a belated recognition of what non-state civil policing has been doing for decades. Problem-solving policing within this account has emerged as a strategy because policing has become increasingly community controlled and organized. According to this narrative, it is the structural changes of global privatization that have been responsible for the shift to problem-solving policing. Here problem solving may use, but certainly does not require, police intervention.

In this account, the loci of control and assistance are reversed. Instead of the police using communities as a resource (as is the case in the anecdote about the skating rink), here, it is "communities" who use the police to assist them to supplement their civil-policing activities. Community policing in this context is given a much more direct and literal meaning. In this narrative, the established role of the police as bandit catchers who use force is not considered as an error in need of correction but as a resource that communities can use when, for example, problem solving does not work or is inappropriate. Thus, for example, the CEO in a tool library company might well want to be able to call on the police to provide a forceful solution to a holdup at the company. In this second narrative, the police are seen as valuable players in a policing network not because they are all-purpose problem solvers but because they have the capacity and legal authority to intervene forcefully in troublesome situations. This perspective is critical of the expansion of the police role, essential to the first narrative, that it regards as a dangerous intrusion into the autonomy of civil society.

What is crucial about the networking of policing the second story describes and advocates is that it is "victims" who are accorded responsibility for the coordination of security resources. Responsibility for this coordination, it argues, should be privatized since it is the communities and institutions that have the local knowledge and resources this requires. To use the example of Disney World that I drew upon earlier, it is the Disney Corporation that manages the problem solving required to secure its property, staff and customers — not the state police.

From the perspective of the second narrative, the policy proposals derived from the first story are viewed as advocating a dangerous expansion of state resources and authority at the expense of civil society. In contrast, the second story advocates a "reversal of power" over policing (Marenin, 1982). Up to this point, this reversal has done much to advance the interests and capacities of the well to do and relatively little to assist poorer communities. This is not because poorer communities do not encounter corporate policing — they are very often policed by private security — but because they tend not (and here I am making a claim that I cannot document here) to direct what private security does in the same way that those with more wealth and power do.

Control over policing has followed the contours of wealth and power. Poorer people do not have (and here, again, I am going beyond what I can document here) as much influence over the new civil policing institutions that the second story identifies as do the wealthy. They have not been similarly empowered. They are more likely to be subjects rather than produces of policing. This state of affairs, I would argue, is not inherent in this transfer of policing power. On the contrary, these developments provide critical opportunities to change this as they recognize that "people — 'ordinary', non-professional people — have competently operated locally-based but extensive legal orders" (Fitzpatrick, 1992:212). They, thus, provide opportunities to shift the locus of policing away from the police to others in ways that will enhance the control of poor, as well as rich, people over their lives. Herein lies the true significance of community policing and the preventive risk-focused strategies it encourages.

CONCLUSION

The two narratives I have outlined reveal a curious feature of our approach toward policing, namely, the bifurcation of its public and its private spheres. We see public policing and private policing as two separate terrains and we think about them separately. Thus, we think about the nature and the trajectory of public policing independently of our thinking about private policing. We study their histories, nature and role separately. We do not study policing. We study policing institutions (the public police and private security) and we study them independently of each other.

Why do we do this? One reason is our division of the world into two autonomous spheres — a public sphere and a private sphere — and we treat each as operating independently of the other. The result is that we study what goes on in each sphere separately and treat what we find in each as unconnected. So we study private policing and public policing, but we do not study policing.

A related reason is that we do not regard the policing that takes place within the private sphere as truly policing because we do not regard anything that happens in the private sphere as governmental. For most of us, only the public sphere is the sphere of government. In contrast, the private sphere is the sphere of the governed, the sphere to be governed. Given this distinction, public and private policing are very different things and so should be treated and studied differently. The one is a governmental activity while the other is not.

This conclusion, as the analysis suggests, is not very sensible. It is not sensible because the nature of governance is changing drastically. If the public sphere ever had a monopoly over governance, it no longer has. Governance now takes place in both spheres.

In recognizing the unrecognized origins of the new policing, we are not only pointing to the roots of what the state police call community policing but are identifying a huge shift in the way policing is being done and thought about. These shifts, if taken seriously, inevitably lead to a new vision of how policing should be organized and practiced.

A critical consequence of recognizing that the private sphere has become a terrain of governance is that we become able to appreciate the extent to which the sphere of business has affected the criminological arena. It also enables us to appreciate the extent to which we should question the assumption that business should look to the public police for direction in promoting safety and security. As the tool library story illustrates so clearly, the skills that people recruited from the public sector bring to the private sector are often as much a hindrance as they are an asset.

A recognition of the private origins of community policing might also encourage a movement of private-sector personnel to the public sector particularly at the managerial and strategic-planning level. There is much that the police can learn from their private security counterparts. This is a lesson that has been learned by many other sectors of the state. It is time for this lesson to be appreciated by the police, not only with respect to police management but with respect to their core task — the prevention of crime.

* * *

NOTES

1. The position outlined here, and developed at greater length in the remainder of this paper, recites arguments developed by Brogden and Shearing (1994).

REFERENCES

Brogden, M. and C. Shearing (1994). *Policing for a New South Africa.* London, UK: Routledge.

Eck, J.E. and W. Spelman (1987). "Who Ya Gonna call? The Police as Problem-Busters." *Crime & Delinquency* 33(1):31-52.

Fitzpatrick, P. (1992). "The Impossibility of Popular Justice." *Social and Legal Studies* 1:199-215.

Johnston, L. (1992). *The Rebirth of Private Policing.* London, UK: Routledge.

Macauley, S. (1986). "Private government." In: L. Lipson and S. Wheeler (eds.), *Law and the Social Sciences.* New York, NY: Russell Sage Foundation.

Marenin, O. (1982). "Parking Tickets and Class Repression: The Concept of Policing in Critical Theories of Criminal Justice." *Contemporary Crisis* 6(3):241-266.

Reiner, R. (1985). *The Politics of the Police.* Brighton, Sussex, UK: Wheatsheaf.

Santos, B. de Sousa (1992). "State, Law and Community in the World System: An Introduction." *Social and Legal Studies* 1(2):131-141.

Sherman, L.W. (1992). "Book Review of *Problem-Oriented Policing.*" *The Journal of Criminal Law and Criminology* 82(3):690-707.

—— (1995) "The Police." In: J.Q. Wilson and J. Petersilia (eds.), *Crime.* San Francisco, CA: ICS Press.

Shearing, C. (1992). "Conceptions of Policing: The Relationship Between its Public and Private Forms." In: M. Tonry and N. Morris (eds.), *Modern Policing. Crime and Justice: A Review of Research,* vol. 15. Chicago, IL: University of Chicago Press.

—— and P. Stenning (1983). "Private Security: Implications for Social Control." *Social Problems* 30(5):493-506.

Skogan, W.G. (1990). *Disorder and Decline: Crime and the Spiral of Decay in American Neighborhoods.* New York, NY: The Free Press.

Stenning, P. and C. Shearing (1980). "The Quiet Revolution: The Nature, Development and General Legal Implications of Private Security in Canada." *Criminal Law Quarterly* 22:220-48.

Wilson, J.Q. and G. Kelling (1982). "Broken Windows." *The Atlantic Monthly* February:29-38.

—— (1989). "Making Neighborhoods Safe." *The Atlantic Monthly* February:46-52.

REAL ESTATE DEVELOPMENT AND CRIME PREVENTION NEEDS

by Richard B. Peiser
University of Southern California

Abstract: *Our understanding of the relationship between real estate and crime is very limited. Cooperation between criminologists and property owners and developers is also at an early stage of development. This paper describes how the real estate industry is structured to help crime researchers better understand the industry and its concerns. As a further aid, the chapter sets out 15 basic questions addressing research issues related to crime and real estate . They are organized according to four areas of inquiry: (1) the impact of crime on real estate; (2) the impact of real estate on crime; (3) educating the real estate industry about crime; and (4) research on crime and real estate.*

Public and private real estate provide the settings for most crimes. Real estate values reflect the impact of crime on neighborhoods and business areas. Its design helps or hinders crime. Property managers and owners are the front line in the battle to keep property secure, protect tenants and customers, and clean things up when crime occurs.

In spite of its critical role in crime and crime prevention, the real estate community has little awareness of research about the interconnections between real estate and crime. There is some awareness, especially in public-housing circles, about work such as Oscar Newman's (1973) book on *Defensible Space.* There is little familiarity, however, with the CPTED — Crime Prevention Through Environmental Design — literature (Crowe, 1991; Jeffery, 1971). Although several social ecological studies have considered how crime relates to local conditions (see, for example, Shaw and McKay, 1942), very often real estate variables are included incidentally or not at all. Consultation with real estate professionals would lead to these variables being included with much more detail.

Criminologists have studied crime with respect to a number of different types of real estate (see, for example, Poyner, 1992; Pease, 1992; Felson, 1994). Research on burglary, for example, has greatly improved the detailed risk statistics for various types of dwellings (Winchester and Jackson, 1982; Bennett and Wright, 1984). However, real estate experts would perhaps modify the ways in which some of these data are organized. For example, they are concerned about the benefits from reducing crime relative to the cost of various deterrents. They are especially interested in prescriptions that help to reduce crime in various product-types, such as those presented by Felson (1995).

Real estate owners and developers have considerable experience in dealing with different types of crime. To date, the major organizations to which property owners and developers belong have had little formal contact with the principal criminology research institutions. The Urban Land Institute held a small seminar in Washington, D.C., in June 1995, which was the first time that many of the largest property owners had ever met the leading criminologists who work in the field of CPTED. The forum, co-sponsored by the National Institute of Justice and the Department of Housing and Urban Development, made developers and owners aware that a large body of research exists about the impact of design on crime (Parham, 1995). It gave CPTED criminologists the opportunity to see for the first time the vast potential data sources that property owners can provide to assist their research.

The fact that the major real estate organizations and companies have little awareness of CPTED research points up the principal problem — lack of communication between the real estate community and criminologists. This paper attempts to facilitate that communication by laying out the issues that concern property owners the most. If criminologists want to have an impact, they will have to find ways to capture the attention of property owners. Surely, the best way to do that is to provide solutions that save property owners money. In the long run, the dialogue should not only save property owners money, but should help to save entire neighborhoods — to stop the ever-quickening cycle of real estate investment, deterioration, property disinvestment and neighborhood abandonment that plagues American cities.

This paper is organized into two main sections. The first section describes how the real estate industry is structured. It is intended to help crime researchers understand who the consumer for their research is and how different parts of the industry are concerned about different crime issues. The second section presents a series of 15 basic questions about crime and real estate. These questions are intended as a guide to future research topics. The final summary concludes the paper.

How the Real Estate Industry is Organized

Altogether the different segments of the real estate industry, from homebuilders to contractors, brokers and developers, comprise almost 20% of the nation's Gross Domestic Product. The real estate industry is composed of many different players (see Figure 1). Developers are the entrepreneurs who create and produce real estate. They may or may not continue to be the long-term owners who manage the real estate.

Figure 1: Real Estate Industry Players and Owners

Players

Developers
Contractors
Lenders
Brokers
Property Managers
Architects / Engineers
Planners / City Council
Government Agencies

Owners

Corporations
REITS
Banks - REO
Partnerships / JVs
Individuals

Each of the players is involved in a different phase of producing or managing real estate. Developers, architects, lenders, planners and city councilmen and women are more involved on the front end. They are the players to address for fixing crime-related problems before they are enshrined in bricks and mortar. Owners, property managers, building departments, police and fire departments and brokers tend to be more involved with the real estate after it is built.

Property Type

The real estate industry is divided into five main product types: residential, office, commercial, industrial, and land (see Figure 2). Crime problems differ considerably from one product type to another. For example, teenage loitering and attendant noise and graffiti problems are much more relevant to residential real estate than to land subdivision or office buildings.

Crime problems also differ by location. Shopping centers in the inner city are more concerned with drug sales, gangs and security than in wealthy suburbs although shoplifting is a concern in both locations.

Figure 2: Understanding the Real Estate Industry — Property Type, Location, Design and Density

Location
CBD
Inner City
Suburbs   *Wealthy*
                 Graying
Exurbs
Rural

Property Type
Single Family Residence
Apartments
Office
Industrial
Retail
Land / Subdivision

Design
Hi Rise
Lo Rise / Garden

Single Story
Parking   *Surface*
                 Structured

Mixed Use

Density
80 + DUs/Acre
30-80 DUs/Acre
18-30 DUs/Acre
3-12 DUs/Acre
350 sf / space
4-5 spaces / 1000 sf
$7-20,000 / space
Shared parking

When one talks about real estate, building design and density is yet another important distinction that influences crime issues. High-rise apartments with structured parking, for example, have different safety concerns than garden apartments (such as in lobbies and elevators and with parking-lot access). Understanding how the industry is organized is necessary if researchers are going to reach the right constituency or know whom to ask what questions.

The following 15 questions address a number of research issues related to crime and real estate. The questions are organized into four main lines of inquiry indicated by Roman numerals. I attempt to answer the questions by estimating their importance to the real estate community and the extent to which property developers, owners and managers have anything to contribute to answering them. Figure 3 shows the major risk factors in developing a project and the related questions about crime.

Figure 3: Real Estate Risk Factors and Questions about Crime

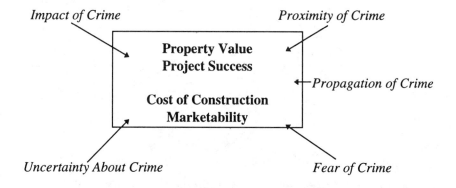

INQUIRY I: THE IMPACT OF CRIME ON REAL ESTATE

Crime has many different forms of impact on real estate. It affects property values, chances for success, cost of money, operating costs and marketability of new, as well as existing, properties. Figure 4 summarizes the various crime issues that have an impact on real estate.

Figure 4: Impact of Crime on Real Estate

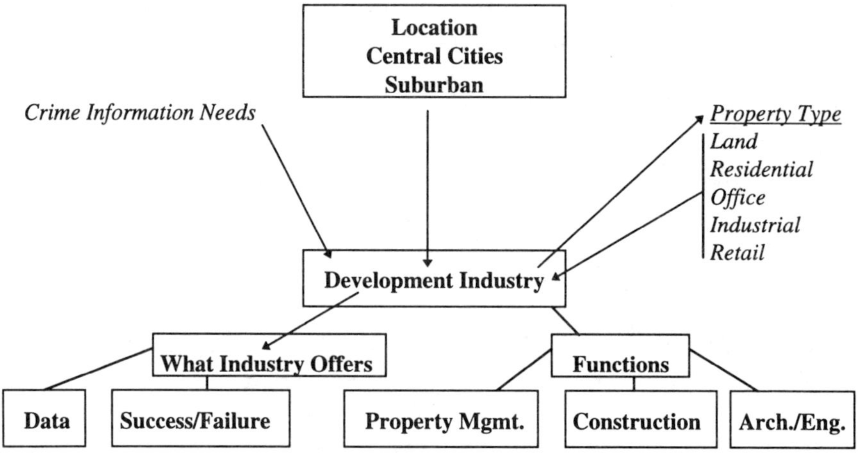

1. How do local increases in crime influence real estate values, project success, costs of construction and probability of failure?

No one knows exactly how crime affects real estate values. Small increases in crime have an impact on construction costs and operating costs in the form of security and insurance. The main issue is where the tipping point is. At some level of crime — or fear of crime — new investment in real estate drops off dramatically. Demand falls sharply, as tenants and buyers look elsewhere. Real estate income falls and, with it, property value. Crime, unfortunately, is correlated with a number of other factors that scare away property buyers, such as lower incomes, racial change, unkempt landscaping, poor property maintenance and neighborhood deterioration. For example, the Hancock Park area of Los Angeles was encircled by the riots in 1992. This event, along with other reported increases in crime, have caused home values to fall more than sharply in Hancock Park than other comparable residential areas.

Buyers, lenders and investors follow a herd mentality. When they become concerned that an area is deteriorating, new investment stops. Loans become expensive and even unavailable. A downward spiral begins that is very hard to stop. How this mechanism works, what the influence of crime is on it, and what types of crime have the greatest impact are among the most important unanswered questions.

2. How does uncertainty about crime affect the above?

Uncertainty about the future — with respect to crime or any number of other factors — directly affects property values. If uncertainty increases, the returns that investors require go up. How crime plays into the equation, however, is by no means certain. The question is, how do property buyers make judgments about crime in an area? Few buyers investigate crime data for a neighborhood before buying, although such data will become more and more available and relied upon in the future. Most home buyers make judgments about crime either from brokers (who "bad mouth" one area in an attempt to steer buyers to another area), or from visual indicators such as property maintenance, homeless people, cars in front lawns and so forth. While uncertainty is important, the mechanism by which buyers incorporate crime into their buying decisions is more so.

3. How does crime in one area affect real estate in nearby areas? How far does the impact travel?

This set of questions is among the most important because it affects the speed of neighborhood change. Neighborhoods that are adjacent to high-crime areas are more at risk than others far away. Property values are likely to reflect the proximity of high crime. However, no one knows how far the impact reaches, how it differs by property type, or what types of preventive measures reduce the impact.

In addition to the propagation of crime from one neighborhood to another, research into how crime travels from one land use to another is also important. For example, industrial parks in Orange County appear to have more crime when they are adjacent to low-income apartments. Planning departments are encouraging more mixed-use developments. Will the presence of more people around-the-clock reduce crime or will the proximity of different uses increase crime? An examination of comparable areas with different mixtures of land uses would shed light on this issue.

4. How does the fear of crime affect real estate development and value, net of objective crime itself.

Developers, home buyers and commercial tenants tend to react much more to the *fear* of crime than the objective crime itself. The key questions are: (1) how do they form their impressions about crime in an area? (2) what types of crime have the greatest impact on their investment and renting decisions? and (3) is there a tipping point above which crime is such that they no longer will consider buying or locating in an area? Research should look at both prices as a function of different types of crime and investment in rehabilitation and new buildings. Measuring *fear* of crime is also very important. Building owners would be very interested in what increases fear because they are dedicated to reducing any negative impressions about their properties.

5. Are real estate developers able to wait for a longer-run success in prevention or must they have fast success? How does their finance timing affect the impact of crime?

Developers have the opportunity to incorporate the most sweeping crime prevention measures because they typically build projects from scratch. Owners of existing property, on the other hand, are more likely to spend money on crime prevention in response to particular management problems.

Developers distinguish the capital costs of building a project from the operating costs of maintaining it once it is built. Capital costs are expended only if the developer believes that tenants or buyers will pay more so that the developer can recover his investment.

"Merchant" builders sell their buildings as soon as they are built and leased. Since they do not incur the operating expenses associated with greater crime, they are less likely to spend money on capital investment for crime prevention. "Investment" builders, on the other hand, continue to own and operate their projects. Since they do realize the operational savings, they are more likely to spend money on capital investment. In both cases, developers must see a direct operating cost savings or an increase in rents if the capital expenditure is to be justified. The burden is on researchers to demonstrate the cost versus the benefit of different crime prevention measures. If the payback period is longer than two-to-three years for an existing building or longer than five-to-seven years for a new building, the crime prevention method is less likely to be implemented. On the other hand, if property owners are concerned about increasing crime, they may tolerate longer payback periods for their investment.

6. Does government play a role in prevention? How does zoning relate to prevention and to developers' concerns? What effects do building codes or other planning activities have?

Government plays many different roles in prevention, from regulatory to code enforcement to ongoing policing. In the ULI Policy Forum on Crime, Diane Zahm discussed how city parking-lot regulations that require hiding the parking lots behind six-foot-high bushes may in fact be *creating* opportunities for crime (Zahm, in press). Developers are frustrated by often-conflicting regulations. Building codes and planning regulations that were conceived long before crime became a major concern sometimes contribute to crime. These codes stay on the books for years.

The research questions are: (1) which regulations contribute to crime? (2) how does one ensure that all city, county and state departments talk to one another before rules are passed? and (3) how can government promote better crime prevention techniques? Private industry is usually ahead of government in devising solutions that work. Developers are distrustful of regulatory approaches to reduce crime. They strongly prefer incentive programs over rules and regulatory requirements.

7. Is prevention of crime and fear possible in suburban as well as urban development?

One must distinguish between older graying suburbs, which are facing many of the same crime problems as inner cities, from new outer-ring suburbs where people are moving to "escape" from crime. One research question is how people in different suburbs perceive crime. As gang and drug problems move even into rural communities, there seems to be a growing perception that one cannot really escape from crime altogether. Certainly, central cities would benefit from statistics that show the likelihood of someone actually being injured either from crime *or* traffic accidents. Articles such as Gerstenzang's (1996) in St. Paul, Minnesota, for example, may help to influence public opinion away from the widely held notion that cities are more dangerous than suburbs.

Crime issues in suburbs differ from those in central cities. Research that highlights the differences in crime would help to raise the consciousness of real estate providers. While the problems differ, the real estate community that serves suburban buyers and tenants tends to be the same one that serves the inner city — especially among retail and office developers. Residential developers are more likely to focus either in cities or suburban areas.

INQUIRY II: THE IMPACT OF REAL ESTATE ON CRIME

Real estate is not just a recipient of crime or the place where it occurs. Different types of real estate are associated with higher incidence of crime, as illustrated in Figure 5.

Figure 5: Impact of Real Estate on Crime

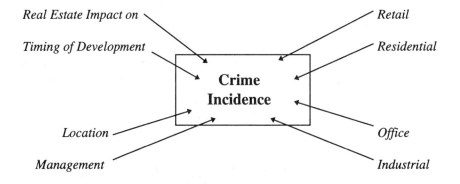

Real Estate Impact on

Timing of Development

Crime Incidence

Retail

Residential

Location

Management

Office

Industrial

8. How do developers and builders themselves contribute to more or less crime by the nature of their design or their organization of the project?

The vast majority of developers have no concept of how the design of their project may contribute to crime. Few have heard about the CPTED research. However, many developers are fascinated by the research when they learn about it. It should not be too difficult to get many of them to participate in future research efforts.

The combination and juxtaposition of land uses is just as important as the design of individual buildings. Bars and liquor stores, for example, are associated with higher crime rates. There has been a concerted effort in Los Angeles to reduce the number of liquor outlets after the 1992 riots.

Most developers are unaware of the real estate uses that contribute to crime.

9. How does the timing of development relate to the timing of crime problems?

The *location* of development is much more related to crime than the *timing* of development. The lead times required to develop property range from one year to five-to-ten years depending on whether the project is a small shopping center, a multi-use urban center, or a large-scale master-planned community. Long-term trends in crime have significant impact on the attractiveness of an area for development but have little impact on the timing. This issue has a low research priority.

INQUIRY III: EDUCATING THE REAL ESTATE INDUSTRY ABOUT CRIME

Figure 6 illustrates the major issues that bear on developers' knowledge about crime and the importance of educating customers and tenants as well as real estate professionals.

10. What part of the building and development industry is most amenable to crime prevention efforts? What parts of the industry will be harder to reach? Why?

The real estate industry is composed of many different segments. Each segment obtains information through different channels. A twofold process must occur. Developers and owners of property should be targeted via task forces and specialized training aimed at each major real estate organization. To get their attention, researchers must demonstrate that their proposals save money either on the capital cost side or on the operating side, or both.

Figure 6: Educating Real Estate Professionals and Their Customers about Crime

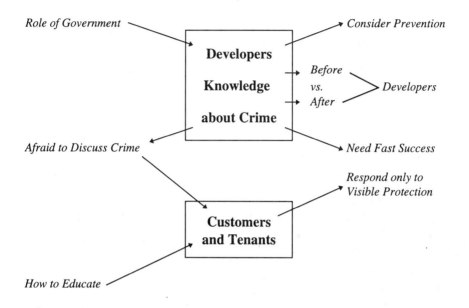

The second group that must be targeted is the consumer. This is the harder group to reach, but when they demand change, then developers will respond.

The building industry is divided by property type. Each property type is served by one or more major professional organizations. They provide the best vehicle for reaching constituent members:

Homebuilding — National Association of Home Builders (NAHB)

Major developers and owners (all property types) — The Urban Land Institute (ULI)

Industrial — Society of Industrial and Office Realtors (SIOR)

Office and Apartment — Building and Owner Managers Association (BOMA)

Apartments — National Apartment Association (NAA)

Shopping Centers — International Council of Shopping Centers (ICSC)

Corporate Real Estate — National Association of Corporate Real Estate Executives (NACORE)

Pension Fund Owners — National Association of Real Estate Investment Managers (NAREIM)

REITs — National Association of Real Estate Investment Trusts (NAREIT)

Realtors — National Association of Realtors (NAR)

Of these organizations, the ones that deal more with property management and sales are likely to be most receptive to crime prevention information — that is, ULI, NAHB, BOMA, NAA, ICSC.

11. Are developers willing to consider crime prevention beforehand or do they wait and put security in after all else has been done?

Developers are hungry for crime prevention information. Programs on crime at ULI annual meetings, for example, have been well attended and the organization is very supportive of crime research and programming activities. The extent to which developers are willing to invest in crime prevention during construction depends primarily on whether they think the measures are cost effective, and whether they think buyers and tenants will pay them for the additional cost. The prevailing wisdom is that home buyers will pay for evidence of security, such as guard gates, even though they may not work as well as other measures. Security is an increasingly important aspect of building design, but new approaches filter down slowly to architects and developers.

The research question is how developers perceive the cost effectiveness of different types of crime prevention.

12. Are developers afraid to discuss crime because they think it scares off customers?

Crime in real estate used to be everyone's "dirty little secret," but that is changing. Buyers and tenants are very concerned about safety, so property developers and managers are becoming accustomed to addressing it directly. Few developers, however, use official crime reporting data to advertise the safety of their projects.

The research question is how developers and managers present security issues to their customers. A second issue is how they deal with tenant relations after crime incidents occur. Research must distinguish between talking about crime before-the-fact in new projects and dealing with the public relations side of crime after-the-fact. While important, I believe the public relations issue has lower priority. Still, it bears on how tenants and buyers form their perceptions about crime, and certain incidents, like rapes and murders in shopping centers, can have dramatic impacts on property value. Puente Hills Shopping Center in Los Angeles, for example, had a well-publicized series of rapes. The loss in business may have reduced the value of the center by as much as $20 million. The incident happened three years ago, and the center has never fully recovered.

13. Do customers respond only to highly visible prevention (for example, guards and iron gates)? Can they be made to understand the more subtle but lower cost and highly effective methods of situational prevention and CPTED?

Conventional wisdom is that customers *do* respond most to highly visible prevention. Otherwise, one would not see guard gates advertised so prominently. This question relates to how customers form their impressions about crime. The answer differs by property type. Home buyers form their impressions primarily from sales people who work for builders while commercial tenants form theirs from brokers and leasing agents. I believe buyers can be made to understand the more subtle methods of CPTED. The question is how to educate them most effectively. I suspect that focusing on the issue of long-term costs and benefits of different measures is the best way to get their attention.

INQUIRY IV: RESEARCH ON CRIME AND REAL ESTATE

14. What information does the industry need to have? How might it obtain this information?

The industry needs information in four main areas:

(1) What are crime statistics for competing properties and what is the experience of other comparable properties?

2) What are the success stories, both during construction and operations, for solutions that reduce crime for each of the different property types?

3) What is the best way to communicate facts about crime to tenants and home buyers? and

4) How can regulatory bodies — in particular, building departments, fire departments, police departments and planning departments — be encouraged to work together to produce regulations that are consistent, avoid conflict, provide clear direction to builders and do not cost money unnecessarily.

15. What information can the industry offer? What proprietary problems interfere with sharing such information?

Property managers have enormous amounts of data that are invaluable to crime research. They are very concerned about releasing crime information, and even more so about publicizing rental and vacancy information. However, larger firms will cooperate, especially if the primary organization to which they belong, such as BOMA or the ULI, collects the data. There is a long tradition of sharing information, even proprietary information among members of the ULI and NAHB. Members will cooperate if they understand how they can benefit from the effort.

CONCLUSIONS

Our understanding of how crime affects real estate and how real estate contributes to crime is embryonic. There is little formal research on the subject other than CPTED's work.

One of the principal challenges is simply one of communication. Few real estate professionals have ever heard of CPTED or know what it may offer to their business. Few CPTED researchers have worked closely with developers and property owners to understand what their biggest concerns are and how their research may be useful.

Because of the enormous attention being given to crime and its impact on real estate prospects, especially in central cities and graying suburbs, real estate professionals are very interested in learning more about how to reduce crime in their projects. They want specific information, not theory. They want specific examples, not general advice.

While the ownership of data is proprietary and few property owners want to publicize their crime problems, they are eager to contribute to studies where they see a clear benefit to their business. A broad outreach effort is needed that familiarizes the major real estate organizations with CPTED and other crime research. These organizations represent the most efficient way to communicate with members of the real estate industry. Whether the industry is supportive of research efforts depends on how quickly they see a payoff from the research.

***

REFERENCES

Bennett, T. and R. Wright (1984). *Burglars on Burglary*. Farnborough, UK: Gower.

Crowe, T.D. (1991). *Crime Prevention Through Environmental Design*. Stoneham, MA: Butterworth's.

Felson, M. (1994). *Crime and Everyday Life: Insight and Implications for Society*. Thousand Oaks, CA: Pine Forge Press.

—— (1995). "How Buildings Can Protect Themselves Against Crime." *Lusk Review for Real Estate Development and Urban Transformation* 1:1-7.

Gerstenzang, J. (1996). "Extra Mileage Cuts Safety in Suburbia down to City Standards." *Pioneer Press*. April 15:1A, 4A.

Jeffery, C.R. (1971). *Crime Prevention Through Environmental Design*. Beverly Hills, CA: Sage.

Newman, O. (1973). *Defensible Space*. New York, NY: MacMillan.

Parham, D.W. (1995). *Crime Prevention Through Real Estate Development and Management*. ULI Education Policy Forum, Series No. 650. Washington, DC: The Urban Land Institute.

Pease, K. (1992). "Preventing Burglary on a British Public Housing Estate." In: R.V. Clarke (ed.), *Situational Crime Prevention: Successful Case Studies*. Albany, NY: Harrow and Heston.

Poyner, B. (1992). "Situational Crime Prevention in Two Parking Facilities." In: R.V. Clarke (ed.), *Situational Crime Prevention: Successful Case Studies*. Albany, NY: Harrow and Heston.

Shaw, C. and H. McKay (1942). *Juvenile Delinquency and Urban Areas*. Chicago, IL: University of Chicago Press.

Winchester, S. and H. Jackson (1982). *Residential Burglary: The Limits of Prevention*. Home Office Research Study No. 74. London, UK: Her Majesty's Stationery Office.

Zahm, D. (in press). "Why Protecting the 'Public Health, Safety and General Welfare' Won't Protect Us from Crime." In: *Crime and Real Estate*. Washington, DC: The Urban Land Institute.

FINANCIAL ANALYSIS OF RETAIL CRIME PREVENTION

by Robert L. DiLonardo

Abstract: *Financial analysis can be critical to the successful implementation and continuation of crime prevention strategies in retail businesses. The utility of this approach is shown by examining the financial impact of shoplifting on a hypothetical men's clothing store. The analysis of the financial impact of this shoplifting includes "tracking" the item from when it was originally ordered to when its replacement is ordered, comparing these losses to other financial losses suffered by the company, and looking at the costs of shoplifting prevention measures. The need for greater links between practitioners and the academic community is discussed.*

INTRODUCTION

Practical financial considerations now drive all decisions regarding asset deployment in retail loss prevention. The skills of internal auditor, financial analyst and corporate controller have become as critical to the successful implementation of crime prevention strategies as the practical law enforcement skills required to enter the field. The profit motive dictates the implementation of retail crime prevention, or its continuance. This assessment requires both a general knowledge of statistical and financial methods and a specific knowledge of the correct ways to employ these techniques within the retail environment. Little information has been published about either statistical or cost-benefit analytical work relative to retail security countermeasures. It is in this area where academicians, retailers and security equipment providers can join together to improve the body of knowledge within the field by undertaking both case studies and by designing and implementing practical methods of cost justification.

USING FINANCIAL ANALYSIS IN RETAIL LOSS PREVENTION

Retailers have a broad range of crimes with which to contend. Some, like employee theft and shoplifting, are more prevalent than others and, therefore, have a more pronounced impact upon the "bottom line" of the organization. This paper focuses upon describing some of the statistical and financial analysis required to conduct a thorough cost-justification study for retail security measures. External theft (shoplifting) of merchandise will be examined because it is a widespread practice and its financial impact is illustrative of the complexity of risk that a retailer assumes. Shoplifting prevention measures will also be studied because they also provide an excellent illustration of the depth and variety of financial analysis required to justify costs.

The discussion will then shift toward the practical matter of linking the valuable work undertaken by academics with the practical problems faced by the practitioners, consultants and security equipment providers. This link can (and should) be provided by statistical and financial benchmarking techniques that can help determine whether something works, how well it works and whether the practical benefits are great enough. The profit motive is a very important driving force behind a theory's practical success.

The Financial Impact of Shoplifting

External theft of merchandise results in a complex series of financial losses for the retailer. Some of these losses are self-evident, but others are quite subtle. These nuances can best be illustrated through the use of an example that "tracks" an item from the time it is originally ordered to the time when a decision must be made whether it should be re-ordered (due to the fact that the original was stolen instead of sold).

Assume that Store A has ordered 12 navy blue men's sport coats in a normal size range. The cost of each coat is $100, and the selling price is expected to be $150. Freight charges from the manufacturer amount to $10 for each coat. The shipment arrives at the distribution center and is dispersed to Store A, where the coats are placed on the sales floor. Assume further that the chain has advertised the arrival of these coats and that four coats in the most common sizes are stolen. The most obvious financial loss is cost of the items ($100 each) and the freight costs ($10 each). Also lost are any costs incurred to process them, move them from the distribution center to the sales floor, or otherwise prepare them for sale. These costs are difficult to assign precisely to the coats and are often termed "soft" costs while the wholesale cost of the coat and the freight charges are termed "hard" costs.

Since the four coats were stolen instead of sold, the opportunity to sell them at a profit was lost as well. The item was part of a planned merchandise assortment that was supposed to generate a certain amount of sales (maximum is 12 coats at $150 each or $1,800). Obviously, maximum sales volume is now only $1,200 (eight remaining coats at $150 each). This lost sales opportunity requires another procurement if possible, which means that *eight* coats (the four original plus four extra) would have to be purchased to achieve the net effect on sales that was expected of the original four coats. The additional procurement means more freight charges and more handling charges.

Suppose that the four stolen coats could not be replaced by the manufacturer. The remaining eight coats are of sizes that would be appropriate for a far-smaller segment of the available market, and it is reasonable to assume that some of these coats might have to be "marked down" to be sold — further reducing the maximum potential sales volume.

In summary, the shoplifting of four coats out of an original assortment of 12 results in a revenue shortfall, an inventory shortage, a loss of the cash invested in the merchandise and freight charge, a waste of time, effort and money on the part of the people processing the coats through the distribution system and a waste of a certain portion of any other fixed or variable costs spent to sell those coats. Additional inventory procurement costs would be incurred if the store needed to replace those four coats. An accumulation of all of these hard and soft dollar losses erodes the store's profitability (DiLonardo, 1985).

To put this into the perspective of the Chief Financial Officer (CFO), if the store is operating under a 5% net profit after taxes, 20 additional coats would have to be procured, processed and sold to generate the profit required to replace each coat that was shoplifted.

Thanks to technological advances in the computer industry, retailers generally have a precise picture of the order of magnitude of overall inventory losses. These losses are now measured semi-annually or annually down to the item level. By comparing sales and inventory levels, they may even estimate the order of magnitude of the sales volume foregone because of the losses. What remains imprecise is the apportionment of inventory loss to external theft, internal theft and document errors. It is in this area where a retail loss-prevention practitioner must use experience, available statistics and academic information to shape risk analysis and countermeasure selection.

Aside from the direct financial implications of shoplifting, there are some other issues that merit some mention. In the case mentioned above, the retailer must decide how much in losses can be absorbed before some remedial activity is undertaken. Clearly, a retail store is in business to make a profit, and, in this example, the loss of four coats represents a significant proportion of the total. Management would use financial analysis to determine whether the loss was significant enough to devote some financial resources in an effort to stem the losses or recover the lost revenue. This is where the decision to implement some type of loss-prevention measure becomes an exercise in statistical and financial analysis.

Financial Comparison of Shoplifting Losses to Other Losses

Statistical and financial analysis is used throughout the business world to assign risk levels. By combining statistical data on the frequency (and expected future frequency) of occurrences, along with analysis of the financial impact of those losses, various criminal activities can be "ranked" to derive a maximum cost-benefit relationship in countermeasure selection. In other words, practitioners have to determine which problem (or problems) presents the greatest opportunity for a positive financial outcome given the opportunity for a deployment of loss-prevention assets.

To provide an illustration, suppose that the men's store mentioned above suffered from shoplifting and occasional burglaries. No other crimes were evident. To provide a firm financial basis for an investment in a countermeasure, the order of magnitude of shoplifting must be assessed and then compared to the order of magnitude of the burglaries. In retail, inventory losses from shoplifting are generally measured in the aggregate using both currency (like dollar amount) and percentage-of-sales measurements. For example, the annual shortage of a 200-store chain of men's clothing stores would be reported for financial purposes as $3 million, or 3.5% of sales. Within the operation, these statistics can be further subdivided into detailed accounts by store and merchandise department down to the individual-item level. So, the average store incurred an annual shortage of $15,000. Additionally, the data would pinpoint losses down to the brand and style level.

While statistical data on the raw number of shoplifting occurrences are impossible to compile, most chains keep track of the number of shoplifting apprehensions (if any are made) and the amount of known losses, which are successful thefts where enough information was left behind so that a probable value could be determined. In our example, if we assume that the average value of the merchandise is $50, and assume further that the entire $15,000 was lost through shoplifting, then we can determine that a reasonable frequency is about six items per week in the average store.

During the past year, the chain has had 40 burglaries, with an aggregate loss of $200,000. On average, only one store in five will be burglarized with an expected loss of $5,000. Clearly, in this case, shoplifting occurrences are statistically and financially more significant than losses from burglaries. At this juncture, management would rank a shoplifting prevention measure with a higher priority provided that it could be demonstrated that the benefits (reduction in loss due to shoplifting) exceeded the costs.

Let us suppose that, in this example, the cost of supplying all 200 stores with burglar alarm monitoring equipment would be $150,000 per year and the frequency of burglaries is estimated to drop from 40 to 15. At $5,000 per incidence, 15 burglaries would "cost" $75,000. Added to the cost of the monitoring equipment, the total cost of providing a countermeasure would exceed the historical financial exposure by $25,000 per year. In this instance, management would not be inclined to invest the money because the cost-benefit ratio is unfavorable — the chain would pay more money to reduce the problem than it currently loses.

Financial Analysis in the Selection of a Shoplifting Prevention Measure

Since it has been determined, in our example, that shoplifting results in more significant losses than burglaries, the loss prevention professional must then select a shoplifting prevention measure that provides the best results (a positive cost-benefit ratio). In so doing, he or she must decide which merchandise is financially "worthy" of protection. In approaching this choice as a management exercise, basic knowledge about the viable countermeasures is gained from experience within the organization and from the various written sources mentioned in the introduction of this paper. Fortunately, a wealth of examples, both expository and macro-economic, provide comfort in the form of positive statements about the effectiveness of various countermeasures. In other words, it is relatively easy to find loss-prevention practitioners who are willing to describe successful experiences with anti-shoplifting devices, such as electronic article surveillance. It is much more difficult to find published research on the statistical strategies and tactics used to select either the counter-measure or the item (or items) that should be afforded protection.

It is commonly assumed that shoplifting protection measures are most easily cost justified when used on items that have a high propensity toward theft. To use our earlier example, if men's sport coats have a history of high shortage, then it makes financial sense to protect them. If another item, such as a chair, has the same price ($150) but has no history of high shortage, then the investment in an anti-shoplifting countermeasure for that item is not indicated. This example is an exercise in common sense.

There are some circumstances that require more financial analysis before the countermeasure implementation decision can be made. Suppose that a drug store contains two items of equal retail value — film, which has a price of $5 per package and a cost of $4, and sunglasses, which also have a price of $5 each but a cost of only $2. Assume that the rates of sales and inventory loss are precisely the same for both items. Assume further that only one of the items can be protected against shoplifting. Which item should be chosen? Merchandising logic suggests that the sunglasses should be protected since they afford the store with the oppor-tunity to make the most per-unit profit if sold ($3). Financial logic suggests that since the cost of the film is 80% of the potential revenue ($4 out of $5), the film is more "dear" than the sunglasses ($4 cost versus $2 cost) and should be protected first.

Very little, if any, of this type of analysis has been published. As the retail environment has become more competitive and less profitable, most large retail organizations have undertaken internal cost justifications for loss-prevention expenditures. For the most part, loss-prevention execu-tives are responsible for identifying the crime problems and suggesting countermeasures. The cost justification exercise has remained (rightly so) in the hands of the financial executives.

In their quest for success, many retail loss-prevention executives have attempted to become better versed in financial analysis or have seen the wisdom of adding some financial capabilities within the loss-prevention department. These activities have resulted in a much more professional approach toward statistical and financial analysis. Today, most larger loss-prevention departments undertake internal studies that can help prove the loss-prevention and financial efficacy of a countermeasure. Unfortunately for loss prevention at large, they are generally considered confidential, so methods and results are rarely published.

Returning to the selection of a shoplifting prevention measure, current prevention activities center around four major ideas — all of which have been well documented as effective (in the expository sense, at least). They are: (1) electronic article surveillance (EAS) systems; (2) employee awareness programs; (3) locks, cables and lockable fixtures; and (4) benefit denial devices (plastic tags containing ink, for example). The primary exercise for the loss-prevention executive is to determine which countermeasure "works best." Statistically, this would be determined by measuring the impact that each has upon inventory losses against a control group. Over the years, an array of retail loss-prevention-specific statistical techniques has been used.[1] To give an example, if ten stores introduced EAS systems and inventory losses were reduced by 50%, and if ten other stores introduced ink tags and losses were reduced by 40%, and if losses remained constant in ten control stores, then it may be reasonable to assume that the savings can be attributed to the countermeasures employed, all other factors being equal. It is this reduction in losses that can be utilized as an economic benefit in the return-on-investment analysis.

Once the most effective countermeasure has been selected, financial analysis is then used to determine its cost effectiveness to aid in the implement-do-not-implement decision. If the statistics showed that EAS systems reduced inventory losses by 50%, and that reduction translates into $1 million, then an investment of $1 million in EAS systems provides a financial "break even" point.

Since two countermeasures have been tested, a cost-benefit analysis might be indicated for the ink tags even though EAS proved more effective in reducing losses. The introduction of financial measurement techniques might skew the decision to select EAS. To demonstrate, assume that the ink-tag test reduced inventory loss by $800,000, but the cost of the counter-measure is only $500,000. Clearly, the investment in ink tags generates a better net return even though the inventory reduction statistics indicated that EAS systems would achieve a greater reduction in inventory loss due to shoplifting. In this case, the choice is complicated by the introduction of some additional relevant facts, namely, the cost differential between the two competing countermeasures. When the analysis reaches the desk of the loss-prevention executive charged with the responsibility for making both the selection of countermeasure and the implement-do-not-imple-ment decision, the one with the best return (financial benefits minus costs) would be implemented — all other factors being equal. These procure-ments are looked upon as investment decisions first because the quality of the investment can influence the countermeasure selection. The avail-able budget has an impact upon this selection. Once selected, and the scope of the implementation decision made, the vendor selection process begins. Increasingly, these three decisions are (can be or should be) made by the executive in charge of loss prevention.

Financial Approvals

Eventually, the anti-shoplifting procurement must be either approved or denied by the appropriate senior financial manager. There are two major hurdles here. First, the investment's pro forma (estimated or expected) return must be attractive enough to exceed the company's acceptable return rate. Often, this is a financial benchmark established as a "right to proceed." To give an illustration, suppose that a retailer can earn an interest rate (rate of return on an investment) of 10% on invested cash. If the expected return on the investment in anti-shoplifting equipment is above 10%, then it makes more sense to invest in the equipment instead of keeping the money in the bank. A rate of return of zero suggests a break-even situation where nothing is lost or gained. This is the type of logic used in valuing investments. If the return on investment (ROI) is attractive enough, the project has the "right to proceed" to the next hurdle, which is competitive in nature.

Second, the countermeasure must demonstrate a return that is at least as attractive as other competing uses of funds. In retail, some management disciplines are more important than others. For example, merchandising and store operations are both deemed critical to the success of the basic retail business. Loss prevention is not. If there were two competing investment choices — one with a direct impact on the basic business, such as an investment in new cash registers for the stores, and one with an impact upon a less critical area of the business, such as our loss-prevention project, then, given an equal financial outcome (positive rate of return that exceeds the minimum hurdle rate), the project with direct impact would be chosen. Neither would be chosen if (a) they generated no profit or (b) their rates of return fell below the minimum hurdle.

Situations like the one described in the last paragraph often force loss-prevention executives to focus upon the cost of doing nothing. As a practical matter, many large, geographically diverse retail chains are making the conscious choice to "live without" certain loss-prevention measures in locations (or situations) where the available funds could be used more profitably elsewhere. This can be described as one of loss prevention's "80/20 rules" — 80% of the problem is concentrated in 20% of the locations. Reverting to the anti-shoplifting procurement exercise, suppose that through the rigorous statistical and financial analysis mentioned above, the CFO determines that it would be most profitable for the chain to install ink tags in the 20% of the locations that exhibit 80% of the inventory loss. The balance of the stores would continue to operate without a shoplifting prevention measure, incurring inventory losses even though it had been proven statistically that such an expenditure was cost justifiable.

LINKAGE BETWEEN ACADEMIC AND PRACTITIONER

Statistical and financial return on investment analysis helps to provide a very useful linkage between the academic disciplines and the loss-prevention practitioners. It provides an even more profitable link between the practitioner and the security equipment provider, whose task is to design, manufacture and sell programs and products that address the needs identified as both effective and economical as crime countermeasures. In a very practical sense, these analytical tools can: set priorities for prevention efforts; aid in the selection of countermeasures; buttress arguments for or against the various theories; and provide the logic required to attract investment capital to put programs in place.

Academic literature provides a wide variety of information relative to the types of theories and programs that are effective in crime prevention. Industry trade magazines provide information on "how to" solve a particular problem and "where to" procure a solution. However, little practical information is published regarding either the financial efficacy of loss-prevention theories and methods or the measurement of the financial impact of the crime and of its solution. Less is published on the correct methods for developing simple, usable loss-prevention-specific financial analysis tools required to make the investment decision. The American Society for Industrial Security Foundation has funded research into a value-added cost-justification model, which seems (to the author) to be overly complex in its practical usage (Gale, 1993). However, the only other organized efforts to educate loss prevention executives in these disciplines are through a few seminars provided as a subset of annual meetings organized by the large retail trade groups, like the National Retail Federation, and a regularly offered seminar on retail loss-prevention operations conducted by a nationally known retail consulting group.

It has been my experience that retailers would be willing to share internally developed data on crime problems and the effectiveness of crime prevention techniques provided that the findings of the study benefited retail in general and not a particular set of competitors or security equipment providers. Also, the confidentiality of the information would have to be assured. Lastly, someone other than themselves (namely the academic community) would, ideally, conduct the analysis and reporting. Since retailer loss-prevention practitioners generally try to implement the "best practices" that they absorb from their academic readings, a sharing of statistical and financial analytical techniques provides a natural quid pro quo. This logic is consistent with the work of Felson and Clarke (1991) and Burrows and Speed (1996), among others.

Twenty-five years ago, retail loss-prevention activities were confined to very basic prevention, containment, investigation and apprehension activities. The classic profile of the professional retail loss-prevention executive was that of an ex-FBI or law enforcement executive. Currently (and in the probable future) retail loss-prevention activities will center around the following activities (Clarke, 1992:5):

(1) identify the type and magnitude of the problem and rank the problems in order of severity, including such concerns as physical harm, financial loss and legal exposure;

(2) investigate possible solutions, consistent with the department head's theories;

(3) identify countermeasures that fit these theories;

(4) test each countermeasure to find one with more benefits than costs;

(5) develop standards for measuring the success or failure of the prevention measure;

(6) present senior management with a cogent, well-documented proposal for implementation;

(7) implement a pilot program and refine it before presenting it to the organization as a company-wide solution; and

(8) set up regular review activities to determine whether it is working. At the core of each of these activities should be a solid statistical and financial perspective.

Establishing the proper loss-prevention controls requires an investment in intellectual skills (such as studying recent literature in the field, systems analysis, auditing, investigations) as well as technology (such as anti-shoplifting systems, closed-circuit television). This is an area where criminologists, consultants, interested practitioners and vendors can contribute to the actions taken by loss-prevention professionals. Enlightened, well-read loss-prevention executives develop their overall protection strategies based upon the crime prevention theories that are most widely practiced at the time. In this area, a wealth of quality information has been published.

It is in the area of follow-up data where the practical link between academic and practitioner needs support. Loss-prevention executives "means-test" academic theories on a daily basis, but little of the data escapes the retail chain that does the work. Means testing in this context is the daily practical activity associated with demonstrating the effectiveness of the countermeasure. A classic example may be the situational loss-prevention technique of alternating the direction of clothing hangers on a rack to deter thieves from grabbing a mass quantity of merchandise (Felson, 1994:127). No formal statistical study (to this author's knowledge) has ever attempted to prove that this method deters shoplifters more successfully than other methods; yet, most of retail loss prevention people in the garment segment of the marketplace make successful use of this tactic because they have first-hand experience with its success. As mentioned earlier, several of the larger retail trade organizations publish the results of annual questionnaires that ask respondents to rank effective loss-prevention measures in order of use, intended future use and adjudged effectiveness. These documents have wide readership, and the comparisons presented probably reinforce procurement decisions.

In addition to researching and espousing front-end theories about criminal behavior, as well as strategies and tactics to contain, deter, apprehend, punish, or change behavior, a major contribution should be made at the "business end." Here academics in partnership with practitioners, or interested security products manufacturers, can develop operational and financial statistics based upon actual performance that can be used to develop empirical proof of effectiveness and costs and benefits (DiLonardo and Clarke, 1996).

SUMMARY

Retail loss prevention has become much more complex over the past twenty-five years. In my view, changes in criminal behavior can explain only a minor portion of the complexity. The real shift has occurred because an extremely competitive business climate has compelled loss-prevention executives to be more thoughtful and thorough in charting the strategic and tactical courses within their departments. This pressure has been brought to bear by an increased intensity toward scrutiny of capital expenditures. If a loss-prevention program cannot demonstrate effectiveness statistically and financially, it probably will not be adopted. Even if it can demonstrate these two traits, it may not compete successfully with other potential expenditures that are deemed more critical to the business.

The academic and business communities have the opportunity and the obligation to use the tools at their disposal to prepare and defend loss-prevention theories and practices. In the future, collaborations among these communities can provide an extremely important new body of knowledge for the security industry.

***

NOTES

1. Very few studies on this topic have been published. Three such studies are: Baumer and Rosenbaum (1984), DiLonardo (1996) and Scherdin (1986).

REFERENCES

Baumer, T.L. and D.P. Rosenbaum (1984). "Article Surveillance." In: *Combating Retail Theft: Programs and Strategies*. Boston, MA: Butterworth.

Burrows, J. and M. Speed (1996). "Crime Analysis: Lessons from the Retail Sector?" *Security Journal* 7:53-60.

Clarke, R.V. (ed.) (1992). *Situational Crime Prevention: Successful Case Studies*. Albany, NY: Harrow and Heston.

DiLonardo, R.L. (1985). *Profits Through Merchandise Preservation*. Deerfield Beach, FL: Sensormatic Electronics Corporation.

—— (1996). "Defining and Measuring the Economic Benefit of Electronic Article Surveillance." *Security Journal* 7:11-14.

—— and R.V. Clarke (1996). "Reducing the Rewards of Shoplifting: An Analysis of Ink Tags." *Security Journal* 7:11-14.

Felson, M. (1994). *Crime and Everyday Life*. Thousand Oaks, CA: Pine Forge Press.

— and R.V. Clarke (1991). Editorial. *Security Journal* 2:4.

Gale, S. (1993). "Value-Added Security." *Security Journal* 4:162-64.

Scherdin, M.J. (1986). "The Halo Effect: Psychological Deterrence of Electronic Security Systems." *Information Technology and Libraries* September: 232-235. [Reprinted in Clarke, R.V. (ed.) (1992). *Situational Crime Prevention: Successful Case Studies*. Albany, NY: Harrow and Heston.]

PREVENTING PAY PHONE DAMAGE

by Cressida Bridgeman
U.K. Home Office Police Research Group

Abstract: *In the 1992-93 financial year, there were 55,000 attacks on the cash compartments of pay phones in Britain, costing British Telecom (BT) some £20 million. By 1994-95 this had been cut to 17,000 attacks, costing £5 million. A major explanation for this significant reduction was the change in approach following the reorganization of pay phone management in the late 1980s. A brief overview of earlier studies provides the context for a description of BT's strategy from the 1960s to date. Data on the effects of its latest strategy, the Security Enhancement Programme, are then presented. A comparison is drawn with Telecom Australia's approach to pay phone damage. Both strategies are related to Clarke's situational crime prevention framework (1992), and general lessons and principles for effective pay phone management are outlined.*

INTRODUCTION

Pay phone damage is a world-wide problem. To the phone company, a damaged phone means loss of revenue, extra costs and a bad public image. To users it can mean anything from inconvenience to actual danger to life.

In Britain, BT's[1] response to pay phone damage has a long history, traditionally involving measures to make the kiosk and phone more vandal-proof. An important development in its approach was the reorganization of pay phone management in the late 1980s. This change in management, with increased emphasis on reducing costs and improving profits, brought opportunities for a new response to pay phone damage. This paper describes the evolution of BT's approach, and presents data on its effects on pay phone damage. Parallels are drawn with Australia, where a synergy of business principles and crime prevention techniques has brought similar benefits.

The Nature of the Problem

Pay phone damage takes a variety of forms.[2] Attacks may be against the kiosk itself, the telephone equipment it contains, or both. Problems suffered by the kiosk include smashed windows, structural damage, graffiti, litter and its use as a lavatory. Incidents of damage to the equipment have included smashed handsets, cut handset cords, coin chutes blocked with litter, plastic keypads being set fire to, and attacks on the cash compartment.

The reasons for attacks can be difficult to determine. Many researchers and practitioners have used adaptations of Cohen's (1973) typology as a framework for understanding vandalism. This typology categorizes vandalism in six ways: as acquisitive, tactical, ideological, vindictive, playful or malicious. While it is difficult to assign the numbers of incidents or costs of damage to pay phones to individual categories, the most serious and systematic attacks in recent years appear to be theft-related and the damage incidental.

Figure 1: A Badly Vandalized Red Kiosk

Early Studies and Their Policy Implications

Considerable attention and resources have been directed at understanding vandalism generally and devising preventive schemes (see Barker and Bridgeman, 1994, for a review of the literature). Three research studies have focused on pay phone vandalism as such in Britain (Mawby, 1977; Mayhew et al., 1979; Markus, 1984), seeking to identify the key factors where preventive effort should be targeted.

These studies have tested several hypotheses concerning the kiosks most likely to suffer vandalism. Mawby's (1977) study of kiosk vandalism in residential areas of Sheffield looked at housing tenures and types and population mix, the level of use of kiosks, and the extent to which they were in public view. Mawby found the strongest relationship to be with the level of kiosk use; the most used kiosks were the most heavily vandalized. This finding, however, was not supported by either Mayhew et al. (1979) or by Markus (1984). One explanation for this may be that Mawby's smaller sample focused on residential areas, whereas the later studies covered a much wider range of settings.

In both Mawby and Mayhew et al.'s studies, natural surveillance, that is, the extent to which kiosks are seen by the public, was shown to have only a small effect on the level of vandalism. The studies suggested that, apart from siting particularly high-risk kiosks in more visible locations, there was little scope for reducing damage through re-siting measures.[3] Focusing efforts on making the kiosks more vandal-proof, for example by target hardening was likely to be more effective.

Markus's work suggested, however, that target-hardening measures should be implemented in parallel with other activities, rather than in isolation. He found that the best predictors of kiosk vandalism were the proximity of schools, the amount of nearby public housing and the general appearance of the neighborhood. He emphasized the importance of developing an understanding of what motivates vandals and how they work, analyzing the problem at its source, and viewing the kiosk and its vandalism as part of the community in which it is sited. This would obviously require joint working efforts between BT and other agencies.

PAY PHONE DAMAGE IN BRITAIN: THE EVOLUTION OF BT'S APPROACH

Early Initiatives

Reflecting its perception of the problem at the time — that is, the need for a defensive program against "senseless" damage (Markus, 1984) — the early BT initiatives all involved design alterations to the original "red" phone kiosks and the telephone equipment inside them. Alterations were aimed at reducing the numbers of attacks against the cash compartments and strengthening the handsets and dialing equipment. The cash compartments were strengthened with 10mm steel and robust locks. These changes still left, among other problems, frequently broken windows and the use of phone kiosks as public toilets.

One response to this was to introduce a completely new design of phone booth in some of the worst hit areas. This was the "Oakham"- type phone booth, formed from an indestructible steel shell, open to the street and containing an armored pay phone. It was said to have had some success in reducing damage, but the problem of graffiti remained. An overall assessment concluded that, nationally, levels of phone vandalism had remained constant despite the design alterations (Markus, 1984).

1985 Modernization Programme

In 1985, BT undertook a £160 million modernization program, which included introducing a number of new ideas to combat pay phone vandalism. The old red phone kiosks were replaced by more open designs, using some of the Oakham design principles, to deter undesirable behavior by making those in the kiosk more observable. This also meant that litter and rubbish were less likely to collect in kiosks, giving pay phones a cleaner, brighter image. To increase visibility still further, 24-hour lighting was installed in the kiosks. To combat the problem of broken glass and to improve visibility into the kiosk, the design of the kiosk was changed to one with fewer, larger panes of toughened glass. This had the incidental effect of reducing the amount of glass smashed, perhaps because of a greater inhibiting effect of smashing a larger pane. The phone itself was also modified, with the introduction of one-piece handsets and of noninflammable metal keypads replacing the plastic keypad, which vandals sometimes ignited to inhale the fumes.

Figure 2: The "Oakham" Phone Booth Introduced in Areas Particularly Badly Hit by Vandalism

1987 Strategy to Improve Serviceability

Despite the modernization program, BT had to acknowledge, following media criticism in 1987, that pay phone service levels were "unacceptably low" (British Telecom, 1988). On surveying the extent of the damage, BT found that a quarter of its pay phones were not working at any one time. This prompted a change of direction in the campaign to reduce vandalism damage, by a new focus on improving levels of serviceability. Influenced by Markus's (1984) findings, this strategy had three elements.

- Faults reported were rectified much sooner than they had been, and instructions were given to all staff visiting pay phones — from the cleaners to the engineers — to report any faults and damage they found.

- To support this effort, research was commissioned to profile who was damaging the phones and why. Interviews with offenders found that a typical vandal was male, under age 20, and from the lower socioeconomic groupings, with the reason for attack varying according to age. Younger offenders were responsible for willful damage, while involvement in damage with the motivation of financial gain increased with age. In some cases, attacks arose out of frustration at finding out-of-order phones. The report made recommendations regarding design, siting and servicing, with particular emphasis on the importance of quick service and repair, and the maintenance of clean, well-maintained pay phones and kiosks (British Telecom, 1988).

- A number of community initiatives were set up, with the express intention of promoting pay phones as valuable community resources, to be looked after rather than damaged. These currently include a variety of "Watch the Box" schemes, where the local community or school keeps an eye on "their" phone kiosk and reports faults to the service engineers, and two educational programs involving videos, posters and leaflets, one for adults and one for children. Both initiatives promote the idea that phone kiosks should be respected.

Reorganization of BT and the Cost of Security Failure Program

In 1990, as part of an overall reorganization of BT, pay phones became the responsibility of one unit, the Pay Phones Division, with a new national policy consolidating the 26 regional agendas. Security teams were created within the business units rather than operating as part of an autonomous headquarters department. These changes were aimed at improving business efficiency rather than crime prevention. They coincided with the introduction of a new Cost of Security Failure program, which included an assessment of the financial losses incurred by pay phones as a result of fraud, theft and criminal damage. This exercise made clear that BT's substantial losses were attributable to theft-related attacks rather than vandalism. A close inspection of recording procedures revealed that engineers' perceptions of the cause of damage frequently resulted in misclassification. Many faults were being incorrectly logged as vandalism rather than theft related. Consequently, BT concentrated its energies on addressing the problem of cash compartment attacks and, on the basis that vandalism, as such, was comparatively minor, decided to discontinue separate records of vandalism.

1992 Security Enhancement Programme

In the 1992-93 financial year, there were 55,000 pay-phone cash-compartment attacks, costing BT £20 million. Perpetrators appeared to be far more mobile than in the past, operating in organized gangs, equipped for the specific task with high-powered cordless drills, guns and, especially, manufactured jacking devices. In one instance, a team from Northampton, targeting kiosks in the South West, collected so much coinage that it had to use the Red Star parcel service to get it all home.

In late 1992, in response to these attacks, the £13 million Security Enhancement Programme was launched. It involved a combination of three basic elements:

- *Target hardening*. BT further improved the cash compartment design by fitting all pay phones with an integral fault-reporting system that automatically notified the area computer exchange of any malfunction. The alarms acted both as a detection tool and as a deterrent. Pilot schemes took place in Gloucestershire using kiosks with audible alarms; attacks on the equipment activated a voice of variable volume giving out a cautionary message.

- *Joint operations*. BT investigators worked with local police forces in operations where selected pay phones were fed marked coins, and were alarmed and monitored by arrest teams in close proximity. Pilot schemes incorporating the undercover operations were first introduced in December 1992 in

Manchester and Liverpool, both areas with particularly high levels of attacks. This was followed by wider adoption throughout the country.

- *Education and awareness.* Strategic use of the media was considered a vital component of the program. BT issued press releases designed to increase public awareness of the impact of cash compartment attacks on serviceability, and to invoke support for the campaign. Details of successful arrests and convictions reinforced the intended warning to perpetrators. Other features of the awareness campaign included two five-minute videos targeted at the police and the judiciary, and an educational comic for schools. In 1994, an exhibition trailer on pay phone crime was introduced for use at police training colleges.

Figure 3: 1990s-Style Phone Kiosks Reflecting BT's New Corporate Image

Figure 4: The Front Cover of BT's Educational Comic

Graffiti

The changes in kiosk design introduced in the 1985 modernization program greatly reduced the incidence of writing on phone kiosks, which often advertised prostitution services. Unfortunately, advertisements on self-adhesive labels began to be used instead, resulting in high cleaning costs. A concerted campaign to remove these labels led to offenders switching to cards (which are not classified as criminal damage and for which offenders are liable for civil rather than criminal prosecution). While this significantly reduced cleaning costs, it did not help BT's image. Some areas are tackling the "card" problem in relation to certain sectors of offenders, for example, taxi firms, by selling them advertising space on display boards in the kiosks. With regard to other sectors, particularly prostitutes, BT is still considering various deterrents.

EVALUATION

Systematic pay phone management was intended to result in more efficient servicing and reporting of faults. BT management claims to have increased serviceability of its pay phones from 75% in 1987 to 95% in 1995. The managers now believe that some of the vandalism in the past may have been the result of frustrated phone users encountering out-of-order phones. This would square with French research, which found that mature adults in both urban and rural areas more frequently took aggressive action against malfunctioning public phones than either the old or the young (Moser, 1984). Improved serviceability would automatically eliminate this sort of vandalism.

Results from the Security Enhancement Programme are encouraging. Table 1 shows the number of cash compartment attacks and the corresponding costs for the last three financial years.

Between April and September 1992 there were 24,662 cash compartment attacks. Over the same period in 1993, attacks fell to 12,478, and, between April and September 1994, they fell further to 8,599. A comparison of the number of arrests made during these periods shows a significant increase of 70%, from 401 arrests between April and September 1992 to 681 arrests between April and September 1993. Over the same period in 1994, 438 arrests were made.

Table 1: Cash Compartment Attacks and Costs*

Financial Year	Number of Attacks	Cost of Cash Compartment Attacks (£)
1992-1993	55,563	19,695,703
1993-1994	22,196	10,474,643
1994-1995	17,111	5,127,456

* *Costs relate to the revenue stolen, supplies and labor.*
Source: BT, 1995

The fall in costs has been due largely to fewer offenses, but also to the improved design and refurbishment program.

Figure 5 presents monthly data on cash compartment attacks nationally between April 1992 and March 1995. A dramatic reduction can be seen from December 1992 onward, when attacks were cut from their peak level of around 6,000 per month to stabilize at levels of around 1,200 to 1,500 per month.

At various times, attacks have appeared to be concentrated on particular areas. In the autumn of 1992, for example, Manchester suffered particularly high levels of attacks. A joint police/BT targeted operation in December 1992, launching the Security Enhancement Programme, resulted in 45 arrests in six weeks, and attacks in the city dropped from 400 a month to fewer than 10. In 1994, kiosks in Leeds were the targets of attacks on the coin mechanism, with losses accounting for the greatest part of the sum stolen nationally. BT investigators mounted a two-month undercover operation with the local police, which included video surveillance of kiosks and dawn raids. More than 140 arrests were made as a result of the initiative, and monthly attacks were reduced from around 400 to fewer than 40.

Figure 5: Number of Cash Compartment Attacks on BT Kiosks (April 1992 - March 1995)

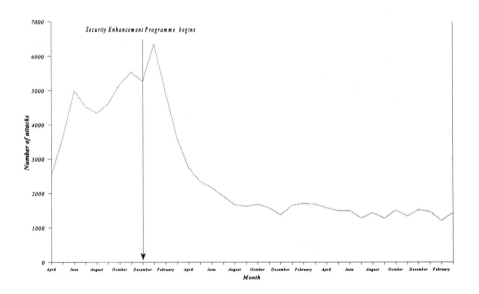

CONCLUSIONS

BT's recent successes in reducing pay phone damage can be seen as a culmination of a series of developments in its approach. In particular, the reorganization of pay phone management in the late 1980s appears to have facilitated better coordination of a more sophisticated range of preventive activities, with increased emphasis on tackling the problem strategically. Accounts of Telecom Australia's experience with pay phone vandalism show similarities to that of BT. These accounts describe how, quite independently, similar problem-solving strategies were devised and implemented.

Pay phone vandalism in Australia was felt to be such a problem that in 1988 a Working Party was established to develop a coordinated national approach. The measures adopted as a result of the Working Party's recommendations included: design modifications; electronic surveillance systems; audible alarms; an educational package; and the introduction of new statistical reporting methods coupled with improved exchange of statistics between the police and Telecom Australia.

After only one year, the cost of repairing vandalized pay phones halved. Two accounts of the initiative attribute its success to different factors. Wilson (1990) argued that the success was due to target-hardening measures that made it more difficult to steal from the cash compartment. Challinger (1991) considered that target hardening alone could not account for the reduction. In his view, the major explanation for the marked decrease was the changes in management resulting from Telecom Australia's privatization, with greater emphasis given to reducing costs and improving profits. In 1987, there were around 16 separate sections of Telecom Australia involved in pay phone management. The problems of uncoordinated policies and lack of focal supervision were addressed by the establishment of the Payphones Division in mid-1988. Challinger stressed that the management change was not introduced as a crime prevention measure to reduce vandalism. Rather, it was introduced to improve performance in the pay phones area, and was part of getting pay phones operational involved tackling vandalism and damage.

In both countries, the changes in management practice followed the privatization of the telecommunications industry. The new strategies might have emerged in any event. In Britain, for example, the public sector has been steadily moving toward a tighter financial regime, but the new management ethos seems to have speeded and stimulated the process. The more general evolution of "multi-agency" approaches to crime prevention will also have smoothed the way for joint working with the police, education authorities and others. The introduction of competitors in the pay phones market also may have added urgency for improvement in BT and Telecom Australia's performance.

The parallel experiences of Britain and Australia highlight a number of key elements in a successful strategy to reduce pay phone damage: the use of situational crime prevention techniques, the development of quality information, and the importance of effective management.

Application of Situational Crime Prevention Techniques

Since the introduction of the concept of situational crime prevention in the mid-1970s (Mayhew et al., 1976), with its focus on opportunity-reducing measures, an array of research studies have demonstrated its effectiveness in preventing a wide variety of crimes in an equal variety of contexts (see Clarke, 1992, for examples). Clarke and Mayhew (1980) developed an eight-category classification of opportunity-reducing techniques, ranging from simple target hardening to more sophisticated measures designed to deflect offenders from possible targets and reduce inducements to criminal action. The classification was subsequently revised and extended to include 12 categories (Clarke, 1992:4) to provide a more "formal and theoretical basis for some practical and commonsense thinking about how to deal with crime."

In common with several of the case studies reviewed by Clarke (1992), the measures adopted by BT and Telecom Australia do not appear consciously to have been developed within a situational crime prevention framework. They are a good example of "practical and common sense thinking" aimed at reducing opportunities for crime. Challinger (1991) grouped Telecom Australia's activities under the headings identified by Clarke's earlier work (1978). Table 2 summarizes this information and also relates the BT measures described in this study to the techniques.

Situational crime prevention follows a standard methodology, a version of action research under which researchers and practitioners work together to analyze and define the problem, identify and experiment with solutions, and evaluate and disseminate the results (Clarke, 1992). Two elements implicit in this process, quality information and effective management, appear to have been of particular significance in the British and Australian experiences with developing successful schemes.

Quality Information

For effective action a precise definition of the problem is essential (see, for example, Ekblom, 1988). In Britain, recognition that some of the earlier damage was due to the frustration of ordinary phone users encountering out-of-order phones suggested a need to improve serviceability, ensuring that faults were quickly reported and acted upon. The importance of rapid repair was highlighted by Wilson and Kelling's (1982) thesis that vandalism is more likely where property shows signs of being uncared for. In Burrows's (1991) commentary on business initiatives, he identified the need for a comprehensive assessment of the losses being sustained from crime, of how these occur, and of emerging vulnerabilities. BT's Cost of

Security Failure program revealed that the cash compartment was the most frequent object of attack and should therefore be a focus for preventive effort.

Table 2: Pay Phone Damage and Situational Crime Prevention

SITUATIONAL TECHNIQUE (from Clarke, 1992)	BT MEASURES	TELECOM AUSTRALIA MEASURES (from Challinger, 1991)
Target Hardening	• Cash compartments strengthened with 10mm steel and robust locks • New tougher handsets and keypads *(early 1980s, local initiatives; 1992→ nationwide implementation)*	• Strengthened handsets, stainless steel cords and redesigned dials • Strengthening of coin box and its security through development of the 'Kirk safe', 'Barker link' and wave door • Modified coin refund chutes that are hard to block • New metal coinheads that restrict direct access to the coin-race *(from 1986→ gradual introduction. By June 1989, all public telephones in South Australia were target hardened)*
Formal Surveillance	• Targeted operations with local police *(from early 1980s, ad hoc operations; 1992→ systematic operations)* • Voice alarmed kiosks *(1992→)*	• Formal surveillance of high risk kiosks by security staff *(best used only where major problems occur, for example in late 1984, special team established in Sydney)*
Surveillance by Employees	• Engineers and cleaners encouraged to report any damage or faults *(1987→)*	• Increased attention from technicians, cleaners, coin collectors *(Sept 1988→)*
Natural Surveillance	• More open kiosk design to make callers more observable *(1985)* • Installation of 24-hour lighting *(1985)* • Resiting of vulnerable kiosks away from dark places *(early 1990s)*	• Resiting of kiosks • Keeping kiosk lighting operational *(1988→)*
Target Removal	• Replacing kiosks in high risk locations with "Oakham" booths *(early 1980s)* • Replacing design of many small panes of glass with fewer larger panes *(1985)* • Installing cardphones which do not use coins *(early 1980s)*	
Removing Inducements	• Rapid repair of faulty equipment and graffiti removal *(1987→)*	• Specialist technicians introduced to ensure rapid repair *(1988→)*
Rule Setting	• Educational campaigns and strategic use of the media reinforcing the message that vandalism is unacceptable *(1985 and 1992→)*	• Adopt-a-phone programme, educational materials, encouragements to report incidents and financial awards *(commenced in Sept 1988)*

Challinger pointed to the need for accurate, specific data on the "victimization" of public pay phones (1991) and reported on Telecom Australia's plans for their collection. BT recognizes that these data must be held in a form capable of sophisticated analysis. The engineer's report is currently being revised to provide more detailed information on: the object of the attack (for example, the cash compartment and the coin mechanism); the method apparently used (for example, was force used or were special tools used?); and information on any equipment failure. This information is being processed on a weekly basis, forwarded to product development staff, and fed into the investigative process. More sophisticated crime pattern analysis (CPA) is in development, including a mapping system to include sitings of all the kiosks. The aim is to use CPA as a predictive tool to enable a cost-effective targeting of prevention resources.

Effective Management

The implementation of preventive measures requires a great deal of commitment, coordination and perseverance (Hope and Murphy, 1983). Efficient management can be pivotal to their success. In BT's case, the changes in arrangements for repairing and maintaining the phone kiosks were necessary for the preventive design alterations to take effect. Furthermore, the restructuring of BT in the late 1980s enabled a coordinated response to be delivered. In Australia, the shift of responsibility from 16 separate sectors into a single new Payphones Division brought similar benefits. The value of this approach has been documented by other research studies. One example is Sloan-Howitt and Kelling's (1990) account of the "Clean Car Program" adopted by the New York City Transit Authority to tackle an escalating graffiti problem. One of the factors identified as responsible for the scheme's success was the creation of a management matrix that coordinated and monitored the activities of the responsible units.

Future Developments in Britain

BT consider the Security Enhancement Programme (SEP) to have successfully reduced what was once an immense problem to manageable levels overall. It is felt that the improved design has deterred opportunistic thieves — in the past, effective amateurs could break into the cash compartments — leaving a hard core of professionals. At the outset, the SEP addressed pay phone crime on a national level, supported by targeted operations, such as those in Manchester and Leeds. For the future, the intention is to direct attention more closely to specific areas with particular problems and to tailor solutions accordingly.

A focused alarm initiative is one line of development. In the past, kiosk alarms have used BT lines to inform the area computer exchange of malfunction or interference. One drawback at present is that if the line is cut, BT does not know about it until an engineer, cleaner or the public notice and report it. In an attempt to overcome this, an alarm system is being developed that will not be reliant on BT phone lines. The idea is that an area of the country will be chosen and alarms will then be fitted in selected kiosks, with other portable alarms deployed to support detection activity.

Another aspect to a more targeted approach is that in the future, Payphone 2000, a multi-payment option phone with the most sophisticated security, will predominate in areas of high usage. The older models of phone will be part of BT's refurbishment program, which includes automatic security upgrading to a minimum level of security specification. Additional levels of security are available for kiosks that have been attacked.

These further initiatives and the continuing motivation of staff to tackle the problem will merit careful monitoring. Businesses have become increasingly persuaded of the need to integrate crime prevention activities into their working practices and procedures, and there is a growing number of documented initiatives that have demonstrably contributed to profitability by cutting crime losses (see, for example, Burrows, 1991). Pay phone damage and its potentially grave consequences in cutting off communications is a worldwide problem. It is also an area in which crime prevention principles and a business management approach are proving to coincide productively.

Figure 6: The Payphone 2000

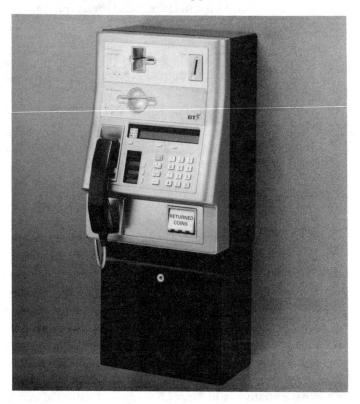

* * *

Acknowledgements: The material in the third section of this article, describing the evolution of BT's approach, is drawn from an earlier case study published in a Home Office Crime Detection and Prevention Series paper on preventing vandalism (Barker and Bridgeman, 1994). All photographs are copyrighted by British Telecommunications plc.

NOTES

1. Until 1984, British Telecom, renamed BT in 1991, was the monopoly supplier of pay phones in Britain. It is still the main operator in the market following privatization, though the government has taken steps to encourage new entrants.

2. There are two main parts to the pay phone: the mechanism control for coin handling and the cash compartment. While a call is in progress, the coins are held

in store in the mechanism. On completion of the call, the coins are transferred to the bottom of the phone to the cash compartment.

3. While natural surveillance did not appear to offer kiosks significant protection against vandalism, Mayhew et al. (1979) pointed out that employee surveillance of rented call boxes in places such as shops, pubs and launderettes results in them suffering far less damage. Rented call boxes, however, do not meet the sort of 24-hour need served by kiosks.

REFERENCES

Barker, M. and C. Bridgeman (1994). *Preventing Vandalism: What Works?* Crime Detection and Prevention Series Paper 56. London, UK: Home Office.

British Telecom (1988). "Vanquishing the Vandal — the Psychology of Crime." *British Telecom Journal* (June):12-15.

Burrows, J. (1991). *Making Crime Prevention Pay: Initiatives from Business.* Crime Prevention Unit Paper 27. London, UK: Home Office.

Challinger, D. (1991). "Less Telephone Vandalism: How Did it Happen?" *Security Journal* 2:111-119.

Clarke, R.V.G. (ed.) (1978). *Tackling Vandalism.* Home Office Research Study No 47. London, UK: Her Majesty's Stationery Office.

—— (1992). *Situational Crime Prevention: Successful Case Studies.* Albany, NY: Harrow and Heston.

—— and P. Mayhew (1980). *Designing out Crime.* London: Her Majesty's Stationery Office.

Cohen, S. (1973). "Property Destruction: Motives and Meanings." In: C. Ward (ed.), *Vandalism.* London, UK: Architectural Press.

Ekblom, P. (1988). *Getting The Best Out of Crime Analysis.* Crime Prevention Unit Paper 10. London, UK: Home Office.

Hope, T. and D. Murphy (1983). "Problems of Implementing Crime Prevention: the Experience of a Demonstration Project." *The Howard Journal of Penology and Crime Prevention* 12:38-50.

Markus, C.L. (1984). "British Telecom Experience in Payphone Management." In: C. Levy-Leboyer (ed.), *Vandalism: Behaviour and Motivations.* Amsterdam: Elsevier.

Mawby, R.I. (1977). "Kiosk Vandalism: A Sheffield Study." *British Journal of Criminology* 17(1):30-46.

Mayhew, P., R.V. Clarke, A. Sturman and J.M. Hough (1976). *Crime as Opportunity.* Home Office Research Study No. 34. London, UK: Her Majesty's Stationery Office.

—— R.V. Clarke, J.N. Burrows, J.M. Hough and S.W.C. Winchester (1979). *Crime in Public View.* Home Office Research Studies No. 49. London, UK: Her Majesty's Stationery Office.

Moser, G. (1984). "Everyday Vandalism: Public Telephones." In: C. Levy-Leboyer (ed.), *Vandalism: Behavior and Motivations.* Amsterdam, NETH: Elsevier.

Sloan-Howitt, M. and G.L. Kelling (1990). "Subway Graffiti in New York City: 'Gettin Up' vs. 'Meaning It and Cleaning It'." *Security Journal* 1(1):131-136.

Wilson, J.Q. and G.L. Kelling (1982). "Broken Windows." *The Atlantic Monthly* March:29-38.

Wilson, P. (1990). "Reduction of Telephone Vandalism: An Australian Case Study." *Security Journal* 1:149-54.

© Crown copyright 1997. Published with the permission of the Controller of Her Majesty's Stationery Office. The views expressed are those of the author and do not necessarily reflect the views or policy of the Home Office or any other government department.

INSURANCE INDUSTRY ANALYSES AND THE PREVENTION OF MOTOR VEHICLE THEFT

by Kim Hazelbaker
Highway Loss Data Institute

Abstract: *This paper focuses primarily on research into vehicle theft conducted by the Highway Loss Data Institute (HLDI). Insurance-claims data from a very large database (73 million vehicles) are routinely analyzed to determine auto theft trends, including types of vehicles stolen, geographic areas of high theft and factors that may work toward theft prevention. Some important differences between the results of theft analyses and similar analyses of HLDI data on vehicle safety are discussed.*

INTRODUCTION

Motor vehicle theft in the United States is a $7.5 billion industry worldwide. Over 1.5 million vehicles were stolen in 1994. But who pays? Much of the loss is paid initially by insurance companies and, ultimately, by consumers who pay higher insurance premiums. Society bears the cost of auto theft through the insurance mechanism (Field, 1993).

The Insurance Institute for Highway Safety (IIHS) and its affiliate, the Highway Loss Data Institute (HLDI), are dedicated to reducing the human and economic losses associated with owning and operating motor vehicles. Both organizations are private nonprofit groups supported by the nation's insurance companies. The primary efforts of both organizations are aimed at reducing fatalities and injuries on the nation's highways. In 1995, there were over 40,000 deaths in vehicle crashes. Reducing vehicle theft is a secondary goal of IIHS and HLDI.

A Brief History of IIHS and HLDI

IIHS was established in 1959 by sponsoring property-casualty insurance companies for the sole purpose of developing driver-improvement programs. The focus was on reducing vehicle crashes by altering drivers' habits. In 1969, the Institute was refocused as a research organization dedicated to finding out what works to improve highway safety based on scientific methods. As a result, over the last 25 years, IIHS has made significant contributions toward reducing fatalities and injuries associated with motor vehicle crashes (IIHS and HLDI, 1994).

HLDI, which is sponsored by the same property-casualty insurance companies as IIHS, was established in 1972 to provide statistical information on insurance losses by vehicle make and model. Until then, there was no aggregation of insurance loss data by make and model. Information from 15 large insurance companies currently is compiled to make up the HLDI database. Over 73 million 1988-1996 vehicle models are represented, allowing HLDI to produce statistically reliable information for use by insurers and the public. Annual reports on insurance losses are published by coverage type: injury, collision and comprehensive, including theft. HLDI also conducts special research studies on a variety of topics to improve vehicle safety and reduce insurance losses.

MAJOR CONTRIBUTIONS TO HIGHWAY SAFETY

The work of IIHS and HLDI has greatly influenced consumers, manufacturers and insurance companies to rethink their roles in safety assurance. The Institute uses vehicle crash testing at its Vehicle Research Center to influence manufacturers toward better occupant protection in a variety of crash modes. Other noteworthy examples are air bags and antilock brakes.

Air Bags

Since the 1970s, IIHS and HLDI have been strong advocates of air bags, based on scientific research (crash test and real world data) indicating their effectiveness. To convince people that air bags reduce severe injuries and fatalities in crashes, the insurance industry has conducted extensive public awareness campaigns. The protection air bags provide has been widely publicized through consumer brochures, films and crash-test footage shown on news broadcasts. Today, all cars sold in the United States have at least a driver air bag, and almost all are equipped with bags for front-seat passengers. Currently, IIHS researchers are working with manufacturers to promote more technologically sophisticated air bag systems with better occupant sensing capabilities.

Antilock Brakes

The overall effectiveness of antilock brakes in reducing crashes is not clear. General Motors and other manufacturers use advertisements showing that antilocks help prevent collisions. However, HLDI research indicates otherwise. In an analysis of HLDI statistics published last year, no overall reduction was found in collision claim frequencies or average collision loss payments for vehicles equipped with antilock brakes (IIHS, 1995).

AUTOMOBILE THEFT

For both antilocks and air bags, IIHS and HLDI's approach has been to evaluate, through scientific research, the effectiveness of the feature and then to disseminate this information widely to manufacturers and the public through the mass media. HLDI is using the same approach in dealing with the auto theft problem.

The most recent HLDI theft study (HLDI, 1996) revealed a significant *decline* in theft claim frequency over the last 15 model years but, at the same time, a significant *rise* in the average loss payment for these claims (see Figure 1). Part of the reason for the escalating costs is the declining recovery rate for stolen vehicles, currently only 62 percent compared with 84 percent in 1970 (NICB, 1995). Export of stolen vehicles has increased dramatically, making the U.S. car theft problem a global issue. The emergence of the newly independent eastern European states has had a dramatic effect on demand for stolen vehicles from the U.S.

Years ago, kids stole many cars primarily for joyriding, and the vehicles later were abandoned. Today, thieves are organized professionals linked to "chop shops," export rings, or both. Several sources indicate this shift in emphasis (for a review, see Clarke and Harris, 1992b). The bottom line is that now car theft is big business.

Figure 1: Theft Claim Frequency and Average Loss Payment Per Claim - By Model Year*

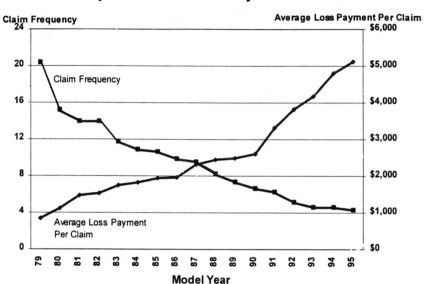

* Losses are based on three years of exposure except 1994 (two years) and 1995 (one year).

In a chop shop, parts are removed (typically from older vehicles) and sold for a sum greater than the overall value of the car. Although attempts to thwart this have included increased marking of parts with vehicle identification numbers (VINs), the problem persists. The deterrent value of parts marking relies on an increased enforcement effort at the body-shop level - a difficult task.

Through major export rings operating across the United States and abroad, "hot" cars, like sport-utility vehicles and luxury cars, are smuggled into foreign countries where they are not widely available. U.S. authorities have discovered the inner workings of some of these export rings. For example, a favorite transshipment point currently is the Dominican Republic for cars shipped from the U.S. East and Gulf Coasts. Hong Kong is favored for cars stolen in California. These export rings are costing insurance companies and consumers $1-4 billion annually (NICB, 1995). The high demand for both parts and entire vehicles has made vehicle theft highly profitable.

Cars with the Highest Theft Losses

The latest theft report from HLDI (1996b) concluded that utility vehicles, luxury cars and sports cars have the highest theft losses. Only three years ago, sports models were the highest-theft vehicles. Now, utility vehicles and luxury cars are in even higher demand. The Toyota Land Cruiser has the highest theft losses — 23 times greater than average. Vehicles of these types are classified as high risk because of both the number of theft occurrences and the actual dollar value of the losses. Regular two- and four-door cars, as well as station wagons and passenger vans, are very low-risk vehicles.

Increasing demand abroad for luxury cars and utility vehicles has magnified the problem. Many of these vehicles never are recovered because they are either driven across the border or shipped overseas. A luxury car stolen in the United States can be sold in a foreign country for as much as three times the U.S. sticker price (NICB, 1995). Clarke and Harris (1992a) concluded that luxury vehicles are more likely to be stolen for permanent retention because of their profit-generating potential.

Where Theft Losses Are Highest

HLDI researchers are able to determine the geographic distribution of vehicle theft using zip code information from the claims database. The clustering of theft around large metropolitan areas is apparent, and this finding is consistent with findings based on FBI data (Clarke and Harris, 1992b).

What may be more surprising are the high theft losses in areas along the Mexican border where overall losses are the fourth highest in the nation (HLDI, 1990b). Miller (1987) also discovered that recovery rates of stolen vehicles generally are lower in the Texas counties that border Mexico. According to Field et al. (1991: 206), low recovery rates along the Mexican border "...indicate thefts for resale, rather than for temporary use or 'joyriding.'" Elsewhere, the Miami and New York City metropolitan areas, both with major ports, also have very high theft losses. Losses in Miami jumped 85 percent compared with only two years ago. Almost half of all insurance dollars paid for theft are accounted for by the six metropolitan areas listed in Table 1. Many of the vehicles stolen in these areas are exported.

Table 1: Areas with High Theft Losses Based on 1993-95 Models

Area[1]	Exposure (Insured Vehicle Years)	Claim Frequency[2]	Average Loss Payment Per Claim	Average Loss Payment Per Insured Vehicle Year
Miami	563,399	8.6	$11,403	$98
New York	1,813,641	8.1	11,723	95
San Diego	254,,977	9.4	8,444	79
Mexican Border[3]	253,476	6.8	9,517	65
Detroit	638,781	21.1	2,835	60
Los Angeles	1,081,040	6.5	6,650	43
U.S. Total	29,453,134	5.3	$4,975	$26

1. Areas are metropolitan statistical areas as determined by the Office of Management and Budget (except the Mexican Border).

2. Claims per 1,000 insured vehicle years.

3. Counties along the Mexican border excluding San Diego.

HLDI also has mapped theft losses by the garaging-location zip code within the metropolitan areas with the highest overall theft losses. Results showed that theft losses tended to be dramatically higher for cars garaged within zip-code areas located near urban centers (HLDI, 1994).

Antitheft Devices

There are a variety of antitheft and tracking systems on the market with costs ranging from basic audible alarms costing $50 to sophisticated tracking systems with $30 monthly fees. Unfortunately, the effectiveness of many of these devices is questionable. The sensitivity of audible alarms to touch or movement, for example, provokes a "boy who cried wolf" reaction. When a car alarm goes off, people tend not to react because the alarms activate so frequently for reasons other than actual theft. HLDI studies show no overall reduction in theft losses for vehicles with such alarms.

The most effective antitheft devices, HLDI has found, are those that immobilize a vehicle when an attempted theft is detected. One system, known as the PASS-Key II in General Motors vehicles, cuts off the electrical power needed to start the engine. Comparing 1994 GM passenger cars equipped with this device and their 1993 counterpart models without the device (no other design changes), HLDI found that the average loss payment declined dramatically for vehicles with PASS-Key II (HLDI, 1996c). According to a new study of 1995 BMWs, average loss payments dropped significantly when a passive immobilizing antitheft device became standard in midyear (HLDI, 1996a).

HLDI has greatly influenced manufacturers to consider installing effective antitheft devices such as immobilization systems, especially on high-theft models. While these systems greatly reduce the chance of a vehicle being driven away, in many cases the vehicle is damaged as a result of an attempted theft. For example, the window or door lock may be broken. But such damage costs insurance companies and consumers much less than the total loss of vehicles.

Vehicle Redesign: What Happens to Older Cars?

HLDI statistics show that older vehicles with no design changes over a period of time are more likely to be stolen than some newer cars. The older cars are stolen primarily for their parts. For vehicles with design changes, a reduction in theft losses usually is evident. The claim frequency and average loss payment for redesigned high-theft vehicles is much lower than for the same vehicles prior to the redesign. The appeal of a vehicle with unchanged sheet metal is that the parts fit a large number of similar vehicles across several model years. In addition, older cars are more likely to be uninsured and the demand for used parts is higher for these vehicles.

Parts Marking — Does It Work?

Under the Motor Vehicle Theft Law Enforcement Act of 1984 and the AntiCar Theft Act of 1992, parts marking is required on high-theft vehicles. This has been one of the most controversial of all antitheft requirements. Manufacturers do not want to absorb the cost of parts marking because they believe it is ineffectual, and there is some evidence for this position. Studies from the National Highway Traffic Safety Administration (1991) provided no evidence that parts marking has a positive effect on theft while a HLDI (1990a) study showed that etching VINs on various parts of a vehicle may have a slight positive effect. Comparison of cars with and without parts marking shows that those with marked parts had lower frequencies of claims for less than $10,000. The average loss payment per insured vehicle year changed little for cars without marked parts while it declined for cars with marked parts. In urban areas, the effect is even more evident. Thus, marking car parts has the potential to reduce vehicle theft, especially in the high-theft urban areas, and it could have more impact if all cars were marked rather the just the high-risk vehicles (Harris and Clarke, 1991).

HLDI Brochure

The most widely known HLDI publication is an annual brochure listing injury, collision and theft losses by vehicle make and model. This brochure has been published since 1982 to help consumers make informed decisions about buying safer and more insurable cars. The goal is to save lives and prevent injuries, and this, in turn, reduces costs not only for consumers but for insurance companies and manufacturers. More than 20 million copies of this consumer brochure have been distributed by HLDI and sponsoring insurers. New car dealerships are required by the U.S. Department of Transportation to make this information available to new car buyers. Consumers Union also uses HLDI information in its various Consumer Reports publications.

CONCLUSIONS

An important component of HLDI analyses of theft and safety data consists of comparisons between models, but there are some interesting differences in the findings. For collisions and injuries, there are relatively small differences between models. Having standardized for the "non-vehicle factors" of operator age groups and deductible amounts, typically the highest-risk models have claim frequencies two or three times those of the lowest-risk models. For injuries, the variation is somewhat greater and is due mainly to vehicle size. For thefts, however, the variation is much greater, with the highest-risk vehicles typically having claim frequencies some twenty times higher than the lowest-risk vehicles.

Some of this variability in theft is the result of design vulnerabilities. For example, Volkswagen Rabbits had high claims frequencies for many years because they were fitted with high quality radios, but the Cabriolet version was especially vulnerable because its soft top could easily be cut open (Braga and Clarke, 1994). Most of the variability in theft, however, is due to the differential attractiveness of models to thieves. Moreover, variations in claim frequencies reflect a mix of motives for theft. Thus, some cars are especially attractive to joyriders, whereas others may be particularly attractive for resale of their parts or for export overseas (see Clarke and Harris, 1992a). Some vehicles, such as certain Cadillacs, have had high claim frequencies simply because of a cult among juveniles of stealing their hood emblems!

Further complicating the picture is that fashions in attractiveness change. A few years ago "muscle" cars such as Chevrolet Camaros and Pontiac Firebirds dominated the theft listings while, at present, the models most at risk are small utility vehicles such as the Suzuki Sidekick. Finally, there are considerable regional variations in attractiveness to theft. For example, models popular among joyriders in Los Angeles at any given period may not be may the same as those popular in New York City or Miami.

These facts make it difficult to formulate a role for HLDI in encouraging preventive action. It is one thing to advise manufacturers of particular vulnerabilities, for example, in the locks of certain models (and HLDI routinely undertakes much work of this kind), but it is quite another to deal with the issue of attractiveness. Manufacturers are struggling to make their models stand out from the crowd. The very features that make their cars attractive to buyers are many of the same ones that attract thieves, and manufacturers will not be willing to change these features. However, they may be persuaded to introduce additional security for the highest-theft models, as indeed was done in the case of Pass-Key II for some GM cars.

In dealing with theft, this may mean that an effective prevention strategy will need to be more "model specific" than in the safety field. There, the general strategy has been to introduce improvements, such as air bags, across the entire model range. For theft, it may be more efficient to protect only the highest-risk models. This would raise the possibility that thieves might displace their attention to other models, and, here, the help of criminologists who have studied displacement in other contexts might be needed. Their help might also be needed in designing and conducting studies of vehicle attractiveness to thieves. Without a deeper understanding of this phenomenon, it may be difficult to anticipate theft trends and act quickly to block them.

* * *

REFERENCES

Braga, A.A. and R.V. Clarke (1994). "Improved Radios and More Stripped Cars in Germany: A Routine Activities Analysis. *Security Journal* 5:154-159.

Clarke, R.V. and P.M. Harris (1992a). "A Rational Choice Perspective on the Targets of Automobile Theft." *Criminal Behaviour and Mental Health* 2:25-42.

—— and P.M. Harris (1992b). "Auto Theft and Its Prevention." In: M. Tonry (ed.), *Crime and Justice: A Review of Research*, vol. 16. Chicago, IL: University of Chicago Press.

Field, S. (1993). "Crime Prevention and the Costs of Auto Theft: An Economic Analysis." In: R.V. Clarke (ed.), *Crime Prevention Studies*, vol. 1. Monsey, NY: Criminal Justice Press.

—— R.V. Clarke and P.M. Harris (1991). "The Mexican Vehicle Market and Auto Theft in Border Areas of the United States." *Security Journal* 2:205-210.

Harris, P.M. and R.V. Clarke (1991). "Car Chopping, Parts Marking and the Motor Vehicle Theft Law Enforcement Act of 1984." *Sociology and Social Research* 75:107-16.

Highway Loss Data Institute (HLDI) (1990a). *Insurance Special Report A-31: The Effect of Vehicle Component Parts Marking on Theft Losses*. Arlington, VA: author.

—— (1990b). *Insurance Special Report A-35: Automobile Losses in Selected Cities and Border Regions.* Arlington, VA: author.

—— (1994). "Atlas of Automobile Theft Losses in Large Metropolitan Areas." *Insurance Special Report*, A-44. Arlington, VA: author.

—— (1996a). "Antitheft Devices in 1995 Model BMWs: Preliminary Results." *Theft Loss Bulletin*, vol. 14, No. 2. Arlington, VA: author.

—— (1996b). *Insurance Theft Report: 1993-95 Passenger Vehicles.* Arlington, VA: author.

—— (1996c). *Theft Loss Bulletin.* vol. 14, No. 1. Arlington, VA: author.

Insurance Institute for Highway Safe (IIHS) (1995). "Antilock Brakes Don't Reduce Crash Frequency or Cost, HLDI Reports." *Status Report* 30: 5. Arlington, VA: author.

—— and Highway Loss Data Institute (IIHS and HLDI) (1994). *25 Years of Work.* Arlington, VA: Insurance Institute for Highway Safety.

Miller, M.V. (1987). "Vehicle Theft along the Texas-Mexico Border." *Journal of Borderland Studies* 2:12-32.

National Highway Traffic Safety Administration *(1991). Auto Theft and Recovery. Effects of the Motor Vehicle Theft Law Enforcement Act of 1984.* Washington, DC: U.S. Department of Transportation.

NATIONAL UNIVERSITY
LIBRARY   SAN DIEGO

NATIONAL UNIVERSITY
SAN DIEGO
LIBRARY

3575